DRAMATIS PERSONAE
in the order, more or less, of their appearing

Charlotte Hagedorn, born Günther
Adolf, her husband
Hermann, their son
Elsbeth ⎫
Alma ⎭ their daughters
Dr. Gerhard Leonhardt, Prussian minister of justice
Friedrich Schwedler, publisher, *New Yorker Demokrat*
Marie, born Stropp, his wife
Anna ⎫
Alwine (Venie) ⎭ their daughters
The spirit of Abraham Lincoln
Annie ⎫
Adolf ⎪
Fred ⎬ children of Hermann and Anna Hagedorn
Elsie ⎪
Irma ⎪
Hermann ⎭
The spirit of Otto von Bismarck
Dr. George Rodemann, principal, Bedford Academy, Bro
Rev. Jacob W. Loch, pastor, German Evangelical Churcl
Nemesis, spirit of retribution
Fritz Kleie, swimming instructor
Lieutenant Colonel Alfred von Mauntz, retired
Gertrud, his wife

Ruby, later Baroness von Wintzingerode
John Meigs, headmaster, the Hill School, Pottstown, Pa.
Marion, his wife, known as "Mrs. John"
Michael F. Sweeney, athletic coach
Dorothy Oakley, later wife of Hermann Hagedorn, junior
Members of the Harvard faculty
Swinburne Hale, student
Dr. Wilhelm Bensen, husband of Irma Hagedorn
Theodore Roosevelt, ex-President of the United States
Ernest H. Gruening, managing editor, *New York Tribune*
An official of the United States Committee on Public Information

For Muriel Smith

in admiration and gratitude —

[signature]

1962.

THE
HYPHENATED
FAMILY

~An American Saga~

by

HERMANN HAGEDORN

New York

THE MACMILLAN COMPANY

Second Printing, 1962

The Macmillan Company, New York
Brett-Macmillan Ltd., Galt, Ontario

Printed in the United States of America

Library of Congress catalog card number: 60–10775

Dedicated
to the memory of those
whose story I have told in this book,
and who cannot tell me now the things
they would have wanted me to know,
to make the story truer, and more kind.

FOREWORD

THIS is a true story. I wish it weren't. I wish it were somebody's book of fiction and I could stand apart from it with an appraising eye and say, "This grandmother and these aunts are overdrawn. The loyalty of the father to his mother and sisters, the self-abnegation of his wife, just can't be true. People don't act that way; and, in real life, destiny doesn't work out its sequences according to the patterns of classic drama." It would be much pleasanter for me, as I look back, if it were fiction. But it isn't. It is fact, told as honestly as I can tell it, with nothing extenuated; nothing, I trust, set down in malice.

It is a story of a family that tried to live in two countries at once; a story of a strong man betrayed at the height of his success by a strain of sentimentalism that brought his triumphs tumbling down around him; a story, finally, of one member of the family, its youngest, who tried to make himself what his German-born mother, rich in sentiment but without a grain of sentimentality, wanted him to be, an unhyphenated American.

The story falls naturally into five parts, corresponding to the canonical five acts of classic tragedy, with its "ascending" and "descending" action, and the final catastrophe of disillusion, disaster and retribution played out against the backdrop of a world war.

THE
HYPHENATED
FAMILY

THE MACMILLAN COMPANY
NEW YORK • CHICAGO
DALLAS • ATLANTA • SAN FRANCISCO
LONDON • MANILA

IN CANADA
BRETT-MACMILLAN LTD.
GALT, ONTARIO

~ Part One ~

CHAPTER ONE

IT ALL began one hot July day in the middle 1880's in a pleasant brownstone front on Berkeley Place in the Prospect Hill section of Brooklyn. Of course, the causes of the tragedy lay away back of that, but what happened that day marked a turning point in our family story. We were on the way to becoming an American family like millions of other American families whose immediate origins lay in other lands, settling into the American scene, sending our roots down into the American soil. What happened that day made us different, forever different, as a family and as individuals, warping personalities, twisting characters; bringing to all of us confusion and inner conflict; separating us one from another by oceans and, at times, more than oceans; finally bringing down on my father's head the impressive structure he had worked forty years to build.

The first memory of my life is of that day. It must have been shortly after my birthday—my fourth—for I remember I was in bed suffering from the effects of too much birthday cake. I can remember my brother Adolf, not quite twelve, yet grave and loving always, bending over me to kiss me good-by; and then Fred, a year younger, was embracing me, less solemnly than his brother, having a livelier curiosity and so being less averse to change.

I don't remember anybody crying. Father had firm control of himself when his conscience wasn't biting him or he did not feel he had to dramatize a sentiment because he did not feel it as deeply as he believed he should; and Mother was never given to weeping, at least when we youngsters were around. I cannot remember, but I can imagine, the defiant brightness of her eyes, that July morning, so blue under her wavy chestnut hair, the eyes brimming but no tears falling. She had imagination and saw ultimate destinies beyond the moment's painful but, on the surface, not too significant expedient.

My father saw just that he was sending his two eldest sons to his mother in Germany for the education that he could not afford to pay for in America, and that the public schools, he believed, could not provide. My mother, I am sure, saw more, and knew that she was giving her sons away to the mother-in-law who had never forgotten that, in the major struggle of a life filled with tempestuous emotional upheavals, this serene, self-effacing young woman had defeated her.

Neither my father nor my mother, I am certain, recognized, that day, that they had chosen to live in two countries at once, though an ocean rolled between.

-2-

I don't know where Father got the idea of going to America, though there is every reason why he should have got it. An uncle had gone to Baltimore in the middle forties and managed, within a few years, not only to establish himself in business but to marry an FFV of the Harrison line, quite an achievement for an impecunious young foreigner in the ante-bellum South. Another uncle who had gone to St. Louis, had done well, too. The air, in fact, was full of stories of American opportunity and German grasp in this "land of unbounded possibilities" across the Atlantic.

Father was nineteen. He would soon have to serve in the Hanoverian army. Prussia was stretching out greedy hands toward its neighboring kingdom, and the chances were that he would have to fight. He had no inclination toward the martial exploits that, over a period of ten years, had carried a grandfather of his crisscross over the face of Europe. Besides, what would he be fighting for? This petty geographical unit, this third-rate kingdom that was the land of his birth, what actually did it mean to him? The boldness of burning his

4

bridges and setting out for the New World would have appealed to him. He was never averse to bold action when the end to be gained seemed worth it.

I don't know how his mother reacted to the idea. Charlotte Hagedorn was an extraordinary woman by any standard. If destiny had thrust her where another energetic young Hanoverian female had been placed, some thirty years earlier, she would, I am sure, have done a very creditable job. But the iron will which might be priceless in a sovereign may be devastating in a mother. I am sure she made a "scene," and that, before it was over, the timbers of the house creaked and groaned like a ship in a storm. Charlotte Hagedorn's capacity to act up, on occasion, is famous in the family annals: and the peculiarly ardent relationship of mother and son might have seemed a valid enough excuse for an eruption. I suspect that, before giving her consent—and he would have done nothing without it—she made him promise that he would throw out no anchors. It would have been like her, in any case, to keep a hold on him through his conscience and his love.

– 3 –

The bitter cold that blew in Father's face as he stepped on the pier at Hoboken, across the Hudson from New York, one mid-January morning in 1866, was no sharper than the wind that had blown apart his Dundreary whiskers as he boarded the ship at Hamburg, but I am sure it seemed more hostile. German folk songs are full of the pathos of youth leaving the homeland to seek fame and fortune in that "outland" that was everywhere where "German speech and German ways and German love" were not; and the gentle melancholy of those songs had sunk deep into his heart. Perhaps the thrill of the adventure on which he was embarked mitigated, on that day, to some degree, the pangs of loneliness and the terror of his first contact with a world that was alien in language, in customs and in political and social attitudes.

With all his sentimentalism, Father had plenty of courage. Obviously, he needed it. The parting from his mother must have been an emotional orgy, from which mother and son emerged, no doubt, shattered and exhausted. The calendar, it happened, had provided further fuel for the grief of parting. It had been on Christmas Day that he had sailed forth into the unknown. For a boy to whom Christmas meant as much as it always meant to him, it must have taken all the stamina he had to go out into the wide and windy world, on that day of all days. I have an idea that Captain Schwensen, master of the steamship *Borussia*, was mindful of the boy's Teutonic sensibilities, for the weather-beaten old sea dog's name is a fragrant memory of my childhood.

The *Borussia*—steam, with sails to help—took three weeks to make the crossing. Barometer and thermometer alike did their worst. Head gales lashed the bucking, rolling old tub the whole width of the Atlantic and, when the vessel finally steamed into New York Harbor, it was into a mass of floating ice. Snow lay over Battery Park and Castle Garden. On Broadway, sleigh bells tinkled in the frosty air.

From a nation about to go to war—a very little nation, it was, the kingdom of Hanover—my father came to a nation stretching in relaxation, as it sought, after four years of civil conflict, to get used to being at peace. Lincoln was dead, and a well intentioned but inept substitute was in the White House, trying to carry out his policies. On the day my father reached New York, Congress was deep in a debate over Southern reconstruction, and talked of bringing Jefferson Davis to trial. In New York City there were murders, political shenanigans, and a performance of Shakespeare's *Coriolanus* in German. West of the Mississippi there were railroads pushing toward the Pacific, towns like mushrooms, a frontier perpetually advancing.

To the newcomer from afar, setting foot on American soil, there was, above and beyond the day's events, something else: a gleaming beacon which shone across four thousand miles of ocean into every window of the Old World. There was Opportunity. Father promptly went after his share of it. He was only a boy, but his black Dundrearys made him look sufficiently adult to win him a subordinate position

6

in a petroleum house, Schepeler & Co., at ten dollars a week, which was munificent, since it was payable not in paper money, elegantly known as "shin-plasters," but in gold.

– 4 –

It was a German firm in which Father found a job. The boarding-house in Brooklyn where he found lodging was run by a woman named Pellerin, but the name was misleading. She, too, was German, as were all the young men she took into her house, and mothered. When Father went out for a meal with his new friends they went to German restaurants; when they went to church they went to a German church; when they wanted to be entertained, they went to the Irving Place Theatre and saw the latest Germany comedy or some Schiller drama or a Shakespeare play, in German.

There was nothing unusual in this hunger of aliens in any land to seek their own kind, and to hear their own language spoken. Americans felt the same hunger in Berlin and Munich, in Paris and Rome.

But there was a difference. The Americans would largely be return-ing to their native land in a year or two or three, and those who remained would be accepted by the people among whom they settled as a foreign colony, detached from the national life. But, with few exceptions, these young Germans in New York would become Ameri-can citizens—"children of the crucible" as, a half century later, a great American would call them—responsible, each, for the fulfillment of the national motto, "Out of the many, one."

If ever a crisis arose involving the Fatherland, where would these men stand?

– 5 –

A photograph of Father, taken shortly after his arrival in New York, shows the black whiskers in all their deceptive luxuriance, with a silken moustache bridging the full, finely-molded lips and the rounded chin that had not yet acquired the firmness I remember.

7

It is not at all the face of the ten-dollar-a-week clerk that he was, or of the masterful man of action he was to become; rather a poet's face, revealing a sadness in the eyes, a wistfulness about the sensitive mouth, that suggests homesickness so devastating that it may have become subconsciously endemic.

It was no hunger for his native Hanover that put that look in Father's eyes.

– 6 –

The relation between Father and his mother went beyond what was to be expected between a loving parent and an affectionate child. His father's premature death had given him, at the age of thirteen, the sense that, so far as he could, he must himself take on the burden of responsibility his father had been forced to lay down. His mother, on her part, had focused on him the impassioned devotion she had given her husband, and the boy had reciprocated with an ardor in which filial love was enhanced by admiration of her beauty and intelligence, and awe of her commanding power.

Charlotte Hagedorn came naturally by her looks, her brains and her emotional intensity. Her father had been a surgeon in the Hanoverian Legion that had fought with the British Army in Sicily and Corsica, Italy, Spain, and finally, at Waterloo. Though the records do not confirm the family tradition that he was on Wellington's staff, his handwriting, curiously like my father's—with mastery in every stroke—indicates that he was a man of intelligence, vigor and will. Nothing is known of his remoter forebears—and Charlotte's daughters, who reveled in titles, threw out hints of a not-impossible connection with a princely line bearing the Günther name—but his eldest son Ludolf who had done so well, so exceptionally well, not only in his marriage, was all the fuel Charlotte needed for her conviction that the Günthers were, socially, at least, among God's elect. Her daughter Elsbeth, at ninety, spoke reverently of her "fabulous pride"—*ihren fabelhaften Stolz.*

It was, in fact, neither the martial exploits of the Hanoverian sur-

8

geon, nor the brilliance and charm of Ludolf, nor the achievements of any of the various clergymen or lawyers who preceded him in the Günther line, which seem to me to justify Charlotte's family pride. There was something else, something very real, revealed in her wide-set eyes and noble brow. A high spirit, creative energy, integrity and loyalty have been characteristic, generation after generation, of men and women in whom the Günther strain was dominant. Charlotte Günther had a right to be proud of her line.

– 7 –

Charlotte and the man she married both grew up in the sleepy little town of Nienburg on the Weser, a narrow stream meandering through flat country until, below Bremen, it deepens, broadens out and becomes something that can carry ocean-going ships coming in from the North Sea. Nienburg, in what was, up to the middle 1860's, the independent kingdom of Hanover, was a picturesque little town of some four thousand inhabitants when Father was born there in the middle 1840's, with timber-and-plaster houses leaning cozily toward one another in the narrow streets, an architecturally impressive town hall, a romantic tower surviving from the Middle Ages, and a shaded promenade constructed on the rubble of the old wall that had once held off the lordly marauders who periodically raided the town. Nienburg was noted for its delicious spongecake, baked in the form of a bear's claw, but, so far as I know, for nothing else.

Adolf Hagedorn's forebears had lived in the town for two hundred years or more, and included an almost unbroken line of bakers, generation after generation, until, early in the nineteenth century, they climbed the ladder, to become merchants, brewers, distillers and churchwardens. There was money in the family by the time Adolf was born, considerable money by Nienburg standards. His father was a successful tradesman, a member of the city senate and a vestryman. Three of his five sons went to the university, one to study theology; one, medicine; the third, Adolf, the law.

Adolf was twenty-seven, tall and slender, with a narrow, thoughtful

9

face, a fine brow and black "fire-escape" whiskers, when he and Charlotte, eight years his junior, were married. They were very much in love. She was an orphan, without the dowry that was regarded as essential to a socially acceptable marriage, but her beauty and intelligence had brought her many suitors and she was a little spoiled. Her father, moreover, had brought home from his military campaigns a knowledge of foreign lands and peoples and the effect of personal relations with British officers of breeding and cultivation that set his home apart from the households of his less traveled neighbors. Charlotte was inclined to look down on the family of well-to-do tradespeople into which she had married. To her, blood, tradition and social position loomed large, but with her husband's people it was business.

My father, Hermann Anton Conrad, was their firstborn. By the time he was thirteen, his father had the best legal practice in Nienburg, was a senator, and a counselor to the royal government. When the blind king of Hanover, George V, came to Nienburg, it was *Landsyndikus* Hagedorn who was chosen to welcome him in behalf of the town fathers. His friends agreed that he was headed for great things.

He glowed, when, after his advancement, he took Charlotte to the spacious house in which he was to have his office, and they and their children, their home.

The house had been built for his own use by a noted architect whom the Emperor Napoleon had called to Paris, early in the century, to lay out parks and boulevards for his capital. It was, in fact, a gem, unmatched in Nienburg not only for dignity but for charm, and Charlotte was carried away by it. "My dear!" she exclaimed. "This is much too beautiful for me!"

"Dearest," he answered, and the words have echoed tenderly down the generations, "I'd give you Paradise if I could!"

Destiny had a different intent. A special session of Hanoverian officialdom met at a banquet in the big house, that December, 1859. *Tante* Elsbeth, seventy-odd years later, remembered how impressive the Herr *Landsyndikus* looked, in his swallowtail and his white embroidered shirt front, and with what dignity and grace he received his guests, and bade them farewell, in the unheated, flagstoned foyer. It seemed to my aunt, in memory, only a few hours after the door had been closed for the last time, that night, that Hermann and his sisters became aware of an unusual stirring in the big house. There was fear in their mother's dark eyes.

A week later, my grandfather asked Father to stay with him through the long Sunday afternoon. Snow was falling in heavy, silent flakes and the thirteen-year-old stood by the window, seeing nothing and knowing nothing except that his father was in the last stages of pneumonia. At intervals, the dying man would call faintly, *"Hermann, wie viel Uhr ist es?"* The boy would tell him the time, and a little later again his father would ask, *"Hermann, wie viel Uhr ist es?"* At intervals, all evening, he repeated the irrelevant query.

That night, after midnight, Christmas Eve, the children were awakened from sleep to stand in uncomprehending misery at the deathbed and see the flame flicker and fail. Elders put such burdens on children in those days. In my grandfather's study, next day, there were no flowers, no wreaths, only four lighted candles in silver candlesticks on the bare coffin. The tragedy released all the young widow's uncontrollable emotions, and she would not let herself be torn from her husband's bier. Through the heavy snow my father walked to the cemetery on foot behind the black-plumed hearse.

CHAPTER TWO

CHARLOTTE HAGEDORN was thirty-three when she became a widow, a full-blooded and beautiful woman still, with her soft brown eyes, that could blaze but could be tender, too; the deceptive serenity of her Günther forehead and the opulent curves of her willful lips.

She did not linger long in Nienburg, after her husband's death. Her father and her brother had, as it were, set her feet where an ocean opened out before her, and life at the edge of a duckpond was no longer tolerable. Living in the big, cheerless Hagedorn domicile with these tradespeople who were her in-laws, moreover, did not appeal to her class-conscious mind, and she had no intention of letting them tell her how to bring up her children. Perhaps they tried it, and the violence of her reaction persuaded them that even so substantial a structure as theirs might not long survive the kind of earthquakes she periodically set going. So, I suspect, it was by common consent that she moved to the little capital in which the blind king was maintaining his precarious throne.

She chose well. The city of Hanover dramatized, even in its external appearance, the breadth of life she craved. Its tree-shaded avenues were wide, and led the eye into dim distances. Its public buildings were stately; its churches held treasures of sculpture and stained glass that travelers came far to see. Its cultural life, if not exceptional, was exciting in contrast to the small-town atmosphere in which Charlotte had grown up, and the German spoken in its streets was recognized as the purest in all the German lands. The city was linked to the great world, moreover, by its ties to England. Its ruling house had given her five kings and, finally, the great Victoria. A public square, with a monument, recalled Waterloo and, in those early 1860's, veterans of Hanover's gallant "English Legion" still sat on benches in the city parks and talked of Blücher and the Iron Duke. In the high-ceilinged, handsomely furnished houses of the aristocrats and the government functionaries, shining Sheffield plate and copper-colored English engravings, framed in austere black, bore further witness to the bonds between the two peoples.

Charlotte, no doubt, was conscious of all these things. In Hanover, too, she knew she could develop for her children those "good connections" that loomed so large in her social outlook. Her husband's closest friend, and her children's unofficial guardian, Dr. Gerhard Leonhardt, lived with his wife and children, moreover, in Celle, barely an hour's journey away, and was always coming to the capital on government business.

– 2 –

Hermann attended the lyceum in Hanover, and, at the age of sixteen, completed all the schooling he was to get. It was considerable, so far as it went, for it gave him standards in his reading and a sense of aesthetic values. Of science he had nothing, or of languages. I suspect that most of what he got in school was drill, but mental discipline came out of it, for he liked to read in later years, and read solid books. His training in elementary mathematics, too, must have been good, or he had a special gift, for his agility at mental arithmetic always entranced me.

His moral and religious training was no less thorough. Lutheran theology might seem sterile as the preachers unfolded it in the bare, icy churches; but in most German homes in the middle of the nine-teenth century, and Charlotte's was no exception, the Deity was a living factor, virtue was practiced as well as approved, and the conscience was assiduously cultivated.

Charlotte was a woman of generous impulses, inclined to be out-

13

going when her self-will was not involved; and it was a God of green pastures rather than of Sinai that she helped her son to find. Father was confirmed in the Lutheran faith when he was fifteen. He was moved by the experience, and kept all his life the pastor's certificate and the autograph album in which his family and friends wrote pious admonitions. His sister Elsbeth, aged thirteen, quoted a famous poem about the pursuit of righteousness even to the "cool grave," but Alma, two years younger, expressed the sentimental hope that Hermann's life might be a rippling brook running through flowers and shady groves with never a storm—which was exactly what that butter-and-honey creature *would* write, even as a child, and was not at all the sort of life that he himself was interested in.

– 3 –

Hermann had no inclination toward a profession. There was, in fact, no money available for a university education, and his mother's brother Anton, who was a shipping and forwarding merchant in Harburg on the Elbe, not far from Hamburg, offered to teach the young man the rudiments of the mercantile life. Father never talked much of this first encounter with the business world, and the only memories that he cared to recall dealt, curiously, not with his experiences as apprentice, but with two American cousins who were in a school for foreign boys in Altona, near-by—sons of his mother's favorite brother, Ludolf. From their Grandmother Harrison's Virginia farm, a faithful old Negro slave had smuggled the boys through the Union lines to Baltimore where their father had shipped them to Hamburg for a taste of German schooling. And here they were, bringing firsthand word of this legendary land beyond three thousand miles of ocean. To a German boy, indeed, they would seem America incarnate, demonstrating in their own charming and cultivated persons what not one German in a hundred imagined, that everything in America was not wilderness, gold rush and whooping red men.

What should have struck Hermann instantly—and I doubt if it did—was that these sons of a German father were not German boys;

14

they were American boys, Virginia boys, who had no interest in kings and were not impressed by the proud family tradition of their Uncle Adolf's meetings with his sovereign. Their heroes were Robert E. Lee and "Stonewall" Jackson.

The Gunther boys—the *Umlaut* had faded quickly in the American air—brought Father his first infusion of the American spirit. What Uncle Anton, tall and straight under his beaver hat, gave him was something with which that spirit was forever at war. Anton had the dictatorial strain which was conspicuous in Charlotte, without the genuine love which served, when she willed, to blunt its edge. At Harburg, I take it, Uncle Anton drummed into my father whatever his mother had not already taught him of that respect for authority, that awe of seniority, position and power, which he retained throughout his life, and blindly passed on to his sons.

– 4 –

While Hermann was discovering America through the eyes of his attractive American cousins, his mother was experiencing emotional upheavals that were to have profound effects in her son's life.

For almost seventy years, I have assumed that the wistful melancholy (*Wehmut* is the word) that lay always in Charlotte Hagedorn's dark eyes, reflected her undying devotion to her husband, and that I was seeing in them an unassuageable grief like Victoria's for Albert. But the packet of letters in microscopic German script that lies before me as I write tells a different story. For they are love letters, written by one of the outstanding German statesmen of the time, whose devotion she obviously reciprocated.

Dr. Leonhardt was Hanoverian Minister of Justice, a man of fifty, and she was thirty-nine when, six years after her husband's death, they spent a week together in the little mountain village of Ballenstedt in the Harz Mountains. Were her daughters with her? I do not know. I know only that the letters that Leonhardt wrote her in the years that followed glow with the memory of the happiness they knew together that week.

In a rare moment of confidence, Charlotte, indeed, once told her younger daughter Alma—more perceptive than her sister Elsbeth—that her relationship with Leonhardt had been purely *seelisch*, a word which the French might adequately reproduce as *spirituel* but English can only flounder over in terms of a mixture of "intellectual" and "spiritual," faintly illuminated by conceptions generally associated with religion. But, Charlotte added, there was no use saying so. Nobody would understand, anyway, or believe it.

The statesman's letters to his "precious Charlotte" are not at all platonic.

Like an infatuated boy, he plans playfully to join Charlotte on the Rhine where she is visiting relatives. "What would I care about your Aunt Marie being around? I can, if necessary, be cold—or seem so." Even if he should not appear, "you can't be sure that, one of these days, I may not, unbeknownst to you, spend a day in your close proximity. You don't know what an unusual, masochistic fellow I am!" But he dismisses the idea. "Fugitive thoughts, presaging fugitive joy. Farewell, my precious friend."

In the house in the country where Leonhardt is staying, a woman tells him that a certain old nobleman who has met Charlotte has admitted that she has given his antique heart a painful jolt. "Is he any happier," Leonhardt writes, "than he who must bleed to death? And who would dare complain? Who ordered the old man to step into your ring if he could not face your magic? Every man suffers his prescribed destiny. Happy is he who has memories of joyous moments." Was she angry with him at this reference? "Surely not. From me you cannot expect polite and tepid letters. Not from me, dear Charlotte! I am glad beyond measure that those last days are a happy memory for you too. I thank you again for your love. As I strive to keep my chin up, do you so, too, my dear, dear Charlotte!"

Two years after their week together in the mountains, Ballenstedt draws him back. "I am living in memories now," he writes, "going my lonely way; drowning in memories. You would think that the problems of my work would absorb my thoughts, but it is not so.

From the first moment of the day to the last, the stream of my thinking is the same!

> " 'Joy-filled
> And sorrow-filled,
> In thought absorbed . . .' "

He does not finish the quotation of Klärchen's song in Goethe's *Egmont*, leaving it to Charlotte to fill in the lines describing the ups and downs of the love-seized heart; one instant "to high heaven jubilant," the next "to death itself depressed," to the final summation:

> " 'Happy alone
> Is the being that loves.' "

He has found no joy, he writes, in his effort to recapture at Ballenstedt some of the happiness he had experienced there with Charlotte. Things had been so different, two years before! How beautiful everything might be "if we had only willed things otherwise and been able to make a great decision. We might all have been happy. . . ."

Had they met at Ballenstedt, removed from public or private responsibilities, to talk, perhaps, about his determination to divorce his wife and marry Charlotte? If it was there that he urged his purpose, so startling in the social group in which they both moved, in any social group, indeed, in that time, he got nowhere with it. Charlotte would not suffer the disruption of his family life, the blight upon her friend's wife—her friend, too, of long standing—and upon the four Leonhardt children. No, it could not be. Apart from her love for Leonhardt, her decision must have fairly torn her apart, since he could have given her security and ease, as well as the social eminence that meant so much to her.

Her decision tore him too. "Now I am back in the flatlands," he writes on his return home, "and whither my thoughts wander, you, my dear Charlotte, know. Who is the poor, forsaken one? You or I?" His letters glow with suppressed emotion. Try as he would to be casual, the emotion he tries to suppress speaks between the lines. He returns to the "joy-filled and sorrow-filled" theme, to say by indirection what he dares not utter, and asks by intimation: Might Charlotte not, after all, relent? She showed no signs of it.

I wonder whether Leonhardt didn't, in fact, have a lucky escape? Intelligent, charming and loving as she was, his Egeria was a good deal of a terror in the home. Her temper was like the blast of an electric torch. Far from having any sense, moreover, of a fault that required disciplined correction, she took pride in it as a kind of natural phenomenon, like Vesuvius or Niagara Falls. Her daughters shared her feeling about it and, sixty years later, still spoke of it with the awe with which the children of Israel regarded the wrath of Jehovah. Her word was law in the little house in Hanover, and the walls rocked if any of the children seemed to transgress it. Her self-will, indeed, was straight in line of descent from Lucifer himself; and when it was crossed she was as hard as the star he fell on when Jehovah himself lost his temper and threw him over the parapet. Her own fate, in the end, was to prove chillingly like the archangel's.

Yet, with all the temper and self-will, Charlotte had what her generation called "character." That is, she put first things first and stood by her judgments. Dr. Leonhardt was not the only one whom the beautiful widow refused to marry. There was a wealthy widower, an industrialist in Würtemberg, her brother Ludolf's closest friend, who, year after year, had been vainly pleading his suit. Like Dr. Leonhardt, he could have given her every comfort, and the scope for her intelligence and her social gifts which she hungered for. But her heart, I am sure, was Leonhardt's. Even if she had been fancy-free, I am convinced that she would have hesitated to let the expectation of personal happiness, with its own obligations and diversions, keep her from the full execution of the duty she owed her children. So she chose to maintain her home on her husband's inherited slim share of his family's business enterprises and the meager pension that the government gave her.

Charlotte's sacrifice was in accordance with the highest moral standards of her generation. But I wonder whether life might not have been a great deal happier for my father and mother, my brothers and sisters and myself, not to speak of the Aunts, if Grandmother had married Dr. Leonhardt or her South German suitor?

Her passionate nature found its only outlet in her devotion to her son, and he responded with a fervor that neither time nor distance would ever cool.

CHAPTER THREE

WHEN Father came to America, he carried his mother, in essence, with him. She was at his side as he sat on his stool in the dingy office of Schepeler & Co.; she was with him at the table in Frau Pellerin's boardinghouse; she was with him as he wandered disconsolately up and down Brooklyn's Fulton Street in the January cold and on over to Fort Greene Park, to find balm for his homesickness in dreams of her. She was with him by day and by night; she was with him at work and at play. She was with him as he walked under the bare trees of Portland Avenue, one Sunday afternoon, to present the letter of introduction that Captain Schwensen had given him.

– 2 –

Two pretty girls in their teens peered out of a second-story window in a substantial square brick house * with a mansard roof, and fluttered as the slender gentleman with the silken moustache and long cheek whiskers opened the gate in the iron picket fence and climbed the front stoop. Their names were Anna and Alwine, but they had been reading a sentimental novel whose lovely heroine rejoiced in the name of Jacquelena, and, in tearful devotion to the peerless one, the

---

* By a friendly trick of fate, the house has survived the changes of the years and the invasion of public service plants and apartment houses, just east of the Flatbush Avenue station of the Interborough Rapid Transit. Four-square in its wide yard, with its covered porch, it stands, shaded by ailanthus trees descended, perhaps, from those that shaded it in the sixties when the Schwedlers lived there. The etched glass of the period is still in the stately, walnut-stained front door.

two girls had split the name between them. Venie, the younger, was "Jacquie," Anna was "Lena." They remained "Jacquie" and "Lena" to each other for the rest of their lives.

"I wonder who it can be?" asked "Lena," mindful that the villain was always dark and, the darker the villainy, the blacker the hair, and this man's tonsorial adornments were jet. "Lena" was sixteen.

"Jacquie," being three years younger, liked 'em young and blond. "Oh, probably just another one of Father's tedious old sea captains." Masters of vessels coming into New York Harbor from German ports had a way of coming to call on the publisher of the *New Yorker Demokrat*.

The doorbell jangled. The girls looked at the card the German maid brought up. "Hermann Hagedorn." The gentleman had a letter of introduction to Herr Schwedler, and he was presenting it on his first Sunday in the New World.

– 3 –

Friedrich Schwedler was a Forty-Eighter; that is, he had taken part in the German revolutionary movement of 1848. It had actually been a European movement, begun with the overthrow of France's last Bourbon king, Louis Philippe, but had achieved meaning as a struggle for liberation mainly through the brilliance and courage of a small but devoted band of German intellectuals. The movement had come to nothing, having no leadership comparable to that of the tough-minded reactionary, Bismarck, beginning, even at thirty-three, to weave the threads of empire. There had been wholesale arrests and wild flights across a dozen borders.

The Schwedlers, cloth merchants in Leipzig, had all been involved. How deeply, I don't know, but, before the year ended, the King of Saxony's police were after them. One of Friedrich's brothers was condemned to death, but escaped in the time-honored fashion of romantic fiction by changing clothes with his wife when she visited him in prison. All took to their heels.

I have never been able to think of Friedrich Schwedler as a revolu-

21

tionary. If he was active in the uprising at all, I am sure he was ineffective, an enthusiastic but inept zealot getting in the way of the real conspirators and captains; and I note that he took time off that year to get married. That he loved liberty and was willing to suffer for it, I know; and it is a part, not of the German but of the American record, that he could fight for it, and fight well.

Sometime in 1851, Friedrich joined the magnificent migration of German liberals to America, the richest gift that a senile feudalism in Europe had made to the New World since the 1630's.

A daguerreotype, evidently made just preceding Friedrich's departure for America, fairly quivers with drama. It shows Friedrich and Marie Schwedler with their two-year-old Anna; Marie, pouting and sullen; Friedrich, angry, too, and stubbornly determined. Marie, twenty years old, is aware that she is going to have another baby and clearly does not think much of the idea of her husband's going off to America and leaving her, and her two infants, a year later, to make the six weeks' crossing in a sailing vessel by themselves. Fritz, thirty-three, thinks she is a naughty child and he is going to take the ship for New York, whatever she says.

Behind Marie's pout is an elemental resentment against this good, able and, on the whole, kindly man. The marriage, I suspect, had been arranged by her thrifty North German parents, who saw a good match in this well-to-do representative of a noted textile firm, coming to isolated, eighteenth century Anklam to get orders from the retailers.

Fritz took ship for New York as he was determined to do. Pending the arrival of what funds he might receive from the liquidation of the family textile business, he taught piano. He was, actually, a businessman only incidentally. At heart and by avocation, he was a musician, who had studied under Liszt, been a music critic on a Leipzig newspaper, known Wagner in his early obscurity, and played duets with Mendelssohn.

Marie joined him with little Anna and a second girl-baby, the following year. She must have been enchanting in the trim, close-fitting garments of the time, her rosy, oval face framed in coal-black hair, parted in the middle of her forehead and tied back over her ears. Fritz adored her, as well he might. Marie, on her side, never got beyond toleration.

– 4 –

The sullen face of the young mother in the daguerreotype does not do justice to the woman she actually was, or, in the course of the years, became. Marie Stropp was born of a line of parsons, and kept her spiritual moorings through good and evil fortune. She had a thoughtful, realistic mind and loved poetry, not as an escape but as illumination. Goethe was her idol and she made his philosophy of self-discipline and renunciation her own.

If the daguerreotype was unjust to Marie it was no less misleading in regard to her husband. A photograph, made, I should guess, in the middle 1860's, reveals a fighter who knows what he is fighting for and who expects to win. It explains why Friedrich Schwedler should have dared to imagine that he, a newcomer to America, and a German idealist out of the storybooks, could run a successful newspaper in the turbulent, raucous New York of the 1850's, even a paper printed in the German language. The fact is, of course, that that was exactly what he did.

The leading New York German-language daily, the *Staatszeitung*, was Democratic, and inclined to appease the South. That was treason against humanity to Fritz Schwedler, as it was to such men as Carl Schurz and the other Forty-Eighters, who were abolitionists to a man. They wanted to bring the German-American elements into the newly established Republican Party, and needed an organ which already had some circulation in the Middle West where the German-Americans were an important political factor. Whether they backed my grandfather financially I don't know, but, in some way, possibly out of his share of the family textile business, he acquired control, in 1856 or 1857, of the daily *New Yorker Demokrat*, established ten years before. He retained the name, since, in the truest sense, he and his friends were democrats—but followed the policy of the dynamic, new Republican Party. With the daily, he bought its weekly publication, *Der Beobachter am Hudson,* which had considerable circulation among the Germans west of the Alleghenies.

Friedrich printed and published the papers in two adjoining houses on Chatham Square. In the dingy, helter-skelter offices, scrubwomen were not tolerated and a broom was regarded as an unnecessary luxury; but the papers published there were models of order and decorum. By present-day standards they were heavy, even dull. A single paragraph might run three-quarters of a column; and the reader, diving into a sentence, would have to be a strong underwater swimmer if, in Mark Twain's phrase, he were to come out at the other end "with the verb in his mouth"; but, for a generation that took its papers seriously, there was solid substance to feed on. With sympathy and imagination the paper sought to meet the needs of the Germans in exile, reminding them of the best of their German heritage, stimulating their thinking, and holding them to their highest as American citizens. It was leadership of an exceptional quality, and in the highest tradition of nineteenth century liberalism.

It was not long before the *Demokrat* became a significant factor in American social and political life. It was the editorial page that made it so. Friedrich's mild-mannered exterior was deceptive. In the campaign of 1860, the *Demokrat* fought for Lincoln with a singularly clear appreciation of the basic principles involved and the special significance of Lincoln's personality. An editorial that it published, late in October, 1860, however, must have made many readers wonder what madness had seized Herr Schwedler's generally sane mind; for it was nothing less than an appeal to the women of German households to come out and take part in the fight against slavery. "We Republicans recognize in women, and especially in German women, our natural allies."

To summon women, and, above all, German women, into the political arena, took both vision and courage in the autumn of 1860. There was, in fact, plenty of both in the musty office of the *Demokrat*, that October. An editorial commenting on the increasing deadliness of the weapons of war suggested the desirability of pre-

24

venting "henceforth and forever such vast destruction of human life"; but the sturdy fighter for liberty hoped it wouldn't happen quite yet, "not until the people of Europe shall have achieved their freedom, and the civilized world an international people's court of justice."

Not bad for October 27th, 1860!

A week later, Abraham Lincoln was elected President, and, three months after, Friedrich Schwedler had a moment of recognition such as has come to few newspaper publishers anywhere. The President-elect sent word to him, during his stopover in New York on his way to his inauguration, inviting him to call upon him at the Astor House.

It was on the afternoon of February 20th, 1861. In a room heavy with black walnut furniture, ottomans, lounges and elaborate hangings, relieved only by a bunch of gay flowers on a table and a fire burning brightly in the grate, a tired but resolute President-elect shook the hands of a steady stream of supporters, and shook them with such heartiness that observers wondered how he survived. The reporter of the New York *Herald* spoke of the "plain, straightforward, honest face, so full of deep, earnest thought, of direct singleness of purpose, of thorough purity of motive and patriotic impulse"; but not everyone saw the prospective President in so appreciative a mood. Democratic newspapers which had supported Stephen A. Douglas and appeasement were caustic, and painted a mountebank with frivolous jests on his lips.

What the Saxon idealist saw that afternoon was his life's one and only hero. Abraham Lincoln had invited him to come, and he came, I suspect, walking on air. The President-elect thanked him for the support the *Demokrat* had given him in the campaign. It had helped, he said, to turn the tide in the Middle West, where most of the German-Americans were and where the weekly edition had many readers.

That, and a handclasp, was all there was, so far as I know. But it was enough to last Friedrich Schwedler for the rest of a very long life.

CHAPTER FOUR

THE parlor in which Herr Schwedler received the lean Hanoverian
with the sallow brow, dark eyes and prodigious Dundrearys, was
high-ceilinged, with an impressive sculptured white marble mantel-
piece. The tall, double-hung windows, reaching from floor to ceiling,
opening on a covered veranda, gave the room a bright appearance
even in midwinter. Between the two, facing the street, a gilt-framed
pier glass reflected the Gilded Age. On one of the walls a print of
Gustave Doré's "Peace," with a flat, gilded frame, decorated with a
Greek design, showed a flock of sheep placidly passing down a village
street, men and women at ease and children playing. On another
wall an oil painting revealed Lake Lucerne as darker and more
mysterious than it seemed to most travelers. On still another was a
dramatic scene from Shakespeare's *Measure for Measure*, painted on
the base of an oval metal tray. On a little ebony cabinet was a white
marble bust of Goethe. The newcomer would note that the Schwedlers were people of cultivation and good taste.

I have no idea what Father and Herr Schwedler talked about.
They were, at heart, antagonists; the younger conservative, the elder
a liberal; the younger a monarchist, the elder a republican (not only
in the political meaning of the word). Sooner or later, I am sure,
they talked of the recent political developments in the antiquated
agglomeration of independent kingdoms, duchies, principalities and

free cities which were Bismarck's pawns in his game of union and empire.

I suspect that, being by this time a good newspaperman, Herr Schwedler pumped his caller. If Prussia made war on Austria, what was the sentiment in Hanover toward an alliance with Austria, to block Bismarck's purpose? The young man would see the big picture and reveal a divided mind. He wanted to see his country maintain her freedom, of course, and yet . . . those self-centered, fenced-in little states, each with its strutting sovereign, its self-important officials, its petty court, were as out-of-date as postilions. Realism dictated, if not empire for Germany, at least unity. The German people, too long the pawns of the great Powers, their soil too long the battleground of contending armies, needed the surrender of petty prerogatives and parochial points of view and a sense of a common national life.

Germans abroad felt the need of a united and powerful Germany almost more than the Germans at home. A Britisher abroad was somebody; a Frenchman, an Austrian, a Russian was somebody; a Norwegian or a Dane was a man with a nation behind him. But what was a Hanoverian, a Saxon, a citizen of the free city of Lübeck or a subject of the Grand Duke of Sachsen-Coburg-Gotha?

All these matters were in Father's mind. He tended to see virtue in power and to respect a man like Bismarck who used it for ends which, if you were a German, seemed so obviously praiseworthy.

Herr Schwedler was not thinking of himself as a German. He was an American and his thinking marched from different premises.

Both being gentlemen, I assume that they let what argument there may have been subside in the ever-convenient conclusion that there was much to be said on both sides of the question.

Or, perhaps, Grandmother entered the parlor, in soft black silk, as beseemed a matron who was all of thirty-five, followed by the German maid bearing a tray with a pot of coffee and a pitcher of hot milk, followed in turn by Annie and Venie, all eyes and ears, bringing in the *Butterkuchen* and the apple cake.

27

There would be no more politics; only polite personal queries, deepening in interest as the caller's background unfolded. His father? A crown counselor, a public prosecutor, a *Landsyndikus?* Dead six years? Alas! A young man would miss a father. There had been a friend who had been a father to him? *Excellenz* Leonhardt? Herr Schwedler would recognize the name.

The girls, meanwhile, would be a-flutter from top to toe. An "elderly sea-captain"? "Jacquie" would do a little quick arithmetic: thirteen, when his father died, only six years ago. Why, he was just a boy! Only three years older than "Lena"! And such sad, sad eyes!

I am sure that, as Father descended the stoop of the Schwedler house, he felt less lonely than he had felt at any time since he had left home.

– 2 –

Determined to establish Prussia's predominance over Austria, Bismarck declared war on his nation's closest ally. Hanover, abutting Prussia on the west and conscious that she was next on Bismarck's program, plumped for the Austrian side, which offered her at least a fighting chance of maintaining her independence.

In the blind king's rickety and doomed domain, Charlotte and her friend breathlessly watched while the brilliant gambler in Berlin played his cards and pushed Leonhardt himself into new and wholly unexpected responsibilities. Bismarck was drawing his lines for a war with France that should consolidate the scattered little states into a nation, and wanted no disgruntled irredentists on his flank. In a move to soften the resentment of the people of the conquered province, Bismarck persuaded the venerable King William to offer Leonhardt the portfolio of Prussian Minister of Justice.

Leonhardt demurs. He knows what he must expect both from the Prussian politicians, who will resent the intrusion of a representative of a conquered people, and from the Hanoverians who will accuse him of having sold out to the enemy. What he really wants, he writes Charlotte, is to live in the country, feed the cows and the chickens and periodically lift the lids off the pots in the kitchen to see what is cooking.

But Bismarck had other ideas, and arranged an audience for him with the King. "I told him candidly with what grave doubts I looked upon his summons," Leonhardt writes Charlotte. "The King did not question my doubts, or the difficulties awaiting me. He recognized, moreover, what a commotion my appointment would stir up, but, he said, he was prepared for it."

"Regard what has come to you as divine Providence," says the King, piously. The words have a "tranquillizing effect" on Leonhardt's apprehensions and help him make up his mind. "And so I must enter upon my difficult task," he writes Charlotte. "Farewell, and pray for me."

It was, indeed, farewell. Now, Charlotte knew, there would be no reconsideration of her hard decision. The scandal of a divorce would now be no mere personal matter; it would be treason.

The trouble the new minister had anticipated came in full measure. Had Prussia annexed Hanover, or had Hanover annexed Prussia? asked the Berlin press angrily. The Hanoverian press, too, was bitter. "Harried, fatigued, nervous, agitated, in deep depression, I sit in the palatial splendor of my ministerial office and think how happy I would be, before the stove in your room and drawing from you deep drafts of new life. Overwhelmed with honors, lifted to dizzy heights, treated with reverence, praised to the skies, I think— and how often!—how much sweeter it was when we wandered together among the Harz hills. Oh, if only for a short time I might see you quietly, alone, and talk with you! How much, precious friend, I have to tell you! Every free moment belongs to you!"

Charlotte asked whether, in the glamour of his high post, he would not be forgetting her. "How could I?" he replied. "You know that could not be. My feeling for you will never change and will end only when everything ends."

29

Charlotte, I am sure, could have said the same. For him at fifty-two, for her at forty-one, the words of the Richard Strauss song, "Die Georgine," were true:

> "Ob spät, ob früh, es ist dasselbe Entzücken,
> Und derselbe Schmerz . . ."

For both, love, though it bloomed in autumn, had the rapture of love blossoming in spring; the rapture, and the pain.

CHAPTER FIVE

WHILE the curtain was descending upon his mother's romance, Father was calling at frequent intervals on the Schwedler girls in the house on Portland Avenue. Alwine, the younger ("Venie" for short, to all except "Lena"), was a vivacious young flirt, all romance and dancing blue eyes. Annie was as lovely, but grave, her eyes steadier and deeper; romantic, too, but rich in reserves of ancestral wisdom. Both Annie and Venie spoke German as a natural mother tongue—not the barbarous, if amusing, patois of Saxony, or the worse hodgepodge of German and English, common among many Germans in America, but the fine, literary German which their parents spoke. They could have passed for German anywhere in Germany, but they had been in America since Annie was two and Venie a baby, and they were to all intents and purposes American. All their friends had a German background, but it was English that they chattered together. And when they thought of their country, it was America that was in their minds.

I suppose it was the impulse behind their migration, made incandescent by the bitter struggle against slavery and dramatized for them by their father's part in it, which, with Annie and Venie, hastened the process of Americanization. Their father and mother, moreover, never looked back. They had come to America for something their own country could not give them and they could not live without, freedom, and they had found it. What, in comparison, was race or soil or blood?

It was a friendly home to which the Schwedlers periodically welcomed the dark stranger from overseas. They discerned shortly that he was mature beyond his nineteen years, but nowhere near as settled as he looked. A charming modesty was coupled with the assurance of a young man who has done well so far and expects to do much better. He knew how to play with abandon and, if he lacked the sense of humor which can turn the laugh inward and is the ultimate balance wheel, he enjoyed a good story and could take a practical joke on himself as though he liked it.

The girls—and their elders, too—found him excellent company. He talked well, never too much and, unlike many young men of brains, kept no dogmas to bark at the unwary. He enjoyed good food —and it was delectable at the Schwedlers'—and drank his wine in moderation. He had manners, moreover, and that quality, better than manners, which is courtesy, and comes from the heart and not from the dancing master.

Venie fell head over heels in love with him and got over it when she recognized that she was really not in his line of vision at all. Annie was much more deliberate; but, when she finally tumbled, there was no getting over it for her, this side of Judgment Day.

My grandfather, I am sure, never realized, until he was told, that this bewhiskered youth had any other than a social interest in the Schwedler home. Friedrich Schwedler was deep in reconstruction politics in the *Demokrat*, backing the Republicans, right or wrong— and they were generally wrong—convinced that the party of Abraham Lincoln, emancipation and Appomattox was the custodian of all the virtues, and the Democrats, the Devil's dependable allies.

My grandmother, having no public duties to perform, could concentrate on personal relationships. She liked this able, maturing Hanoverian, who, in spite of his truncated education, was so obviously a cultivated man. And she was enough of an artist to enjoy the outward graces of his masculinity. Grandmother, at thirty-seven, was away beyond the age at which mothers were supposed to dance, but she enjoyed watching young people in the dizzy whirl of the German waltz or the mingled formality and abandon of the lanciers. Father put dignity into his dancing. He seemed never to forget that dancing was not merely an opportunity to embrace a pretty girl, but an art.

Grandmother liked that. But, as matters began to look serious between Annie and this self-assured young man, I can see her lips pucker and her blue eyes focus sharply as she watched him, thinking, "Young man, what have you got inside?" Grandmother had few illusions about life in general and none whatever about men. How deeply she looked into her elder daughter's suitor, I have no way of knowing, or how much she saw of the weaknesses that were there. But I know that she interposed no obstacle to the course of true love and, when the Schwedlers were abroad in 1869 to visit the Paris Exposition, they made a point of calling on *Frau Landsyndikus* Hagedorn in Hanover.

– 4 –

I should like to have been at that meeting, when the two women— one just below, the other just above the forty mark—dressed in their best, with billowy skirts and tight-fitting, buttoned bodices, turned their penetrating eyes on each other, exchanging casual remarks over the *Kaffeekuchen*, and wanting to tear each other's hair out.

"What will this self-assured woman with the masterful features and the sentimental eyes do to my daughter?" Grandmother Schwedler may well have asked herself.

"Who are these people, anyway?" Grandmother Hagedorn, I know, did ask herself. "What are their family connections, their background, their position? Revolutionaries, rebels against authority, fugitives from justice, refugees, without recognizable background or social connections. What is this little man with the dreamy blue eyes? A newspaper publisher? A journalist; probably a two-penny hack! And this girl? Pretty enough and well mannered—on the surface. But what does she know? Has her mother taught her anything? This free America, this equality, this barbarism, with no sense of class and social position. . . ."

Some way like this, I am sure, ran Charlotte's thoughts as she welcomed her guests from America. "This mother, this father, this girl, are trying to hook my son! That is clear. Well, I shall see about that!"

Storms raged in her, though, on the surface, she was urbanity itself, indicating with the most gracious of gestures the right-hand corner of the sofa—sacred place of honor—for Frau Schwedler, and directing interested queries to her husband about newspaper publishing in New York, with philosophic comments on the sacred mission of journalism to guide and instruct the ignorant masses.

I am certain that she did not fool Grandmother Schwedler for a minute, or Grandfather, either.

Charlotte's daughters played their assigned parts, reflecting their mother's outwardly gracious hospitality, fluttering around the guests from America—the short, wiry Elsbeth with the thin lips and snapping eyes, just twenty-one; the taller, dramatic Alma, two years younger, all stateliness, poses and sugar. They entertained Annie and Venie excitedly and, I suspect, a little fulsomely. I have an idea they really liked the Schwedler girls (who were easy to like, with their attractive American clothes, their good looks and generous, open ways) and, when they had gone, cried *reizend!* and *entzückend!*— charming, entrancing; and I am just as sure that they hurriedly toned down their expressions of pleasure under their mother's sultry gaze.

Grandmother Hagedorn's house was rich in that kind of theater.

- 5 -

The determination of the high-spirited lady that her son should not marry the girl he was in love with was no passing mood of an emotional woman, which might be trusted to peter out in lamentation and self-pity. It was part of the Günther strain that you not merely wept or raged, you did something about it. She knew enough about strategy to know that you can't beat somebody with nobody. So she picked another somebody.

The young woman she chose was, so far as I ever knew, somebody only by courtesy—a big, raw-boned girl named Bertha, with a face like a horse and a tongue that murdered the German language in the best Swabian tradition. But to Grandmother she seemed ideal. She had not only the domestic virtues—which, no one could gainsay, were also Anna Schwedler's—but she was the daughter of Grandmother's old admirer, the South German industrialist, and might anticipate a tidy fortune when her father's time was up. Most important of all, she was Charlotte Hagedorn's own creature, who could be depended on to flutter or lie still, as she was told, think what her mother-in-law wanted her to think, and obey orders before they were uttered.

Father knew the fair Bertha. Her family had a way of coming in a body to visit the Hagedorns, arriving invariably by a train that reached Hanover at three in the morning, expecting to be met at the station, and always staying longer than they were expected to stay. But none of those things bothered Grandmother. It was Hermann who had had to meet the trains.

I don't know what negotiations went on between Grandmother and her adoring industrialist, but Bertha proved willing. As for Father, Grandmother knew the hold she had on him, through his conscience and his sense of duty.

The battle was on.

Whether Grandmother sent for Father, or Father went to see his mother on his own initiative to overcome her opposition to his courtship of Anna Schwedler, I don't know. I know only that, in the summer of 1870, he was in Germany. I don't know whether his mother invited the equine Bertha to Hanover, or tried to persuade Hermann to see her in Stuttgart. All I know is that his response to his mother was determinedly negative. The anti-Anna, pro-Bertha campaign left scars behind it, but no records, except the few hints that Mother gave me. Knowing something of my grandmother and more about my father, however, I am sure that there was noise and there were tears, with the Günther temper finally in eruption, and Elsbeth and Alma tiptoeing around, shocked, solicitous, tearful, thrilled at the drama; and hurrying out, at the first opportunity, to share the details volubly with their friends.

There is only one thing about that struggle that I am sure of and that is, that, in order to take the edge off his defiance of the will hitherto regarded as sacrosanct, Father made promises which subsequently he could not keep. He may have told his mother that, within a certain period, he would return to Germany with whatever family God had given him, and settle down somewhere not too remote from the matriarchal eye.

Before Father bade her farewell, to return to America and the girl he loved, his mother, I am sure, was all tenderness and Christian renunciation; and I am equally sure that, in the days and weeks of brooding that followed, she made up her mind that it was she and not Anna Schwedler who would rule her son's heart and home.

Father arrived back in New York late in September, and took the first train he could get north to Lake George, where the Schwedlers were spending the summer. He and Annie became engaged on the closing day of the month.

– 6 –

That summer was notable in the family history, also, for a psychological catalysis that affected the future course of Father's life and the lives of his wife and every one of their children.

Living in Hanover, that epochal summer, Father experienced, at first hand, the Franco-Prussian War: the doctored telegram that precipitated the conflict, the enthusiasm of the mobilization of armies, in Hanover and elsewhere, the sudden thrust into France, the victories on victories. Six weeks from the declaration of war to the surrender of the French armies and of the Emperor himself! In all history had there ever been so swift, so glorious a triumph?

Father saw the figure of the Iron Chancellor, Bismarck, grow that summer to mythical proportions as the shaper and maker of a German nation. He saw the end of the ignominious insignificance among the nations of the world, of twenty-odd petty, impotent states, and the emergence of an empire that had proved its right, by the immemorial test of armed might, to assert itself on an equality with other empires whose word was law over vast territories, and whose wealth and splendor dominated the imagination and the political action even of nations not directly under her sway.

Father saw those things, seeing not only Bismarck but the Hohenzollerns—the venerable Prussian King William and his able and attractive son, the Crown Prince Frederick—as the instruments of a great destiny, the fashioners of a great future. Whatever allegiance he may have retained to the Hanoverian kingdom that Prussia absorbed, and to its exiled king, faded forever in the fierce blaze of the nationalistic enthusiasm that took possession of him. His imagination was seized by the picture of German power, German glory, German splendor, and subconsciously identified with it everything that had been part of his life since his boyhood—German virtue, German piety, German song—to make a single, glamorous and compelling object of idolatry—*Deutschland*.

– 7 –

Father's impassioned discovery that he had a country cannot have fallen lightly on the heart and mind of his prospective father-in-law. To Father, Bismarck was the German hero of heroes; to Friedrich Schwedler, he was anathema. In the house on Portland Avenue, Abraham Lincoln symbolically confronted the man of "blood and iron."

I don't know what arguments passed back and forth in that sunny parlor. I suspect that both, being men of ideals coupled with sound sense, recognized that their differences were so profound that no

37

words would ever bridge them, and talked of the weather and the newest German comedy at the Irving Place Theatre, and the future, if any, of the petroleum industry on which Herr Schwedler's future son-in-law was depending to keep the budget balanced in the home that he and Annie were beginning to dream about.

– 8 –

They were married in front of the white marble fireplace in Portland Avenue the middle of May, 1872, with all the mixture of frolic and solemnity that was as traditional in Saxony as in Hanover, the long-drawn Lutheran marriage service, sermon and all, followed by the elaborate, ten-course dinner, with a different wine for each course, interminable speeches, sly references to possible offspring, and *Hoch sollen sie leben!* sung with more and more gusto as the evening advanced.

Of Mother, that day, I can be sure only of her demure beauty and her shining eyes, with the tears ever imminent and never falling; of Father, only of his outward grace and inner gravity; and, in both, a passionate love and a sharp sense of responsibility to God and to each other.

In Hanover, Father's mother darkly brooded, unreconciled. Years after, she said that that day had been the unhappiest of her life.

– 9 –

Was it Father's brilliant idea to invite his sister Elsbeth to the wedding, to help in the preparations and stay on afterward, or was it his mother's? Perhaps there were hints which Father, already a little uneasy in his mind, could not resist. His mother, no doubt, felt that she must have someone in the new household who represented her point of view. There were ways of doing things—her ways —and this unwelcome daughter-in-law-to-be might as well learn them at once. So Elsbeth came, with the expectation of staying a year and helping the young couple get settled.

My mother was the most amenable of brides, but she had steel in her spine and she had a mother of her own who knew her business and could fill in whatever chinks remained in the training in domestic economy that she had been giving both girls for years. As for Elsbeth, she was a capable young woman, but, as a plenipotentiary she was no success at all. She never saw the new home, so far as I know. She had all the energy of the Günthers and nothing to spend it on, all the practical sense of the Hagedorns and no philosophy to direct it. She proved to be a busybody and a gossip; she meddled, tried to run everybody; said sharp things and made trouble generally in a social circle which regarded good will not only as good politics but good manners and wanted nothing except to live and let live. Father stood up for her with stubborn loyalty, but he saw well enough that she did not fit into this new world which was rapidly becoming his world, and shipped her home when the wedding was over.

CHAPTER SIX

THE young couple settled down in a little house on Carlton Avenue, not far from the Schwedler home, and scandalized their friends by having a baby a year for four years running, and a fifth after an interval of a further twenty-five months.

The birth certificate of the second of my three sisters indicates a pathetic and futile attempt on Mother's part to assert the loyalty to the American tradition that was in her heart. With a new baby on the way, Father and Mother went to the Centennial Exposition in Philadelphia in the summer of 1876, not dreaming, evidently, of the possibility of a premature delivery. My sister was born in the Trans-Continental Hotel. The exposition had apparently set Mother's patriotic pulse beating as never before, for the doctor's birth certificate gives the baby's name as "Martha Washington Hagedorn." Alas, the name did not stick. When the baby was christened, a few months later, she bore the name of Father's sister, Elsbeth.

Grandmother's spinster daughters were a continuing menace. Elsbeth having failed as an influence, Grandmother Hagedorn sent her second daughter to see that everything was being done as it should be. Alma, who, like her sister, had many excellent qualities of mind and heart, did not fit into the American picture any better than Elsbeth. She was rather handsome, but over-dramatic in her bearing, warmhearted but inclined to be effusive, and clever, but not as clever as she imagined. What made her insufferable to Mother was the way she gushed over Father and waited on him. Father himself didn't like it, and saw that she was making him ridiculous before his friends. He suffered her loyally until her year was up, but I'm sure he joined in the general sigh of relief when she departed.

– 2 –

The visitations of Elsbeth and Alma were the major ordeals of my mother's early married life. But there were others. A year after her marriage her father was taken ill and went abroad for a year with Grandmother and Auntie, leaving the *Demokrat* and the *Beobachter* in care of a conscientious but inexperienced brother-in-law. The panic of 1873 was too much for him, as it was for my grandfather's farsighted but premature ventures in Brooklyn suburban real estate. By the time the Schwedlers returned from Europe, the tidy fortune they had brought over from Leipzig with all that Grandfather had added to it, was swept away, and they were penniless. Grandfather, in his middle fifties, lacked the energy, and perhaps the courage, as he lacked the funds, to engage in any new business, and was satisfied to solicit small-scale advertisements for the paper he had for so many years controlled and directed. My father accepted the responsibility of supplementing the meager pittance that Grandfather managed to earn, and, when that too failed, supported his wife's family, as a matter of course, through good and evil fortune, uncomplainingly, as long as they lived.

He was doing well financially, though he was no longer in petroleum. His Uncle Ludolf in Baltimore, whom he had visited at intervals before his marriage, had told him sapiently that there was "no future in oil" and had persuaded him to go into cotton. Father joined the recently organized New York Cotton Exchange, operating in a single long, narrow room not far from his own office in Pearl Street. The New York business directory which called him a "cotton broker" in the early seventies was shortly referring to him as a "cotton merchant," which was something else. Father was never one to play safe, and was beginning to buy and sell on his own. By the time Grandfather's financial reverses made it necessary for the

41

Schwelders to give up the comfortable Portland Avenue house, Father was in a position to take it over.

– 3 –

He was twenty-eight and establishing himself economically and socially, making lasting friendships in the cotton world, and, with his lovely wife, taking the social position their backgrounds and their social graces merited. There was an exceptional group of German-American families, many of them scions of patrician families of the old free city of Bremen, who were living on Brooklyn Heights, overlooking the East River and the harbor. They all belonged to the German Evangelical Church on Schermerhorn Street, where the women did their share in the *Frauen Verein*, and, Sunday mornings, the men, in Prince Alberts, with their top hats under their pews, dutifully sang *"Lobe den Herren, den mächtigen König der Ehren,"* and listened to dull stretches of Lutheran theology not too closely related to what Republican "stalwarts" were doing in Washington, William M. Tweed was doing in New York, or Otto von Bismarck was doing in the Empire he had so brilliantly and ruthlessly established.

The social life of this German-American "upper crust," as it might be called, naturally reflected the background of the men and women who constituted it. At the dinners which the Vietors and the Achelises, the Hoppenstedts and the Dreiers, the Fleitmanns, the Dommerichs, the Rasmusses, the Lichtensteins and the Spies gave, not only was the food deliciously prepared, in the best German tradition, and the Rhine wine and Moselle the most delicate that importers could provide, but the talk was on a high level. The group was as different in outlook and manner of life from the intellectual revolutionaries of my grandfather's generation as it was from the German tradespeople who ran the grocery stores and the butcher shops. They were given neither to splitting Hegelian hairs nor to joining *Sängerbunde* or swinging on parallel bars at *Turnvereine*. They were men and women of conservative disposition and consid-

42

erable cultivation, who enjoyed good books and good music, and thought nothing of the long journey by horsecar, ferry and again horsecar, to take in a performance of Schiller or Shakespeare (in German) at the Irving Place Theatre, or whatever German opera company came to New York to perform *Tannhäuser* or *Die Hochzeit des Figaro* or, happily, *Die Fledermaus*.

There were whist parties and, for the men, *Skat* evenings; celebrations of anniversaries, dinners and more dinners and occasionally dances at the *Germania*, a large social club which some of the patricians looked down upon as too much on the lower middle class side, but the rest enjoyed for its German atmosphere, and its imported Munich beer.

It is noteworthy that all the gatherings were limited to the "German set." The attractive, socially congenial group was self-contained, and seemed to be content to have it so. The children who came to the heavy, sedate, handsome houses talked German as their native tongue, had German governesses and nurses, ate German food, played with boys and girls who were to all intents and purposes German. The five who were young in the Hagedorn house on Portland Avenue during the seventies were as German as *Apfeltorte*.

– 4 –

In the case of my family there was, indeed, an element, which was unique, working for the perpetuation of a German consciousness and a German culture. That was Grandmother Hagedorn. Gifted with sympathetic understanding and the power to inspire, but prohibited by conscientious scruples and social taboos from using her intelligence to enlarge and enrich the life of the man she loved, she tried to be to her son what she could not permit herself to be to Dr. Leonhardt, clinging to him with a tenacity of love and pride that Father could not resist, and Mother had no defense against.

And defense was needed. From the red brick house that Grandmother had built in the pleasant old university town of Göttingen, she dominated our home. She wrote my father once a week, and once every week he wrote her. Everything that happened in my father's and mother's house came, in a sense, under Charlotte Hagedorn's eye and was subject to her comment. It was not that Father deliberately laid Mother open to Grandmother Hagedorn's penetrating examination. But when a man writes any one individual from four to eight pages once a week he must either be a philosopher, elaborating abstractions, or he must deal in the details of daily living. My father was no philosopher. There was, in consequence, nothing about the household or the children which, sooner or later, his mother did not know.

Grandmother Hagedorn was a masterful person, capable of managing large affairs, with only a house, a garden, and two intimidated daughters at hand to use her executive talents upon. So she exercised them on the household on Portland Avenue. The four-thousand-mile finger was in every pie. The clothes the children wore, the food they ate, their schooling, their friends, nothing was too large, nothing too small, to call forth her minatory injunctions. She sent over nice little German suits for the boys and dresses for the girls, and the poor creatures had to wear them, to the wicked delight of their American playmates. She told my mother her duty and waited for reports to make sure that it was accomplished as she desired it. Twenty-five years later Mother handed my sisters a packet of Grandmother's letters. "Read them," she said quietly, "and then destroy them." The girls read three or four with mounting anger; then, overcome by the famous Günther-plus-Hagedorn temper, threw the lot in the fire in disgust.

Grandmother had never got over her initial anger against this young woman who had defeated her in the one matter that was important to her, and she made no effort to conceal her abiding resentment. "How can you have a single quiet moment," she wrote on one occasion, "knowing that you have robbed me of my son?"

I don't know whether Mother showed that letter to Father. As a rule, letters from Germany were passed from hand to hand, but this one she may have suppressed, for Father's peace of mind. But she did not destroy it.

Mother bore her mother-in-law's remote control with saintly patience. It was not only that, according to the custom of her generation, her husband's mother was a privileged character, to be respected and obeyed, or that she recognized that Charlotte Hagedorn's temper, or even her irritating strain of sentimental melancholy, were not to be overborne by any outburst of independence. Mother had a philosophy. It turned about a proverb I heard from her lips again and again—*Der klügste giebt nach.* The idea that, in any controversy, the one who gives in is the wiser, has a close affinity to the Christian injunctions about turning the other cheek, agreeing with your adversary quickly, and by meekness inheriting the earth. Mother found, I think, that if you didn't make too much of a fuss, things came around, more or less, your way; not altogether, but as much as anyone had a right to expect. She never manipulated hidden strings to make them come; that was not in her nature. She was silent, and waited, and smiled, though often, I am sure, her blood boiled.

It was so she dealt with her mother-in-law, and very definitely, with Father. He had a tender and loyal heart, but, like his mother, a hot temper. The plates would rattle on the table when he brought his fist down with the exclamation (in German, of course), "I should like to know who is master in this house!" Mother never disputed his dominance, but her gentleness, her courageous nonresistance generally overcame him in the end. Not always, alas! I am sure that the course she took with Father was the only one that she, loving and sensitive as she was, could possibly have taken without betraying her own nature, but I am not sure that, by her submission, she did not let Father down and keep him from the growth he might have experienced if she had occasionally let the steel that was in her flash out and thrust home.

CHAPTER SEVEN

IN THE spring of 1880, Father took his family to Germany to spend
a year and a half with his mother.

His friends on the Exchange shook their heads. Father was establishing himself in the cotton world; he was on the way up; he was
making money; and it seemed to them misguided to the point of
folly to cut the web he had for a decade been laboriously spinning,
and absent himself for so long a period. His action seemed all the
more surprising since the man they knew at the India House in
Hanover Square, where the Cotton Exchange was now operating,
was nothing if not hardheaded. They did not know the strain of
sentimentalism that was in his heart.

His mother, no doubt, had been at work on him, reminding him
that she had not seen him for ten years; reminding him too, I gather,
that he had always said he was planning to return to Germany to
live. Perhaps he actually did think of settling definitely in Germany,
for the pull of "the old country" was strong, and he wanted a full
year to look over the ground. I know few of the details of that year,
except that the Schwedlers moved back into the Portland Avenue
house for the time being and Father and Mother and their five children—the eldest, seven; the youngest, not quite two—settled in
Grandmother's big brick house in Göttingen.

– 2 –

Mother was not in a frame of mind to enjoy the beauty of the
old university town or its picturesque environs. She was living with

her husband and children, crowded together in the home of a woman who had hated her and, for all Mother knew, hated her still, and resented her presence. Outwardly loving and gracious though Charlotte may have been, slave to her emotions as she was, her spirit lay over the household like a thundercloud, and no one ever knew when or where the lightning would strike. There was, for Mother, no escaping her, in her own bedroom or even in the garden. Her mother-in-law's personality and her moods projected themselves into every recess. Her customary melancholy hung like a heavy scent in the air, and when, as too frequently happened, it deepened into depression, it filled the house for days and lay upon the spirits of children and grownups alike, like a black fog. With all her piety and sharp moral sense—both, I am convinced, wholly sincere—Grandmother, emerging from her glooms, seemed to have no contrition over the ordeal to which she had subjected those who had to live with her. Like her temper and her pride, she accepted her depressed moods as phenomena of nature and even, I suspect, took pride in them as evidence of personal force.

Elsbeth and Alma were terrified of her disapproval and blasts of temper and did nothing to ease the situation for their brother or his wife, counseling abject submission where only red-hot opposition to an emotional bully could have accomplished anything.

For Mother, that year and a half in Grandmother's home was an ordeal that might have scarred for life a woman with a less equable temperament or one less endowed with inner resources. For she had not only her husband's mother to face and to endure, but his sisters. Elsbeth and Alma were basically good women, fairly saintly, indeed, in the way they suffered their mother's domination, her touchiness, her shifting moods, and her devastating depressions; but their slavish devotion was drained of any joy by their fear of her. Their only outlet for any free and satisfying emotional life was in relation to their brother, and they poured their love out on him in uninhibited sentimentalism.

Like any self-respecting male, Father disliked gush, but he was grateful for his sisters' devotion and hesitated to suggest limits to its expression for fear of hurting their feelings; and feelings, in that household, were easily hurt. When Mother, by a word, revealed her impatience or disgust, Father was instantly on the defensive. The result was a rift which, slight as it might be, held a potential menace, since it revealed Father and his sisters on one side and Mother on the other. Neither Elsbeth nor Alma would have dreamed consciously of separating their brother from his wife by the minutest measure, but he was the one great passion of their lives, as he had become their mother's, and their hunger to possess him wholly was insatiable.

With Father a doubtful ally in her relations with his mother and sisters, Mother and little Annie, going on eight, drew very close to each other. Annie, the eldest of her five, was a mature and responsible child, and kept a motherly eye on the others. She had the kind of intuitive perception that required no explanation of her mother's difficulties in this always tense and too often turbulent household. Mother, I am sure, told her nothing of her relations with the child's grandmother or her aunts; that would have seemed to her disloyal to Father; but, sitting alone together in one of the bedrooms or in the garden, or walking desolately together down the Weender *Chaussée*, without exchanging any words, they would understand each other.

– 3 –

Mother went to coffee parties and dinners with Grandmother and the Aunts, said the correct things and showed a correct interest in the people she met, but their formality was alien to her outgoing nature and she made no lasting friends. Father was restless and journeying hither and yon, looking into business possibilities, but his heart was not really in his investigations. He had felt too keenly the largeness of life in America, the scale of thinking in business and the informality of intercourse in the business world, not to feel impatient with the pettiness in German business methods, and the formality and stuffiness of the merchants and bankers he met. He did not realize how definitely he was on his way to becoming an American.

On the other hand, his mother's pressure on him to settle permanently in Germany with his family was, I am sure, unremitting. It was sharpened, no doubt, by the death, in May of that year, of her friend Leonhardt. They had remained in close correspondence and, year after year, he had let his family spend Christmas Eve alone, while he sat at Charlotte's feet in Göttingen. "How she ever managed to keep this visitor shady from the Göttingen gossip-girls," my sister Irma wrote me, fifty years later, "is beyond me."

With Leonhardt dead, Charlotte would be more dependent than ever on her son for that assurance of devotion which her nature demanded. Her pressure would have been expressed less in direct adjuration than in not-quite-suppressed sighs and eloquent glances out of her soulful eyes, in whispered words of resignation, and, though she was only in her middle fifties, reminders that her lonely life must soon be nearing its end. Itching though he was, I am sure, to get back into the big game on the Exchange, his mother's campaign of unuttered beseechings would tear Father, for he was naïve in many respects, and intensely loving. It would never occur to him that his mother was a selfish, self-centered woman who, as a girl, had been spoiled by too much attention and had never wholly grown up.

If Charlotte was exercising pressure, there was pressure, too, of a wholly different sort, from across the sea. In Göttingen, in April, 1881, Annie was about to celebrate her eighth birthday, and Grandfather Schwedler, known as Opa to the children, took his pen in hand. It was too bad that he could not be with them, he wrote in his microscopic script. How much they would all have to show him and tell him, and how many different things they would want to do with him! "You, my Annie, would say, 'Oh, dear Opa, please play the piano and sing the song about *lieber Augustin*.' Dolfy would say, 'Oh, no, tell us stories,' and Freddie would beg that I play blindman's buff, and Elsie that I play school and Irma that I dance ring-around-a-rosy with her." Well, there was no use quarreling about what he was going to do with them because he couldn't come for his dear little Annie's birthday, anyway. "He has to stay with Oma and *Tante* Venie at 149 Portland Avenue, guarding the house to see that no thieves and no cats come in, and you find everything in perfect order when you come back in the fall with Papa and Mama. My, but we shall all be terribly happy when that time comes! Then, I hope, when there are birthdays, Opa, Oma and *Tante* Venie can be there, too, and clink glasses with you so they ring, and play and dance with you, so it's a delight!"

The tender simplicity of the letter was in sharp contrast to the formality, the sultry mood and the theatrical poses of the Göttingen household. I don't suppose it had the slightest influence in turning the faces of the Hagedorn family westward. But, in a choice between Grandmother Hagedorn and Grandfather Schwedler, I have no question which way the votes of the children would have gone.

–4–

In this first struggle between America and the Fatherland, America won. Father and Mother decided that Germany, as a permanent place of business and a home, was not for them, and, in the autumn of 1881, the family was back in the Portland Avenue house. Another baby was on the way: myself. My journey was stormy and uncertain, and encompassed with tragedy. Whether Father had been too detached from New York to watch over his investments properly, or his perspective had been blurred by his long absence, and his judgment slipped, I don't know, but, before he knew what was happening, he had lost everything he had made—"a fortune," I have been told—and was deep in debt, to boot.

But financial disaster was nothing to the blow that struck the family when, the day before Christmas, lovely little Annie, her mother's confidante, the children's vice-mother, died of pneumonia. The house was filled with preparations for Christmas. The *Weihnachtskuchen*—those delicious crisp brown molasses cookies—were all made, piled deep in flour tins, piled high on platters. The bureau drawers and closets were filled with toys for the children. Anticipation was at its peak. Annie had been sick for no more than a week; she had been the kind of thoughtful child who naturally awakens affection and responds to it; and her death brought the sort of grief that time does not soften. A quarter century later, Grandmother Schwedler said to me, "I grieved over *liebe* Annie as I have grieved over no other loss in life, and I am grieving still."

Father was beside himself, lying for days, wildly sobbing, absorbed in his own loss, forgetting that it was also Mother's, and that she, with a new baby coming in seven months, needed any support he might be able to give her. It was his heritage from his mother, letting itself go; emotionalism, proud of itself and its capacity to feel, opening all the sluice gates. But, I believe, it was also something else. His mother had begged him to stay in Germany. He had thwarted her wish, returned to America, and lost his firstborn. Knowing Father, I am sure it was his conscience more than his inherited emotionalism which tore him so desperately after little Annie's death.

Mother, herself devastated with grief, was unable to rouse his will. He came back to the realities only when Grandmother Schwedler's younger sister, our beloved *Tante* Liese, only a few years older than Mother, told him sharply that he had better pull himself together and give his wife a husband's strength to lean on, if he did not want to lose the unborn baby too.

∽ Part Two ∽

CHAPTER ONE

I CAME the following July.

If anything could partially assuage such a loss as Father and Mother had suffered, it was a new baby. As far back as I can remember there was no sense of desolation in our home, such as must have been in Father's and Mother's hearts, but *"liebe Annie"*—and the two words were invariably linked—was an integral part of our family life. She was never idealized to me, never painted as a paragon. But I came to realize that she must have been an exceptionally loving and lovable creature, sensitive and responsible, as Mother's firstborn *would* be. As long as I can remember, I felt a personal relationship to her, as though we had met in passing, she on her way out of the world, I on my way in.

My first memory, as I have indicated, is of the day, shortly after my fourth birthday, that saw the curtain rise on the second act of the family tragedy.

Father's finances had never recovered from the effects of his misguided defiance of Destiny and the vagaries of the cotton market; and two years after his return to New York he was still barely earning enough to support his family. Business was at a standstill. Competition among the brokers on the Exchange was sharp, and Father, who had dreamed of providing his mother with luxuries in her declining years, was forced to ask her for a loan from her own limited resources. The question of adequate schooling for the older boys, moreover, was becoming acute. Private schools in Brooklyn were expensive and public schools slipshod and, in Father's mind, too much of a melting pot. Father had a good deal of inherited class feeling, and neither he nor Mother shared or had, indeed, been given a chance to learn, the American point of view toward the public school as an agency for preparing boys and girls for life in the American community. There was really no way they could have got it, for they had no American friends; no friends, that is, with enough background of life in the United States or acquaintance with American ideals, to interpret the American way of life.

I don't know who fished out of obscure and poisonous depths the idea of sending my brothers to Göttingen for their education, but I suspect it was Grandmother Hagedorn; and I am sure she missed no argument that might make it seem plausible. The large house; the spacious garden, ideal for growing boys; her daughters, living at home, eager to do everything a mother would want done for the two boys; the excellent *Gymnasium*—the government-directed secondary school in Göttingen; Father's own straitened circumstances and the debts of his financial smash still to be paid—did they not all point to this simple, this ideal solution of an otherwise apparently insoluble problem?

I can imagine the painful hours, weeks and months before the decision was made, but no evidence of that excruciating struggle reached my consciousness. The financial crisis that Father was facing must have been desperate, indeed, to make him consider sending the boys to their grandmother to be educated, and to paralyze the functioning of his feeling for home and family which was his most conspicuous quality. If ever a man knew what a mother meant to a boy and a boy to his mother, Father knew it. How then could he give ear to a project that left out of consideration the instinct of the mother to look after her young, and the need of boys for their mother—not to speak of their father—during their adolescent years? There was yet a third consideration, almost as important as the other two: Grandmother was sixty years old and her daughters were cowed and stuffy old maids without any life apart from hers. How Father could have disregarded these factors, how indeed, after the death of

Annie, he could have brought himself even to suggest to Mother that she surrender her two eldest surviving children to her mother-in-law during their most impressionable years, is beyond me; but how Mother could have acquiesced is beyond me, too.

Incredible as it seems, it happened, and was Grandmother Hagedorn's perfect revenge for that 16th of May, 1872, when Anna Schwedler married her son.

In her heart, I am sure, Mother knew that the project was not only foolish but wicked, though she may not have been able to say so in convincing terms, even to herself; and, being sure, I am thrown back upon my old bewilderment how she could have given her consent. *Der klügste giebt nach?* Was she really wise this time in giving in, avoiding a basic conflict in the faith that, in the long run, the meek inherit the earth? It has always seemed to me that this was the moment, the supreme moment, when she should have put her foot down and said, "Over my dead body!" Why didn't she say it? She had plenty of courage. But conflict was not in her nature.

So it happened that Father took the boys away from their mother, who was all gentleness, sympathy and understanding—not that she was ever soft; you never got away with much, with Mother!—and placed them under the despotic direction of their self-centered, neurotic grandmother and her two daughters, none of whom knew any more of boy nature and the inner tumults and confusions of adolescence than they knew of *The Origin of Species.*

– 2 –

I have been told that Father became an American citizen in order to give the boys the protection of the American flag. He had been, for twenty years, as he was to be again, in a later, darker period, a man without a country. When the kingdom of Hanover had been absorbed by Prussia, he had not sought Prussian citizenship, fearing, perhaps, that the fact that he had left his country partly to avoid military service might lead to a call to service in the armies of Prussia. If he actually became a naturalized American in order that his sons might be under the American eagle in Germany, the irony is bitterly obvious; for he became a citizen at the moment when he was committing the act that would forever keep him from being wholly an American himself, an act that would alienate completely from his American birthright one of the sons he was asking the flag to protect, and leave the other plagued by conflicting voices.

– 3 –

I never heard how violently Grandmother Hagedorn reacted to Father's naturalization. She may not have reacted violently at all. She could afford to acquiesce. She held hostages.

She must have recognized shortly, moreover, how little Father's American citizenship affected his devotion to his fatherland. I remember the day the news came of the death of the ruling Emperor, the venerable William I. He had been a great man, Father told me, to be revered always. My recollection of that March 9th, 1888, is confirmed by the successive letters that Father wrote his mother that week.

I find my hackles rise as I read the evidence of Father's bland ignoring of his recently acquired American citizenship. "Like every German," he writes, "I too am deeply moved by everything that has been happening during the past ten days in our imperial capital." *Our* capital? Had Father forgotten so soon the oath of allegiance he had taken? A few months after the old Emperor's death came the death of his son, the Emperor Frederick, and the succession of the *junge Kaiser*, Wilhelm II. I was made to feel that I should regard it all as frightfully important to me.

CHAPTER TWO

WHEN Mother permitted Father to send Adolf and Fred to his mother, she knew, of course, that the experience would be hard for the boys, but I am sure she never guessed how hard it would prove to be.

The unhappy venture got off to a bad start. Grandmother had promised to meet the boys in Bremerhafen, and was not there when the ship docked. The boys, wide-eyed and heartsick, were alone in a strange land, and filled with foreboding. Grandmother finally arrived, God only knows how late. I am sure the Aunts' subsequent welcome at the Göttingen railroad station was eager and warm, but the initial impression of aloneness had cut deep.

Two households could scarcely have been in sharper contrast than that from which the boys had come and that into which they were so abruptly thrust. From the brightness and color, the fellowship of children with each other and with a warm-hearted and understanding mother, and a father who wanted, above all, to be his children's friend; from the perpetual action, the boisterous fun in the company of their contemporaries, the singing around the piano; from all this the boys were transferred to a home in which a self-centered, frustrated and melancholy old woman set the mood, the tempo and the daily pattern of living. Spacious and airy as the house was, it must have seemed to the boys unbearably cramped and chill in contrast to the narrower bounds of a house where the prevailing mood was happy and free and bright with expectation. There was no happiness under Grandmother Hagedorn's rule, and no freedom.

The household was in a perpetual state of tension, caused in part by Grandmother's sultry moods, in part by her daughters' terror of her, but mainly by the hair-trigger touchiness of all three. Somebody's feelings were always being hurt, one or the other of the women was always running out of the room in tears or going into sulks; somebody was always "making theater," as the German phrase has it. The relations of Elsbeth and Alma to each other deepened the habitual strain. To the world they gave an impression of sisterly devotion. That was the proper attitude of sisters toward each other and that was the picture that, at all costs, people must see. Actually, Elsbeth dominated the gentler Alma with ruthless acerbity, smiling on her sweetly in public and lashing her with her tongue when they were in the privacy of their room. Alma took it, as, together, they took their mother's hot-tempered outbursts, and consoled herself with dramatic poses and the assurance of her superior mentality.

What the boys caught of all this was only the tension, the electricity in the air, the roll of distant thunder, the momentary expectation of lightning. There had been tension in their own home, for Father was a thoroughgoing Günther and the inheritor of more than his mother's noble brow, stately bearing and shapely hands; but Mother's sunny nature had generally served to clear the air. Nothing but time or some outward circumstance cleared the air in Grandmother's house.

– 2 –

It was into this charged atmosphere that the two boys, neither yet in his teens, and both, since birth, sheltered from the harshness of life by every consideration of loving devotion, were set down. The relations of children to their elders had been interpreted to them by Mother in terms of love; love that was without demand; love that taught discipline out of its own nature, without threats or rumblings from Sinai. I have no question that Grandmother and the Aunts were loving according to their lights and filled with a Christian resolve to do their best, but, unhappily, their conception of that "best" included no provision for any outlet for the boys' desperate homesickness, or for any child's need of freedom to be himself. Discipline, moreover, was in terms of those primary conceptions of the Prussian mind—duty and obedience.

The world outside the house in no way mitigated for the boys the ordeal of their transplanting. The school in which they were enrolled was alien to them in method, routine and spirit, the teachers, in the main, unsympathetic and lacking any tradition of fellowship with their pupils. Their schoolmates were different, moreover, from any boys the two brothers had known; all impeccable in the presence of their elders, many outrageous when they weren't watched; and merciless to the *Amerikaner*.

It was hard, moreover, to get up at six in the morning, or earlier, to be at school from seven or eight until the middle of the afternoon and then to have to do chores in the house, or the garden. Grandmother and the Aunts believed in discipline and no coddling. Any resistance, any balkiness, was *unerhört*—unheard of—and handled with severity.

– 3 –

Under the most favorable circumstances, the boys, abruptly separated from their home for reasons they could not grasp, and forced to live four thousand miles away with three strange women, would have had difficulty adjusting themselves. As it was, they were desperately homesick. They longed to write Mother as they felt, not to complain or to beg to be allowed to come home, but to talk to someone who would understand, and to get the pain and the poison out of their systems. But they learned soon that that was not to be permitted. They must write only how tender and kind their grandmother was, how marvelously *Tante* Alma helped them with their

61

lessons, how wonderful the meals were under *Tante* Elsbeth's guiding hand; and how very, very happy they were.

To Mother, hungering for her boys in our Brooklyn home, it must have seemed almost as though they were dead, so far as living contact with them went. She must have realized quickly that they were not writing freely. Indeed, every letter of theirs was read and censored, in order that nothing should mar the picture that Grandmother and the Aunts were painting of two happy little boys, at peace with themselves and their surroundings. No doubt the three women justified their censorship by telling themselves that they were saving the boys' mother from "useless" worry. They did not, or perhaps would not, recognize that what a mother felt she was not being told might disturb her more acutely than anything she might actually hear.

Why the boys did not surreptitiously write their mother the facts of their life in Göttingen, I don't know, except that they were given no allowance, not so much as the price of a stamp. They would not have dreamed, in any event, of writing Father the truth, and, possibly, they felt that Mother, too, would reprove candor.

— 4 —

Father would have resented passionately and with amazement any suggestion that the boys were prisoners. Yet prisoners they were, prisoners not only to an old woman and her frustrated daughters but to a tradition and a system. For they were subjected daily to a kind of brain-washing which the Teutonic mind seems to have understood long before it dawned on the Russian or the Chinese. Was there anything at their grandmother's, or at school, or in Göttingen's little world that the boys were inclined to comment on, without the proper appreciation? *Impertinente Burschen!* Boys of eleven or twelve did not know what they liked or didn't like! What made them think they might have opinions? Opinions were for their elders. Children did as they were told, and thought as they were supposed to think.

Tante Alma, I am sure, put it all in sugar-coated capsules, with unction, smiles and a soft pat on the shoulder. But not *Tante* Elsbeth. She tore into them, waspishly, and left them drained and limp.

Adolf was like the Schwedlers, sensitive, high-minded, dreamy, tender, peace-loving, wanting only to live and let live. Fred was like the Günthers, having an exceptional mind, emotional intensity and a strong will. Adolf took the ordeal philosophically, and survived intact, but Fred resisted. "Fred was more pig-headed," Irma writes. "Adolf was Grandmother's favorite. Fred had a hell of a life." In the course of the struggle, the three women drove him in on himself, making him reticent, almost secretive; but he survived, living his independent life in a world they knew nothing about.

Grandmother found a way to compensate herself for her failure to break Fred. Adolf was a good boy, she wrote their distant mother, but Fred, Mother could be sure, would never amount to anything.

I don't know why Mother didn't hold that letter before Father's eyes and command him to take her straight over the sea to Göttingen to have it out once and for all with her mother-in-law, except that, if she had, it wouldn't have been Mother; she couldn't operate that way; and anyway there was no money available for ocean trips in those late eighties—not in the Hagedorn household.

– 5 –

Fred never quite forgave Father for denying him his right to a home, not to speak of a father and a mother, during the years that he needed them most. Thirty years later, Father defended his action in a long letter to Fred's wife, on the basis of the "dire need" that "left him no choice." Yet there *was* an alternative. Could six hours of rubbing elbows with the good and the evil in American society in a Brooklyn public school, and, for the other eighteen hours, a lovingly disciplined home, providing corrective influence, as needed, possibly have had worse effects than eight years of autocratic domination in an alien land?

63

The homesickness of those years, the frustrated longing for a mother's love, remained an aching memory for Fred as long as he lived. When he became engaged, he made his fiancée promise that, if they should have children, they would never, never, never, make one of them live away from home.

– 6 –

Grandmother and the Aunts watched over the boys' education with devoted concern. Education was taken with deadly seriousness in the German family in the 1880's. More was involved than the intelligent parents' desire to see their son make the most of his opportunities. Failure to be promoted from one grade to the next brought a stigma not only on the boy but on his family. "Have you heard? Hans Schmidt is stuck in the third grade." The whole family felt itself socially downgraded. This social responsibility was added to the other burdens the two young exiles were made to bear.

Tante Alma, who was primarily in charge of the boys' education, saw to it that no blot fell on the Hagedorn name. Grandmother wrote Father happily of their progress. Father's letters, in turn, were full of appreciation of what the three women were doing. The boys were getting a sound education, and would be grateful for it, he wrote, the rest of their lives.

The thought that his sons might have needs which these women could not meet seems never to have occurred to him. He wrote of his own longing for his mother, of moments of almost overwhelming homesickness for her. "I have such infinite longing for you, my dear, dear Mother," he writes. Year after year, he "yearns and prays" to be able to visit her, looks forward to it, "like a child," and agonizes when his hopes are dashed.

The pain, I am sure, was all that he said it was, but it never apparently crossed his mind that his boys might be suffering kindred agonies; or that all was not sunlight and roses for them.

"We are always so thankful that our sons are having such a happy

64

boyhood," he wrote. "What a blessing their grandmother's home has been for them!" When Adolf was confirmed, Father wrote, "What the boy knows and what he has become thus far is due wholly to you and your motherly love and vision."

Wholly to her? Did the boy's years under their own mother's care mean nothing?

CHAPTER THREE

WE WERE a truncated family after the boys were sent away; each of us, in his individual way, impoverished beyond analysis or measurement. It is idle to speculate how our family life might have developed if there had been five of us children in our home instead of three, what effect the older boys might have had on the girls, or the girls on the boys, or how our very numbers might have affected our characters and personalities. I am sure that I myself might have been spared much of the bewilderment of adolescence if I had had two elder brothers at my side. When I think of our family life, moreover, during those late eighties and early nineties, the love, the mutual solicitude, the world of books and good talk and gracious hospitality that Father and Mother and the Schwedlers made for us, the music —no note was ever heard in Grandmother Hagedorn's house—the Christmas magic, the carefree summers in the country; when I remember these things, I rage at the folly that robbed the boys of their birthright.

– 2 –

It must have seemed to Mother a very small household with the boys gone. Elsie was six years older than I, Irma four; Elsie tall, slender and delicate, with blue eyes, a nervous temperament, and a generous nature; Irma, shorter and inclined to weight, which worried her frightfully. Her eyes were brown like Father's, and she had the fine broad brow of the Günthers. She also had more than her share of the Günther temperament. She sulked, she raged; she wanted what she wanted when she wanted it. Happily, her tempestuous emotions were balanced by an exceptional mind and a gay humor that took on an engaging sparkle as she grew older.

Irma and I were always in each other's hair, and I, being the baby, and coddled for that reason, seemed to Irma created to be her meat. She teased me unmercifully in all the ways that eight knows how to tease four, or ten learns how to tease six. Her persecution became so notorious that, though she might be in the basement when I started bawling on the top floor, Mother, somewhere in between, would shout, "Irma, leave that boy alone!" It was probably all very good for me. In any event, I survived, and, about the time Irma was sixteen and I twelve, our feud suffered a happy transformation, developing into a friendship which, in the course of the years, became, for both of us, second only to the relationship which came to each of us through marriage.

– 3 –

For financial reasons, Father had had to give up the comfortable, roomy house on Portland Avenue in the early eighties, and, at the time the boys went to Germany, we were living on Berkeley Place, just off the informal green stretches of Prospect Park. We moved a good deal in the course of those early years—every three or four years, and, until the middle nineties, on a descending scale. We always lived in rented houses. Father would never buy a square foot of real estate in America. He had promised his mother to keep himself foot-free, so we never knew the stability of a home of our own to be cherished and worked for because it was our own; and he held to his promise even after her death. Wherever we were, we were birds of passage.

– 4 –

It was in the Berkeley Place house that I became conscious of my Schwedler grandparents and "Auntie."

67

If a novelist were inventing the story of our hyphenated family, he could not conceive a more dramatic foil to the autocracy and the tensions of Grandmother Hagedorn's household than the free and relaxed spirit of the Schwedlers. They were living, those years, in a little house in the next block. They had practically no money except what Father was able to give them, and lived very frugally, but that never seemed to bother them. They moved even more often than we did, but they managed to give every home they occupied—even the smallest—the same flavor of dignity and cultivation. Certain pieces of furniture, certain pictures, alabaster figurines and knick-knacks went with them wherever they went: the vast oil painting of the Lake of Lucerne, very dark and rather haunting, one or two engravings of Goethe, a large engraving of Torquato Tasso reading "Jerusalem Delivered" at the court of Ferrara, and that other engraving, from the Portland Avenue house, depicting the blessings of peace. I remember, too, the little ebony curio cabinet with the tiny bust of Goethe to which, later, one of Richard Wagner was added; and the books—not many, but always some volume of Goethe's and some collection of his letters, or of Wilhelm von Humboldt's—or was it Alexander's?—or the poems or short stories of Paul Heyse.

Grandmother Schwedler was an arresting person to look at, with her shiny hair, still jet black, and laid in flat braids over the ears in what seemed to me a very intricate web. On the top of her head she wore a little cap of black lace with narrow black velvet ribbons. Her skin was sallow, finely lined, and a little like parchment.

It was always a party to go to the Schwedlers. They treated you with respect. At home, I was just the baby, but at Grandma's I was a guest, an honored guest. Grandma, early, had the pathetically unwarranted notion that I might amount to something, and made me feel that perhaps I had better. Poetry loomed large in her life; to be a poet, the voice of your time speaking to the hearts of your generation and the generations that followed—that was the supreme achievement. I am not sure Grandma did well in planting an ambition in my subconscious which such endowments as the Lord gave me were so inadequate to satisfy.

I think of Grandma with a book in her hand, or a copy of the *New Yorker Revue*, the successor of the weekly *Beobachter am Hudson*, which she consumed from the first page to the last, travel articles, book reviews, serials and all, particularly the serials. How, with her love of the best in literature, she could find those soap operas of the day as absorbing as she did, I never quite understood. Perhaps it was that, in any German of her generation, the romantic died hard.

– 5 –

Grandpa was afraid of Grandma; and when she called "Fritz!" he jumped. I have before me, as I write, a torn and faded clipping which I found among Venie's scanty treasures, sixty years later. It is an editorial, published by his successor, when Grandfather retired from the *Demokrat*. "Education, purpose, zeal for the great political movements of his time" had, it runs, been united in this fighting humanitarian. "Independent and resolute, in the shifting storms of the time," faithful to his higher calling as he conceived it, "a hater of special privilege, filled with the noblest sentiments of justice and brotherhood," he had maintained his paper on a level "on which brutality and common malice could find no foothold."

I assume it was all true, but I assume it on faith.

When I became aware of Grandfather, he was in his late sixties, and so gentle that he would not have striven with a mouse for a piece of cheese. The fight had long gone out of him and he who had been "independent and resolute" was just a dreamy old man with long, silky white hair, watery blue eyes and skin as pink as a baby's. His slender little body was always cased in a rusty frock coat from whose tail pocket a red silk handkerchief would generally be dangling. He took snuff and I can still see him drawing the little silver snuffbox out of his vest pocket and applying a pinch of the black powder to each nostril. I don't know why he did it, but, for that matter, I don't know why anyone ever took snuff.

Grandma ruled him with a firm hand, not too obviously, and

never publicly, but definitely, and beyond appeal. I suppose she blamed him for his financial failure, and he knew it and felt ashamed and inferior; or perhaps it was just that, being a capable woman, his dreamy ways annoyed her. The relationship created no tensions, for Grandfather had never dared display in his home the fighting qualities that were evident in his work as a publisher. I suppose that he was basically a man of peace and that the idealism of the struggle for freedom in Germany and in the United States had driven him beyond his natural capacity for battle and left him spiritually drained. There are few idealists who have more than one fight in them. It was from Grandfather, I am sure, that Mother derived her philosophy of nonresistance.

I cannot remember him ever angry, except when Father questioned the Republican Party's divine right to rule forever. Then he would sputter.

Grandpa came into his own with us grandchildren. He was himself, at heart, a child, and we welcomed him as a comrade, as eager to play with us as we were to play with him. I remember his thin old fingers on the keyboard of our Steinway upright, playing a Mozart minuet, and his faraway look as he played some bit of Chopin that sent one hand rising and dipping like a gull over the other to pounce upon some dark b-flat.

Grandpa was never disciplinary, he never said *don't*, so we were never afraid of him.

– 6 –

We were never afraid of Grandma, either, yet I don't remember that we were ever *ausgelassen* with her, ever out of hand. There was an unobtrusive dignity about her which commanded our respect. The very thought of being afraid of "Auntie," would never have occurred to us.

Auntie was the mainstay of the Schwedler household. She had not married and, though she was at that time only in her middle thirties, she had already, I am sure, given up any serious thought of marriage.

70

She accepted cheerfully the position in the Victorian convention of the younger daughter who gives up her life to take care of her father and mother; a tradition as definite among Germans as among Anglo-Saxons.

She had had her devoted swains. There had been some sort of "understanding," in fact, with Father's cousin, attractive, gay-hearted Harry Gunther, who had spent a year or two, prior to Father and Mother's wedding, working in a tobacco house in New York. Venie, who at heart was true as steel, never could learn to make her eyes behave and, for that matter, never did, even at eighty. Another young man called on her. He meant nothing to Venie but she could not persuade Harry of it and he stormed out of the house and never returned. "I shall never marry anyone else," were the last words she said to him. She never did; nor did she see him again for almost thirty years. I remember how flustered she was when she encountered him unexpectedly at our house with his beautiful southern wife on their silver wedding journey.

When she was in her middle seventies, writing him to ask his help for a cousin of his in Germany who was destitute, she recalled "the Sunday when Hermann brought you to our house in Portland Avenue." She and Anna had been "gowned in pink Paris dresses with a train attached," and when she and Harry parted that evening she had felt "as if I had known you for years." She recalled his abrupt departure—"my first big heartache that took years to heal." We youngsters never caught the slightest intimation of the lovelorn in her.

There wasn't a grain of starch, or solemnity, in her make-up. She treated us youngsters as though we were her contemporaries, and, with enchanting mimicry, used to reduce people of the adult world to dimensions we could deal with. Never Father or Mother or the grandparents or any others who deserved respect, only the pompous casuals who fluttered or strutted in and out. Auntie took them off with a sure touch and thereby did more than she ever knew to reconcile the ways of God to childhood.

I suppose Auntie was often serious with us and told us to do this or that in no uncertain tones, for she had a clear sense of what was proper and what wasn't; but, when I think of her in those early years, I think of her dancing, china-blue eyes, her puckish smile and the bounce that set her tail feathers waving. In what might, with almost anyone else, have been an occasion of terror and heartbreak, in the spring when I was going on six, she put Elsie, Irma and me into stitches of hilarious merriment. Mother was desperately ill with diphtheria, and Auntie, who had been nursing her, took us children to the boardinghouse of a stately old maid, Fräulein Kröhnke, on Staten Island, to get us away from infection, I suppose, and spare us the agonies of seeing the Shadow hovering near.

Mother was everything in the world to Auntie but it was life and not death she made us think about. I suppose it was her imitation of the Kröhnke's best boardinghouse majesty which bowled us over, or some other bit of gorgeous mimicry. I don't remember what it was. All I know is that we laughed till we rolled on the floor, and forgot all about Mother, which, of course, was the main object of our Staten Island exile. But our gaiety ceased abruptly when Auntie herself came down with the diphtheria. I don't know how we children escaped unless it was that Auntie laughed us out of it.

CHAPTER FOUR

GRANDPA, Grandma, and Auntie—inseparable and precious trio—were a Godsend to us children, providing us a refuge of relaxation from the tension that seemed to possess our own home. Not that our home wasn't happy. It was. Father and Mother were devoted to each other; they never quarreled in our hearing, and neither wanted anything so much as to make our home a place where we would be at ease in body and mind. But the tension was there. It was there for breakfast and it was there for dinner. The fact that, weekdays, it wasn't there, in the hours between, was due to the fact that Father was in his office in New York.

For it was Father, of course, who was the source of the tension. He set the mood of the household. If he slept badly, we were made to feel it instantly at the breakfast-table; and, if anything went wrong in business during the day, and something went wrong pretty often during the depressed 1880's and early nineties, the dinner was a gloom. It was not that Father sulked; he seldom did. He occasionally exploded; but he did not even explode often. Our affliction was that he was what the Germans call *empfindlich*; he was easily hurt; and we never knew what would set him off.

It is a peculiar German trait, this touchiness. *Es hat mir Weh getan. Ich birn auf's Tiefste gekränkt. Der ganze Tag ist für mich verschmerzt.* The phrases come ringing back, telling of hurt feelings, of the heart bruised, the day ruined. Father was so much a man in his relations with other men and in his struggle for a living that I am at a loss to account for this feminine hypersensitiveness, except that it was an inheritance from his spoiled and self-centered mother. His sisters had it, too, and gloried in it. Father's *Empfindlichkeit* was at its worst—on a veritable hair trigger, indeed—where his mother and sisters were concerned. If any one of us said, or appeared to imply, something which his imagination could twist into the slightest reflection on his three feminine adorers across the sea, then the day was definitely lost.

The spirits of those three women floated monstrously over our home. So and so many times a year they appeared to descend, and, for a boy of five or six or eight or twelve, became a present cataclysm. That was a few weeks before Christmas or when a birthday was imminent and letters had to be written. German letters. The German part of it was not so bad; I was five before I spoke English. But to indite a proper epistle and to do it in German script! Those letters, so polite, so formal, ruined my epistolary style for life, and my letters today reflect those early suppressions of everything that was individually myself.

I can still see myself, my face bent close over the paper, following the penciled double lines that Father or Mother carefully ruled for me, and laboriously drawing those capital H's with the big loop above the line, the saddle on the line, the other big loop below. Reading Gothic script is nothing to writing the German. Always, moreover, the labored epistles had to pass inspection. Woe unto me if I messed up the page, if the careful erasures left their mark! I was sure to hear paternal thunders. Once, in fact—and I remember it vividly—I felt, on the seat of my pants, the paternal hand.

Father never did things by halves. He was intensely loyal to his mother and sisters, and wanted them to know that they were important to him and that he was bringing up his children to love them and pay them respect. But he never realized—Germans of his generation as a rule didn't—that, when certain things can be done only by coercion, they had better not be done at all. Duty and obedience are valuable ideals, but, beyond a certain point, they create blind spots. We children were ready to do our duty, and we were perfectly willing to be, and generally were, obedient; and in one of his letters to his mother, Father bears witness to it. We were, indeed, scared to be anything else. But to compose messages of affection under the shadow of the club, and do it as though we meant it, was beyond the capacity of flesh and blood. The pain, vexation and tears those letters cost all of us, Father included, served effectively to prevent the very sense of kinship and understanding that Father was seeking to foster. In those years, we hated Grandmother Hagedorn and the Aunts with a fervor deeper than that love of his for them, which made all the trouble in the first place.

Apart from the ridiculous commotion about the letters, I had occasion more than once to feel the lash of what seemed Father's instinctive urge to command first, and think afterward, if then.

There was one instance, in the winter before I was six, that left an impression on my mind which seventy summers and winters have been unable to erase. Snow had been falling for days. It lay three, four, five feet deep on the sidewalk and the street, completely darkened the rooms on the street level and lay drifted to the parlor windows on the first floor. The weather was making history.

Father had been down with a bad cold and was glad of the excuse the Great Blizzard gave him to stay home an extra day or two to complete his recovery. I remember sitting on the floor of the parlor playing with a miniature dumpcart, about two inches long, drawn by a piebald wooden horse. I suppose I thought I was carting away snow, for I was depositing in the cart the lint lying on top of the carpet. Father saw what I was doing and commanded me to stop it at once. I was destroying the carpet, he said. I supposed he imagined I was plucking out the threads, but a moment's thought would have told him that anything like that would take not only a man's hand but a pair of pliers. I didn't explain that I was merely removing the fuzz that lay in little balls on top of the nap, or ask, as I might have, how its removal could possibly affect the carpet. One didn't talk back to fathers in the world that I was living in. One merely felt crushed and bewildered, and very small and weak.

I wish I had known then what I know now, from a letter of Father's to his mother, that he was "tired and on edge," that day, or could have read the devoted and deluded nonsense he wrote her later that spring about my supposed qualities and probable future. His mother mustn't think he was soft with me, he added. "I can be stern," he assured her, "but when I really have to punish him, the whole day is clouded over for me."

So that March day was clouded over for us both. He forgot all about the episode, I am sure. I never could; and I am a little ashamed of that now. But little boys seem to be like that.

– 2 –

In Father's letters to his mother, in those late 1880's and early nineties, his strength and his weakness alike are laid bare. There, glowing on every page, are his intensely loving nature, his devoted caring for his wife and children as well as his mother and sisters, his clear sense of duty, his unremitting, day-after-day industry, his courage in the face of successive disappointments in the ten-year struggle to keep his head above water, his magnanimity toward the friend who failed him in his hour of need. In the letters, too, are his absorption in his physical aches and pains, meticulously described to his mother, his lapses into self-pity, the occasional emotional outbursts— sincere, I am sure, when they were written but reflecting only a small corner of him, not the whole man: "If I could find rest against your heart from the cares and perplexities of life, to be with you in your garden, if it were only at first for a few weeks or months and, later, yes, later, perhaps, again for always."

Sentiment or sentimentalism?

The fact was that, when Father did go to visit his mother, one summer, taking Irma and Elsie with him, "he was generally somewhere else," Irma wrote me, sixty years later, "leaving us alone with Grandmother and the Aunts, three grim, prim dames who seldom laughed; life was too serious. Father adored his mother but I noted that he never seemed to miss a chance to go off somewhere with Uncle Harry Gunther, who was in Germany that summer, or patch up feuds with Hagedorn relatives in Hanover and elsewhere, feuds which had been going on for years and years because Grandmother could never condescend to acknowledge a mistake she had made, or a hurt she had suffered."

In Father's relations with his mother, the compulsion to do and say the "proper," the conventional thing, was as strong as in the Aunts. "How dear and kind" it was of Grandmother to stand at his side with advice, he wrote on one occasion. "Ah, Mother mine, had I always accepted your loving counsels, had I followed them blindly, how many cares and sorrows I would have spared myself!"

He did not mean that at all, really, for, if he had, it would have meant that he regretted his marriage which, I am certain, he never did, and would never have dreamed of admitting, if he had. I suspect he was about to side-step something Grandmother was advising him to do. Such solemn antics were a part of the Hagedorn theater.

– 3 –

Mother was a darling, firm with us, yet tender and gay, soothing our bruises, laughing off our hurt feelings with her quiet sense of humor, smoothing down Father, avoiding conflict at any cost to herself, nursing no grievances. Father might storm out of the house, in a temper, in the morning, but when he returned, at night, Mother's welcome would be as loving and cheery as though no cloud had lain on her day.

She had a clear, religious faith, but seldom, if ever, talked to us about religious matters, her faith and her love ascending as an emanation of her daily living. I remember the lullaby she used to sing me to sleep with when I was four or five, a verse of a peasant song, set by Carl Maria von Weber to tender music that brings a lump to my throat when I hear it today.

77

"Schlaf, Herzenssöhnchen, mein Liebling bist du.
Tue die kleinen Guckäugelein zu.
Alles ist ruhig und still wie im Grab.
Schlaf nur, ich wehre die Fliegen dir ab."

She taught me to sing a little four-line song for my bedtime prayer, and it brings her vividly back to me in all her tenderness and simple, inarticulate faith:

"Müde bin ich, geh zur Ruh,
Schliesse meine Augen zu.
Vater, lass das Auge dein
Ueber meinem Bette sein."

I imagine that her own prayer, when she sank, at night, into her big, black-walnut bed, may have been just as uncomplicated as that.

Mother could be stern, but never for long, and, as a disciplinarian, she was successful only by going against all the rules. When I was ten or thereabouts I remember her pursuing me with a slipper with the intent of applying it where it would do the most good. I dashed down the hall, into the back room, and through the passage where the washstands were, with Mother after me. Two or three times the Imp and the Avenging Angel made the circle of the hall, the rooms, and the inner passage, with the Imp sticking his head around the corners, grinning, and the Angel finally grinning, too. It was all very slack, from the German standpoint, but it made for fellowship, and fellowship made for discipline of a sort that Father's thunders never could achieve.

– 4 –

I don't know when German poetry and German folk songs entered my consciousness. I suppose the folk songs came first—the best of them not actually folk songs at all, having been written by Goethe, Uhland or other recognized poets, with music composed by trained composers, but adopted by the *Volk* as their own. *Heidenröslein* was among the earliest I knew, *Ich hat einen Kameraden, Freut euch des Lebens,* and the haunting *Muss i denn.* A younger cousin of Father's, a dear, warmhearted fellow, not overbright, but loyal and true, who came to New York to get a job and became a kind of elder brother to us children, had a good voice that filled the house when he bellowed *Still wie die Nacht.* With "Vetter Wilhelm" leading, Sunday evenings, we sang all the familiar old songs. Their simple words and melodies, reflecting the raptures and the brooding, the merriment and the exaltations of ordinary men and women in their passage from the cradle to the grave, entered into my innermost parts, leaving an emotional influence that seventy-eight years of life in America have not wholly overcome. The heart of the German people as I knew it, at its best, as a boy—warm, compassionate and true—speaks to me through them still.

Certain quotations of Schiller's poems were such time-worn *clichés* of the family talk, that I can't remember when the poems themselves first entered my world; but a letter that Mother wrote Father from Tannersville, the summer I became six, indicates that, one rainy day, she was keeping us children occupied by reading Schiller to us. The old classic standbys became part of me early and I can't remember the time when *Der Handschuh* wasn't familiar:

> "*Vor seinem Löwengarten*
> *Das Kampfspiel zu erwarten,*
> *Sass König Franz . . .*"

How I thrilled to the knight's return from the arena with the glove his lady had dropped to test his love:

> "*Und er wirft ihr den Handschuh ins Gesicht:*
> '*Den Dank, Dame, begehr' ich nicht!*'
> *Und verlässt sie zur selben Stunde.*"

and so on. *Der Taucher* was another favorite, *Die Bürgschaft* still another, ballads of heroism and loyalty, good for children, boys or girls; and I am grateful that they were drummed into me young.

Goethe's *Erlkönig* gave me the cold shivers, and does still. As a part of my personal discipline *Der Struwelpeter* was read to me. It was a lengthy doggerel about a horrid little boy who wouldn't eat his soup or let his hair or his nails be cut, and finally committed the ultimate crime of playing with matches, and went up in smoke. *Max und Moritz*, I suppose, came much later. They still seem to me the most satisfying pair of boy-demons I know anything about in literature, and it is too bad they have never been acclimated in English-speaking lands. Perhaps they and their environment are too completely German. Anyway, inspired doggerel is unexportable. You can translate Lucretius or Dante or the second part of *Faust*, where you can't translate Wilhelm Busch.

CHAPTER FIVE

It was a German world in which we lived. Whether it were in the pleasant house on Berkeley Place, or the narrower, dingier house on Hancock Street, in the Bedford Heights section, it was as German as Bingen on the Rhine. The girls and I generally talked English with Mother, but, when Father was around, and especially at the dinner-table, the language was German. Occasionally, if we were forgetful or obdurate, slipping into English, or returning to German too tardily, the paternal fist would make the dishes rattle with an emphatic but good-natured *"Hier wird deutsch gesprochen!"* Talking German seemed to us somehow strained, but Father was right, of course, when he said that someday we would be glad he had been strict about it.

The meals were German, from the grace, which was my job, as the youngest, to pronounce—

> *"Komm, lieber Herr Jesu, sei du unser Gast*
> *Und segne was du uns bescheret hast—"*

to the *Gesegnete Mahlzeit!*—which everybody said when the meal was over. The food itself was as German as *Sauerkraut*, though *Sauerkraut* itself was never on the menu, being regarded as distinctly lower middle class. I suppose it is romantic nostalgia but it seems to me that I have never tasted such soups since, such asparagus (white and portly, like Brünnhilde's arms, not spindly and green, such as the

81

heathen use!) or such sauces and salads, *Kompots* and desserts! In our leanest days we seem always to have been able to afford a good cook; and, if the cook didn't know her job when she came, she learned it speedily under Mother's capable direction.

Those, of course, were the days of free immigration when German girls arrived from the homeland by hundreds every week. We paid our cooks twenty-two dollars a month and, when we could afford a second girl, we paid her eighteen or, at most, twenty dollars. Once, while we were in the Hancock Street house, and finances were sour, we engaged a general housekeeper from a German orphanage for sixteen dollars a month, and she wasn't worth it. But she was an exception. Most of the girls who worked for us—twelve to fifteen hours a day for some five cents an hour and their keep—were smart and capable and worth five times what they got even by the standards of the nineties; and each stayed with us for many years.

When finances permitted, Father and Mother entertained; not lavishly, of course, but generously, with heavy linen napkins and crystal goblets and lovely thin-stemmed wine glasses, sparkling on the satiny tablecloths. Father and Mother would look in on us children upstairs before the party began and I retain vividly the handsome sight Father made in a dress suit. Mother, too, was lovely in her open-neck gowns. They were, incidentally, never low-neck. Father was finicky about that. I remember, standing in my white night gown (it was before the days of pajamas) leaning over the banisters to watch the guests arrive. It was almost as exciting for us youngsters when Father and Mother went out to other people's dinners, or to weddings—they were generally in the evenings in the German social group—or to the opera. They would look in on us when they came home and, finding us awake occasionally, tell us about it. More than once I remember Father diving into the pocket of his swallow-tail coat and fishing out some delicious sweetmeat he had surreptitiously wrapped in his handkerchief and secreted for us. I don't know why it was not squashed, but it never was. He must have folded those tails over his knees when he sat down. I recall late returnings from the opera—horsecars were slow—and mention of Schott, the great tenor, of Anton Seidl, and of Walter Damrosch, the young and gifted new conductor.

The most notable party of the year was always on Mother's birthday in November. Father used to call the day *den grössten Feiertag in den Vereinigten Staaten*—and we children agreed that there was no anniversary—except Christmas—that meant so much to us. The festivities began at the breakfast table, where Mother's place would be ringed with flowers and her chair garlanded in smilax. Then, while Mother waited at her place, Father would set out her presents in the parlor. I remember the linen sheet on the table and the multitude of gifts, never "gift-wrapped," but open in all their manifold colors. They were usually very practical gifts which Father himself generally selected—dress silks and scarfs and gloves and a dressing gown, perhaps, and—when there were funds—some inexpensive brooch or a set of wine glasses and, tucked away somewhere, perhaps, a new purse with a twenty-dollar gold piece in it.

The table was never skimpy that I can remember, even in the leanest years, and, in flush times, it was opulent. Father could feel dreadfully poor when things went against him, but, when the tide turned, he was lavish. I remember Mother protesting against his habit, during such lush periods, of buying gloves for her not by the pair but by the dozen.

The presentation of gifts was important but not the really memorable part of the festivities. That was the *Festessen* at night, the one adult dinner party of the year in which we children, even myself, were included.

I can still feel the excitement of that long, glittering table and the dressed-up splendor of the friends who gathered round it. The Hoppenstedts, that stately pair, were there, as a matter of course, and I can see the handsome figure of Mr. Hoppenstedt rising after the dessert with his glass in his hand, to make the speech of the occasion. Generally it was a gentle tribute, graciously phrased, now and then it was a poem, with clever, excruciating rhymes; always it was witty and memorable. When the speech was over, everyone would get up and chant

"Hoch soll sie leben!
Hoch soll sie leben!
Hoch soll sie leben!
Dreimal hoch!"

Then we would all walk around the table clinking glasses with everybody else. There would be other speeches, with toasts to the boys in Göttingen and more *Hoch sollen sie leben,* and more clinking glasses, and finally a speech from Father—and he had a gift for such things—generally about the blessing of friendship.

The food at those birthday parties was bountiful by present-day standards—soup, fish, meat, vegetables and fruit compote, salad and dessert; and the wine was the best Moselle, Rhine wine and Burgundy Father could afford. There was always enough and never too much. And at the dessert always came Father's pineapple punch.

That punch was famous among our friends for its flavor and its mildness. There was a quart of light claret, poured over canned pineapple, a quart of mild Rhine wine, a quart of champagne, a quart of Apollinaris. That was all. You could drink it like water. Even we children were allowed to have it. Only you mustn't eat the pineapple. The pineapple absorbed the alcohol, and was potent.

I remember Father telling his friends an amusing incident when he was staying at Fräulein Kröhnke's in Staten Island one summer while Mother was in the Catskills with us children. The Kröhnkes gave a lawn party one Saturday evening and Father contributed his punch. Among the guests was the Episcopal rector whose church was across the street. He drank the punch like lemonade, commending its mildness and, I suppose, being innocent, he consumed the pineapple too. The next morning, Father, looking out of his window, saw the rector walking up and down his walled garden, a towel round his head. Evidently the towel didn't really help, for, at ten-thirty, the verger appeared at the church door to tack up a notice. Father went over to investigate and read to his glee that the rector would unhappily be unable to conduct services "because of a sudden indisposition." That was enough to make a good story, but it wasn't all. A couple of weeks later Father heard that the vestry of the church had come to the conclusion that the rector had been overworking, and voted him a year's leave of absence and a trip abroad. "And all that because of my punch!" Father would say. "Isn't that a punch?"

– 2 –

Mother's birthday may have been for us, in Father's phrase, "the greatest holiday in the United States," but the most exciting festival, of course, was Christmas. Queer things happen to my spine, even after seventy years, when I think of it.

It was so gorgeously long-drawn-out a thrill! Not just a matter of a golden Christmas morning, standing at the fireplace, reaching up for long black stockings, mysteriously filled. Christmas began for us about the first of December, when Father and Mother would suggest that it might be prudent for us youngsters to make a list of things hoped for, to be a guide to the busy *Weihnachtsmann*. Was that a moment!

A week after the making of the *Weihnachtsliste*, Mother would casually remark some morning that she was going to start preparing the dough for the *Honigkuchen*. Those golden-brown cookies were an essential part of the show. You couldn't imagine Christmas without them. Mother made them by the barrel and though she gave them away generously, we generally had some until well into February, even with three hungry children reaching into the deep tins.

I don't know what went into the composition of the *Honigkuchen* except that, paradoxically, honey was not among the ingredients and it was molasses which contributed the color. The dough was mixed and set aside for two weeks to ferment; *gären* was the word. It was another great day when Mother finally rolled out the dough, dusted it with flour and stamped it with little tin forms into diamonds and circles and stars. We youngsters had a share in that, and in the further business of plastering an almond in the center of each cookie.

85

We might help bake the cookies, but, when the pans went into the oven, that was the last we saw of the *Honigkuchen* until Christmas. There was no such thing as anticipating the occasion. This particular kind of cookie was a part of Christmas, never made at any other time of the year and never, under any circumstances, eaten in advance of the day.

The day, of course, by German tradition, was not Christmas Day itself, but Christmas Eve. The time between the baking of the cakes and the Day of Days seemed months, in which excitement mounted from hour to hour. There were our gifts to buy, or to make, for one thing. Then there were the packages arriving, to be stowed away by Mother in closets ostentatiously locked. There were, too, the mysterious references that Father and Mother made across the breakfast table, intended to heighten the suspense. We always had a Christmas tree, of course, but I never saw it arrive at the house or being borne into the "Christmas room." It was a part of the thrill that there should be mystery about it all. Father and Mother, I am sure, enjoyed the enchanting hocus-pocus as much as we.

The Christmas celebration was always in the evening and I don't know how we lived through the day. We peeked into closets, of course, and peeked through keyholes, but Father and Mother were generally two jumps ahead of us and we never saw much. Father generally came up from the office by three o'clock. Dinner was at five-thirty and, shortly before, Grandpa, Grandma and Auntie would arrive, laden with gifts, and frequently Grandma's sister, *Tante* Liese, whose vigorous words had been effective in keeping me from possibly slipping out of life before I entered it.

The glittering splendor of the dinner table of those far-off Christmas Eves! The suspense of that final hour before the giving of the gifts, the *Bescheerung!* Just before the dessert, Father would excuse himself. "Come up in about half an hour," he would say. We knew that he would be bringing Mother's presents to her table in the Christmas room, the *Weihnachtsstube,* and then lighting the tree.

Long before he was ready for us, we would be in the corridor outside the parlor, sitting on the stairs. Mother would begin to sing

> *"O du selige,*
> *O du fröhliche,*
> *Gnadenbringende*
> *Weihnachtszeit!"*

and we would all join in, even to Grandpa. Then one of us would strike up with

> *"O Tannenbaum,*
> *O Tannenbaum,*
> *Wie grün sind deine Blätter!"*

"Singt doch Stille Nacht," Father would call from the *Weihnachtszimmer,* and we would sing a verse or two of the lovely old carol:

> *"Stille Nacht, heilige Nacht,*
> *Alles schläft, einsam wacht . . ."*

"Where's the water pail?" Father would interpose, prosaically, "the stick and the sponge?" The pail, and the stick, with a sponge attached, constituted our fire-extinguishing apparatus, and did we need it, with dozens of candles burning on an inflammable evergreen? The preventive equipment would be set near the door, while someone would start on another carol.

"Are the maids there?" Father would call. They generally were, decked out in clean white starched dresses. There would be another *"Stille Nacht"* or *"O du selige"* . . . and then the tinkling of a little silver bell.

My heart acts up as I write the words. If ever I get to paradise—if I do—St. Peter had better tinkle a little silver bell as he opens the gate or I won't believe that it's heaven. I can still hear Father's little silver bell, and, when I can't hear anything else, I think I shall still hear it. For, through the tinkle, I would become aware of a dazzling scene, as Father, beaming, opened the door: every gaslight on the crystal chandelier blazing, a Christmas tree sparkling with a hundred little living flames and, roundabout, on all sides, a splendor of gifts.

Each of us had his own table and, of course, made a dash for it.

Most of the gifts would be useful, the sort of thing Mother would have had to buy for us in the course of the winter anyway, but, finding it there, under the blaze of lights, gave it an aura. And then there were always things that were not utilitarian, a sled, perhaps, and lead soldiers and stamps and books; and on every table, always a soup plate full of the *Honigkuchen* and another full of nuts and raisins and tough, jaw-cracking *Pfeffernüsse* and *Aniseplätzchen*.

I remember the relaxing of the tension, sitting on the floor with a new toy or a new book, and looking up at the tree. A more cautious generation, stringing hard-faced little electric bulbs up and down and across its Christmas trees, knows nothing of the enchantment that was in those wavering little yellow flames, making the tinsel sparkle and the gold cheeks of the walnuts glow fitfully.

There was always the danger of fire, of course, as no one knew better than I, for I backed into the burning candles once when I was two or three, and my flimsy dress went up in flame. It was Auntie who rescued me—Father and Mother were too paralyzed with horror to move—throwing some rug or garment about me. Knowing the danger, we kept one eye constantly on the tree and the other on our fire-fighting apparatus. Now and again we would hear the sudden ominous crackle of pine needles and would pounce with the sponge on the burning twig, always happily in time. That was all a part of the thrill.

Father hovered over it all, warm and tender and, I am sure, completely happy.

– 3 –

German speech, German music, German servants, German food; German friends, German festivals.

All these were to the good. Unfortunately, they were not all. With them went a conception of human relations that ran directly contrary to American tradition and custom: an insistence, so continuous that I never dreamed of questioning it, on uncritical respect for the judgment and opinions of my elders.

The first duty of a young man, Father told me, was to be *bescheiden*—modest—in the presence of his elders; respectful, and aware that any opinions he might have were negligible, and, if pressed, an impertinence. I was led to gather—though not consciously, on Father's part, I am sure—that years were the measure of respect-worthiness and that intelligence was the product of time. When age was backed by position—social, economic or administrative—I was expected to reduce correspondingly my conception of my own significance.

I did not consciously accept this fantastic perversion of intelligent human relations; I merely absorbed it. It was the air that I breathed, and, by the time I got deep enough into the American world to learn something of the supreme need of the individual to be himself, I had developed a sense of awe of my elders, especially when they had "position," a blind trust in their intelligence and a consciousness of my own inferiority that made me shy and diffident in my dealings with them. Ridiculous as it may seem, I was actually in my thirties before I fully realized that a man with gray hair might conceivably know less of a given proposition than I, or be less dependable in judgment.

There was a further element in my boyhood that drew my mind and imagination away toward Father's fatherland. In our dining room on Hancock Street—and they went with us into our other homes—hung life-size photogravures of the three Kaisers, Wilhelm I, Frederick III and Wilhelm II, beside a reproduction of one of Franz von Lenbach's sinister portraits of the man who had raised them to imperial power, the man of blood and iron, who had achieved the supreme glory by the application of military might.

If Abraham Lincoln was the presiding genius of Mother's childhood home, Bismarck was the tutelary deity of ours.

CHAPTER SIX

IT WAS shortly after we moved into the Hancock Street house when I was seven or eight—and a slit of a house it was, only sixteen feet wide, three stories, brownstone front with basement and steep stoop —that I met the two boys who lived in the more modern cut-stone house, next door. They were Bob and Will Manning, Bob my own age, Will a little younger, sons of a most attractive couple, of Scotch-Irish background, ten years or so younger than my father and mother. The boys and I were always running in and out of each other's houses, playing in each other's yards or mingling with the other boys on the block for such games as prisoner's base that we could play on the rough cobbles. They introduced me to *Youth's Companion* and *St. Nicholas*, the Alger and Henty books, Kirk Monroe, the Castleman series, and the rest, which carried my imagination out of my German environment into the American scene.

The Mannings, indeed, were the first door that opened to us into the American world. Father and Mother liked Americans of the older stock, admired them and, I am sure, were eager to know more of them than they did. The height of praise for Father about this or that man was that he was a genuine American—*ein echter Amerikaner* —and he took pride in the friendship of the Mannings and his special intimates on the Cotton Exchange. The latter, alas, all lived in New York or in the suburbs, so we had no social contact with them or their families. That was a great loss for us. Our social group remained

German and never expanded beyond the small, rather exclusive circle that had a common center in the Schermerhorn Street church.

– 2 –

The church loomed large in our lives. Father was fond of its minister, the genial, bewhiskered Reverend Jacob Loch. "Jakey," as we children irreverently dubbed him, loved a good glass of wine and an evening of cards, but his heart was sound and he was a hard-working, kindly soul; and Sundays he was all gravity and unction.

Pastor Loch confirmed Elsie, Irma and myself, in succession. Confirmation in those days was a serious business, preceded by three or four months of weekly lessons in Christian doctrine and Lutheran theology, culminating in a public examination before the whole congregation. This ordeal was actually not as grim as it sounds, for the test was rigged by the parson to prevent any failure, embarrassing alike to the confirmee and the congregation. "Jakey" knew what each of us knew and didn't know, and adjusted his questions accordingly. The gravity of the sacrament of confirmation was impressed on me on Palm Sunday morning by Father's bringing the big German Bible to breakfast and reading his favorite psalm, the 103rd.

– 3 –

The most intimate friend of my boyhood belonged to the group that had its focus in the Schermerhorn Street Church. Bernard Recknagel was an exceptionally bright redhead and for five or six years he and I were inseparable, at work and at play. His home, too, was a German home.

Bedford Academy, the school that we attended, was owned and conducted mainly for the sons of German-Americans by a certain Dr. George Rodemann, a stiff Prussian with black hair, a black cavalry moustache and a left cheek heavily gashed as a result of students' duels in some German university.

We learned nothing from him about the American way of life,

democratic processes of government or the responsibilities of freedom, but few boys learned anything of that sort in any school in those days. Freedom was taken for granted and the citizen was supposed to absorb from the atmosphere any wisdom, discipline and self-control he might need to be a useful citizen. Dr. Rodemann was no more derelict in regard to training for citizenship than the other schoolmasters of the country. He was merely in his own person a particularly glaring example of what the American spirit wasn't.

– 4 –

It was when I was ten that I first realized that people of German stock were disliked by Americans of other stock because of certain qualities of character they were supposed to possess and from which other Americans presumably were free.

The Manning boys and I had built a rough shack in my back yard. It wasn't much of a shack, being just a lean-to, built of such stray boards as we could pick up in our cellars or in vacant lots; but it had walls and a roof and fulfilled that ultimate dream of the ten-year-old, a lodging all his own, a hideout and a clubhouse.

It was a shock, therefore, when a neighboring boy, also of German parentage, came to see what we had and started literally tearing it to pieces. "You've done it all wrong!" he cried, tearing off board after board. "You should have done it this way"—and he told us how buildings should be constructed. He was technically right, I am sure, but we hadn't built for eternity or even for next month or to satisfy the city building inspector. He devastated our shack and didn't even offer to rebuild it according to his own ideals of efficient construction.

As we viewed the wreckage, Bob Manning made a comment which sank deep: "These high-and-mighty Dutchmen that want to run everything their way!"

"Dutchmen." That was us. I was fully conscious of it. I was something different from the other boys on the street. I was a "Dutchman." It never bothered me particularly, except as it made me peculiarly toothsome to the gang of "Micks" which, at intervals, invaded

92

our section from the less genteel regions farther north. These tough Irish boys were a source of real terror to me. My German background of ordered lives in ordered communities had no philosophy to meet the situation, no tradition of the free man defending his right to pursue his orderly way.

I had been given the impression that only low-class boys used their fists, and no one challenged the child's natural timidity or made me see that it was cowardly not to stand and resist. Nor was I given any other suggestion, as to what I was supposed to do when a gang of Micks surrounded me on my way to school, called me "Dutchy!" and threatened to beat me up. They never did beat me up, and were probably perfectly decent youngsters, terrorizing me because I was easy meat and deserved to be terrorized. They would lie in wait for me outside the house after luncheon to nab me when I was returning to school, but I found I could avoid them by climbing the back fence and crossing a vacant lot, and remember, with ignominy, being frequently boosted over the fence by the cook.

The Micks, I can see now, were America's first challenge to the nice, timid little German boy that I was.

– 5 –

I first really began to have a feeling for America when I became conscious of its physical beauties and experienced its freedom and its wildness. In the summers, in the late eighties and early nineties, we used to go to Sullivan County, west of the Hudson, and to the Catskills. I can remember the thrill of piling, bag and baggage, into a day coach of the West Shore Railroad at Weehawken (itself a Sabbath-day journey from Brooklyn, those days) and the rapture of the arrival at Liberty or Tannersville or Hunter. In those premotor days, those were villages where the bearded farmers were still the guileless but warmhearted "hicks" of *Puck* and *Judge*, buying gold bricks from the crafty "city feller." They proved kind to little boys. For the city child there was magic in the springy softness and the fragrance of a load of hay, crawling home to the barn on a hot day;

93

the deep dust of the roads in the midsummer heat; the tangled woods and tumbling brooks of the Kaaterskill Clove where bears still wandered; the expanding beauty of wooded hills and fertile farmlands as we climbed Hunter Mountain.

There was a brook, Schoharie Creek, fringed with bushes and patches of woods, which was my particular joy. For there were fish in it and occasionally they permitted themselves to be deluded by a worm craftily wound over a hook. The fish were very small, but, for a city boy, it was something rapturous to jump from rock to rock and dangle the hook before young fish only a little less experienced in the nature of hooks and worms than himself.

We had a swimming hole, of course; no more than four feet or so deep and only some fifteen feet across, which was plenty good enough for me who could not yet swim. The slimy, slippery rocks at the bottom cut your feet; but the water was clear and cool, and overhead was a wide-spreading oak, and you and your friends were miles from anybody, without a stitch on, in and out of the water, through the long summer hours. What more could any boy ask?

Bean-shooters played a great role in my life in the Catskills. I found a succession of tough hickory crotches and equipped them with three-quarter-inch rubber bands, fastened to the arms of the crotch with infinite care. I never hit any of the birds, the squirrels or the chipmunks that I shot at, but hitting things wasn't the point. Shooting itself was the thrill. My bean-shooter was to me what a real six-shooter would today be to a million synthetic Hopalong Cassidys. It made me a brother to Tom Sawyer.

One summer a gang of us twelve-year-olds conducted a little private war across Schoharie Creek, with an army of us—three or four—on each side, firing BB shot with our bean-shooters at each other through the brush. It was an exciting game that would have put our mothers into no mean dithers if they had known about it, and quite rightly. I don't know why some of us weren't hurt; we might have shot one another's eyes out. Perhaps we were all very bad shots, or too thrilled to aim accurately at the skinny spiders we saw jumping around behind the bushes on the other side.

Those summers along the Schoharie were American summers and they did something to make a German boy into an American boy. But the year that I became twelve was the last for me of such delectable savagery.

CHAPTER SEVEN

IT WAS some four years after the boys were sent to Germany that the consequences of that misguided venture began to show. The question of Adolf's future arose. Addie wanted to go into business. Father agreed, and made plans to find him a job in New York at the foot of some ladder that promised an ultimate and profitable ascent.

Grandmother stayed his hand, as her devastating possessiveness reached down into the next generation. If the boy wanted to go into business, let it be in Germany. She could offer no hopeful prospects. The point was—and she stated it shamelessly—how, in her old age, could she be parted from this boy she had come to love? The thought that the boy had a life's work to prepare for, or that his mother might want to recover her child, does not seem to have occurred to her.

This time Father stood firm. His heart "bled" for her, he averred, but the boy's future came first. Suppose he did get Addie a start, say, in Bremen? The boy would have no real future there and would be away from Grandmother anyway.

Father stood up to his mother again when Fred expressed his ambition, when the time came, to go to the university in Göttingen, and study law. That frightened him, as he recognized for the first time the implications of what he had done in sending the boys abroad, and saw, lurking in the shadows, the stern face of Nemesis, spirit of retribution. "Any other profession," he wrote his mother, almost in

panic, "only not law, for then he would be lost to us completely."
Any knowledge of law the boy acquired in German universities would
be useless to him in America, Father pointed out, and, if he returned
home, he would have to begin his studies all over again. Or was he
planning to become a German subject? I can imagine the dismay
with which Father raised the question. Here was a possibility he had
not taken into account when he sent his sons to his mother. If
Grandmother discouraged the boy's predilections, there is no evidence
of it. Anyway, Fred was taking no directions from his grandmother,
his father or anybody else.

– 2 –

Five years after the boys had been sent from home Father was
finally in a position to visit his mother and see his sons again. Possibly, his journey had a further purpose, to bring Addie home himself
in case Grandmother proved obdurate. He took me along.

I was nine that summer, old enough to enjoy the strangeness of the
German landscape, the storks in the chimneys, the orderly fields, the
ruined castles and tile-roofed houses; and young enough not to feel
the tensions of Grandmother's household.

I remember the impressiveness of the old lady, dressed always in
black, with a cap of black lace on her head, a picture of power, soft-
ened, in my memory, by an expression of unrelieved sadness and by
what seems to me to have been genuine tenderness toward the little
boy who was her youngest grandchild. I see her in memory, sitting in
the right-hand sofa corner in the *beste Stube*, that was the parlor,
under an enlarged framed photograph of a fine-looking, rather stern
old man with clear-cut, intellectual features whom the Aunts always
spoke of with a respect that was near to reverence, as *Onkle* Leonhardt. The name, of course, meant nothing to me, but I was told
that he had been a close family friend.

Grandma, on her throne, was kindly enough so far as I was concerned. My sisters, who spent the following summer with her,
admitted they felt only fear of her but "never the desire to love her or

97

feel near to her." I remember no thunders, that summer. Once, moreover, I discovered that, underneath the solemnity and the melancholy, she had a faint approximation of humor.

She was entering the house with Father and pointed out to him the worn sandstone step before the door. "The tooth of time," she commented with a sentimental sigh. I was with them and rolled the phrase on my tongue. The next time I entered the house with one of the Aunts, I repeated it, with proper unction. The story got back to Grandmother, of course, and the way she gently kidded my borrowed philosophy, happily brings a shaft of sunlight across the somber portrait of her which other hands have painted.

There must have been endless discussions, that summer, of Addie's future, and Fred's, but I was not conscious of them; and there must have been hours on hours when Father, alone with Fred in one of the shady arbors in the garden, probed the tenacity of his determination—his portentous determination—to study law in Germany. Fred had come to terms of a sort with Grandmother and the Aunts. He had become obedient; he did as he was told, but he gave no one his confidence. Father did not get far with him; the independence of spirit which Fred had, in desperation, developed in relation to the three women who tried to break his spirit, proved as resolute in relation to Father. The only concession he would make took the form of a promise that, before making any irrevocable decision to study law in Göttingen, he would return home and look into some American law school.

My happiest memories of that summer center around Addie, whose tender heart and gentle spirit—so like Mother's—enveloped me with an elder brother's responsibility.

Father remained steadfast in the face of Grandmother's sighs and her eyes' piteous appeals. My newly acquired big brother went home with us.

– 3 –

Three years after Addie's return to the family, a mysterious and disturbing climax brought the curtain down on Grandmother Hagedorn. One spring, when Grandmother was in her late sixties, she had some kind of quarrel with her daughters—perhaps for once they stood up to her—and she left them in a blaze of temper to go to the Harz Mountains, ostensibly because she hoped the mountain air might relieve her asthma. The place she chose was a sanatorium in Ballenstedt, the little watering-place where she had spent a week with her friend Leonhardt, almost thirty years before.

There was always a veil of mystery over what followed. Suddenly, and for no adequate cause so far as her physical condition was concerned, she died.

The date?

I always got the creeps a little when I thought of the date. For it was the anniversary of Father's and Mother's marriage which she had so desperately resented. There was something a little terrifying to me in the coincidence.

– 4 –

I remember vividly when the news of her death reached us. There were no telephones for middle-income familes in Brooklyn in the middle nineties, or for any families, for that matter—and our cook came to my school to call me home. Father was in a terrific state, letting his emotions have their way, as though the very excess of tears were a tribute to his mother's memory. I suppose he blamed himself for many things that had nothing to do with the case, remembering maternal adjurations he had disregarded, maternal plans he had failed to fall in with. For days our house was like a mortuary. At the actual hour of the funeral service in Göttingen, we had a service in our back parlor, with all of us in mourning, of course, even the servants present, and the Reverend "Jakey" unctuously officiating. It was all pretty awful, but I think it comforted Father.

– 5 –

It is sixty-five years since Grandmother Hagedorn died, it is five since I have learned what actually happened, at the time of her death;

and the mystery is darker than ever. My brother Fred, happening to be in the neighborhood of Ballenstedt, some twenty years ago, decided to find out, if he could, what lay behind the hush-hush over Grandmother's death. At the sanatorium where she had died he asked to see the records, and was shaken and appalled by what they revealed.

Grandmother had committed suicide.

Why did she jump from the upper window to her death? Was it a sudden aberration in one of her periodic orgies of depression? Was the struggle to breathe suddenly too much for her? Was she filled with renewed bitterness over her son's marriage? She had returned to Ballenstedt, no doubt, as Leonhardt himself had once returned there, to nurture the sweet illusion that, for a moment, the happy past might come to life again. Had the memories that, for three decades, she had shared with no one, proved too poignant for her emotional nature, and, in a black moment of utter emptiness, overcome her? I shall never know.

The final ironic touch was the black-bordered announcement of her death which, according to German custom, her daughters issued "in the name of the deeply-sorrowing children and grandchildren." "After great suffering," it reads—and I have it before me as I write— the Lord had, "by a serene death," drawn *Frau Landsyndikus* Hagedorn into his heavenly kingdom.

The words, "serene death," stick in my crop. Granted that any hint of suicide would have started an unbearable clatter of tongues, need the lie have been quite so barefaced? The words throw a blazing light on the part that the conventions played in the lives of Charlotte's daughters. When anyone in Germany died it was customary to say that he had died a "serene death"—*einen sanften Tod*. So, of course, these good women, these fundamentally (I believe) honest women, must by every social compulsion say that their mother had died so, though the facts were such as to make the words a fraud and a mockery.

She deserved better of her daughters than that. With all her possessiveness, her self-will, her temper, her jealousy, her resentments, her autocratic spirit, she must have had great qualities. Four men loved her devotedly: her husband, her son, Dr. Leonhardt and her South German suitor. There must have been exceptional qualities of heart and mind in her to attract and hold such devotion, not for a year or two but for decades. Yet a fifth, one of Germany's leading economists, a professor at the University of Göttingen, was her warm admirer and friend. "She kept such friends," Irma writes, "and they worshiped her to her dying day. She was treated in the town like a saint, and her memory, for a long time, was almost a legend." Her descendants are the losers insofar as the qualities that inspired devotion are an assumption, based on indirect evidence, but the qualities that confused and disrupted our family life are a matter of record.

Who really was this woman with whom one of the leading personalities in the mid-century German world should have wanted so much to share his thoughts and aspirations? What was the "magic" that he felt, the spell to which he perpetually hungered to submit himself? What poisons were generated in her by her renunciation of the love he offered her and by the sorrow, through the years, she could not or would not share? What kind of Aspasia *was* this beautiful, high-tempered grandmother of mine?

– 6 –

On the surface, life went on as before in our little German world; but actually, that year that I became twelve, our family life took a new direction.

Fred had passed his matriculation examinations for the university, and, in fulfillment of his promise to Father, returned to America to consider the possibility of entering some American law school. He was just short of nineteen when he came to resume his place in the family circle, and almost a stranger. Mother had not seen him for eight years, and it was hard for her to identify this tall, reserved young man with the eager, affectionate, outgoing boy she had parted with so long ago. It must have been no less hard for Fred to pick up the threads so abruptly cut, and tied in knots for him by Grandmother's taboo on candor in his letters, and by his resentment against his long exile. That actually the threads were united again was due to a quality in Mother which was irresistible to a boy who, for eight years, had lived in an atmosphere of play-acting, and conformity at any price. It was her sheer integrity. Her emotions were true, to the last faint vibration. There was no sham in her, no cant, no trace of sentimentality. There was no sham in Fred either. The fellowship they developed was clear and deep and steadfast.

Fred seemed very foreign with his little silken moustache and his German ways. He had completely forgotten his English; but in Hunter, where we spent the summer, there happened to be an exceptionally attractive young lady from Norwich, Connecticut, named Jennie Carew. Jennie, as I remember her, was the perfect Gibson type, tall and slender, with golden hair; and, by the end of the month, Fred's English flowed like a brook.

The first hurdle in the way of Fred's return to American life being thus overcome, he faced the second, his professional training. Father got him an introduction to Seth Low, at that time president of Columbia University, and Fred went to see him about the possibility of entering the Columbia Law School. His credits proved ample and, for some time, the matter was touch and go. But Fred felt the lack of an American college background and of the associations which he knew were important in the practice of law in the United States. Try as he might, moreover, he could not see himself in the American picture. He had been away too long, and had, in his thinking and feeling, become too definitely a German. In October, he returned to Göttingen to enter the university.

His return widened the cleft between our family and the country of which Father was a citizen, the country in which all six of us children had been born. For now that an intimate relationship with Fred had been re-established and he had decided not to remain in the United States, it became clear that Father and Mother would want to take every opportunity to be with him in the land he had chosen, the land that had once been their own, and Father, for one, had never really given up.

~ Part Three ~

CHAPTER ONE

I SUPPOSE it was just coincidence, but after Grandmother Hagedorn's death the family finances took a sharp turn upward, and that, in spite of the 1893 panic. Perhaps subconsciously, Father felt his mother's resentment that he was in America at all, felt it as a kind of drag, as, I am sure, he felt as a spur his responsibility to his sisters, now that his mother was gone. Whatever it was, he, who in the late eighties had been financially unable to make the journey alone to visit his mother, was able, the year after Grandmother's death, to take not only himself but Mother, the girls and me.

We went straight to Göttingen; we scarcely ever went anywhere else, indeed, on our successive and, before long, our annual trans-Atlantic journeys, except for a few weeks once or twice to the Harz Mountains, a couple of hours away by train, to Pomerania where Mother's people came from, and once or twice to the Bavarian Alps. We never went to London or Paris or Rome; we didn't even go to Berlin until much later, when we were all grown up; or to the Rhine, or to Weimar where Goethe had lived, or to the Wartburg where Luther had translated the Bible and thrown the famous inkwell at the Devil. It seems never to have occurred to Father that visits to historic shrines might widen our horizons or deepen our conceptions of life or of that German cultural atmosphere in which we spent our childhood. We went to Göttingen straight from the boat landing at Bremerhafen in June; we left Göttingen to return straight to Bremerhafen in September. We went to Europe, that is, with blinders on.

We saw Göttingen but we saw practically nothing else. If Father had had any conscious thought of making nice little Germans of us children, he muffed a thousand opportunities. But I don't believe that that idea ever occurred to him. He took us to Göttingen because his sisters were there.

Once, indeed, he took us because he wanted to keep them there. According to German custom, Father and Mother were planning a big celebration of their silver wedding anniversary. The date was in the middle of May, 1897, and we expected, in late June, to go for the summer to Lake Minnewaska, just south of the Catskills. Unexpectedly, came ecstatic letters from the Aunts saying that they had decided to come over for the silver wedding. Father received the news at the office and, before he returned home, that night, had made steamer reservations to Bremen for us all, and had written the Aunts in effect: too bad about their dear intent, but he was planning to bring the whole family to them. Even after a quarter-century, Father had not forgotten the strains and stresses of his "beloved sisters'" visits. There was to be no repetition of anything of that sort. Elsbeth and Alma were wonderful in their own environment, he was prepared to assert to all and sundry, but he would not try to set them in an American frame. Not again!

- 2 -

Remembering my summers in the Catskills—the Schoharie, the swimming hole, the bean-shooters, the boys I ran with—I was inclined to consider Göttingen an arid wilderness, unfit for human habitation; I considered it thus, that is, for our first two or three visits. So long as I compared my activities there with my free, exuberant life in the Catskills, I was miserable; and it was only after I came to recognize that Göttingen summers might have qualities which, though different from those I longed for, were not without their charm, that Göttingen began to seem bearable and finally attractive.

Grandmother's house was situated at the northern edge of the town where the residential section gave way to open fields. She had built it with a legacy left her by one of her husband's brothers, designing the square, three-story structure herself. The house was spacious and comfortable, the living rooms large, high-ceilinged and well proportioned, the stairway fairly palatial in its breadth and easy ascent. The upper hall from which the bedrooms opened was eight or ten feet across, and the casement windows in all the rooms were high and wide. The huge porcelain stoves in the bedrooms had the impressiveness of an oriental tomb but did not come within shouting distance of American standards of heating; and the toilet, off a landing, halfway between the first floor and the second, was such as may still be noted in ruined castles, built out over the cliff's edge. Actually, it was less hygienic than the mediaeval, since a huge tun in the cellar received what, in the case of the castles, earth and sun, and wind and rain absorbed. The periodic, professional transfer, pail by pail, of the contents of the tun to a truck on the street was torture to the sensibilities. The facilities for bathing were only a little less primitive. There was a bathroom in the cellar with a huge stove to heat the water and you had to give the Aunts notice, days ahead, when you planned to take a bath. In my case I suppose it was Mother who made the date for me, since I was at an age when bathing is not a voluntary act. For reasons of thrift, *Tante* Elsbeth and *Tante* Alma generally directed the girls and me to take our baths in the water in which one or the other of the Aunts had just taken hers. There were no bath towels such as we know them today. You wrapped yourself in a sheet which, I assume, was subsequently hung on the clothesline to dry and used on a bed.

The garden, surrounding the house on three sides, was a glory of mottled shade and sunlight, of winding paths and benches in hidden nooks, of shrubbery and fruit trees and berry bushes and comfortable arbors—three of them!—and little islands of soft lawn. There were peaches and apricots on the wall of the square, solid house, Seckel pears on a tall tree that dominated the garden like some elder spirit, cherries—when the sparrows did not see them first—on a small tree near a garden patch which I was allowed to regard as my special own. Altogether, it was a garden for a boy to eat, drink and be merry in. Birds loved it, nesting undisturbed under the thatched roofs of the arbors. The heavy shrubbery made numberless coverts for hide-and-seek.

The garden played a substantial part in the life of the household. The three arbors were located in such a manner that one or the other provided shelter in any wind. Whenever the weather was even reasonably fair—the Aunts could stand astonishing amounts of chilliness—we had our afternoon coffee in one of these arbors. This fourth meal, served at three-thirty, was as much a part of the day's routine as any of the others. I can see the maid, now, bearing the tray with the steaming coffee, the pitcher of hot milk, the luscious, buttery *Butterkuchen* or the open *Apfeltorte* with the apple slices folded against each other and baked on the lightest of piecrusts.

At the arbor nearest the house, and the one most often used, was the post and the four-foot-square platform for a *Kegelspiel*, a nine-pin variant of the more familiar alley game, which, for some reason that I have never been able to understand, has, so far as I know, never been taken up in any other country. From a kind of gallows, about a dozen feet high, a typical bowling ball, some eight inches in diameter is suspended by a rope. The pins on the platform are set around a kingpin, and the object is to swing the ball around a three-foot post, just beyond the platform, in such a way as to knock down eight pins and leave the kingpin standing; failing that, to knock down as many pins as possible, including the king. It's the best garden game I've ever played, for, though it takes considerable skill to play it well, any tyro can have fun at it. I have happy memories of young and old leaving their coffee and cake to take their turn, and can still hear the clatter of the pins and the shouts as the great "strike" was made, or just missed. There was one element in the game which, I remember, was more taken for granted than stressed; it was a good idea to keep out of the orbit of the ball. I don't know yet why, at those casual afternoon-coffee-and-bowling sessions, someone wasn't occasionally knocked cold.

The only exercise I got was walking, generally by myself, and an occasional riding lesson from a stocky and perennially grouchy riding master with a square gray beard, who used to drive through town in a minute landau with an eighteenth century air, drawn by two little white ponies. His name intrigued me. Baron Münchhausen, for such he was, was, in fact, a descendant of the immortal liar, as well as of a later, more constructive baron of the same name who had been, in effect, the creator of Göttingen's university.

Now and again I had a swim.

The *Göttinger städtische Badeanstalt* was an awful comedown from my Schoharie swimming hole. It was a good deal larger, of course, but where the Schoharie was crystal clear, the River Leine was muddy brown. And cold! Suffering Moses! I don't know what the temperature was but I don't think it was ever over 55. Yet I recall the place with feelings of considerable gratitude, for it was there that I learned to swim. The method of teaching was odd and I have never seen it tried elsewhere, but it did what it was supposed to do and did it rather quickly and under what seem to me still distinctly adverse conditions.

The bathing establishment was built across the river so that the swift, coffee-colored waters flowed under it. Along the covered piazza in front of the bathhouses ran a heavy rail supported at proper intervals on posts. Upon this rail the swimming instructor rested a seven- or eight-foot pole, about two inches thick, with a rope at the end of it and at the end of the rope a canvas band that was fastened under the pupil's armpits. The instructor was a nice old fellow named Fritz Kleie who prided himself on his ability to call the strokes in several languages. As he moved the pole with its human fish across the river he would chant, *Eins, zwei, drei!* On *eins* I was supposed to shoot my joined palms forward; on *zwei* sweep them to either side, and on *drei* bring them to my chest. What the legs were supposed to do, except on *drei* to shoot back, I don't remember. *Eins, zwei, drei,* it went, *un, deux, trois—* Don't ask me to reproduce his French as modified and orchestrated by purest *Jöttingsh—vann, too, t'ree, uno, duo, tre, eins, zwei, drei,* and so on, for twenty minutes, while my flesh congealed. When the time came for my first solo swim without the support of Fritz Kleie's fishpole, I was sure that the river was twice as wide and twice as cold and the current twice as swift as ever before.

CHAPTER TWO

THE girls and I agreed that Göttingen was the "jumping-off place" and, summer after summer, with mounting exasperation, bewailed its boredom; but, as I look down the long perspective, I recognize that actually I was never half so bored as I told myself I was. Göttingen wasn't the Catskills, but it wasn't Brooklyn either. The little town had exceptional charm and interest within itself, and environs which kindled my imagination and left nostalgic memories.

There were character and tradition in the gently winding Weender *Strasse*, with its line of brick-and-plaster structures on either side, broken only by an occasional narrow side street where residences nestled in hidden gardens. The tablets on the walls related the houses, moreover, to great worthies in the German past, and, curiously, the American past, too. In this house the Grimm brothers had lived, in that other, Henry Wadsworth Longfellow; in yet another, George Bancroft, the American historian, and, a generation later, J. Pierpont Morgan. (Anyone in Göttingen who knew anything could tell you that the financial colossus might have had a professorship in mathematics at the University if he had been willing to wait for it.) You went down a kind of Avenue of Fame, going down the Weender *Strasse*. But Göttingen was more than a pantheon of the illustrious dead. Many of the living were no less notable. Again and again, on the Weender *Strasse*, I must have passed—in my ignorance, without a tremor—some of the world's greatest men in the field of science and mathematics, among others, Walther Nernst, whose

113

work in thermodynamics anticipated Max Planck's, and Planck himself, whose *quantum* theory was a chief steppingstone to nuclear fission.

The heart of the town was the market place to which, three times a week, the heavy-set muscular peasant women came from the farms round about, carrying on their backs huge baskets of produce, or striding beside little wagons drawn by shepherd dogs. In their stalls, they sold live fowl, eggs, cheese, vegetables, fruit and dried fish. The crowing, the cackle and the quacks mingled with the chatter of the peasant women and the occasional shrill haggling, punctuated at intervals by the solemn boom of the *Rathaus* clock. I can still see the mingled colors on the stalls, the bright greens and vermilions and yellows, and smell the dubious fragrance of the fish, cheese and decaying vegetables and the body odor of the earthy peasant women.

The *Rathaus*, sturdily built of cut gray stone, had a long slate roof with a turret and occasional dormers. It also had a *Keller* where the town fathers were wont to meet for what was known as a "second breakfast"—beer and sandwiches—against a background of huge tuns in which wine matured "in the wood." The *Keller* brimmed over on the sidewalk where broad awnings kept off the sun. Near-by, and the focus of interest in the market place, was a lovely fountain on which a graceful little bronze goosegirl herded her bronze wards under a canopy of interwoven metal boughs.

I used to enjoy going to market with *Tante* Elsbeth who ran the household at 41 Weender *Chaussée*, and watch her match wits—and tongue—with the peasant women. I can still hear her shocked exclamations as she heard the day's price of a bunch of carrots or a quart of peas, her strident incredulity that anyone could be so brazen as to charge such a price. "*Na, Frau Kopp*"—she knew all the peasants by name—"*das hätt' ich von Ihnen, weiss Gott, nicht erwartet dass Sie mich so schinden würden!*" (God knew, she had never expected so to be cheated, not by Frau Kopp!) The peasant woman would answer with hot shot in best *Jöttingsh*—a patois distinct to the region but related to the *Plattdeutsch* of the North—and *Tante* Elsbeth, who was as good a haggler as any peasant, would come back with a fresh reproach. At last, a compromise would be reached and my aunt would open her little black purse and reluctantly hand over the forty or fifty *pfennig*—ten to twelve and a half cents—that the war had been about. Then, with a firm set of her thin lips and a snap of satisfaction in her coffee-colored eyes at having got what she wanted for five *pfennig* or ten less than the peasant had asked, she would move to the next stand and repeat the performance. After an hour of this you would have thought she would drop into one of the *Ratskeller* chairs, exhausted, but she strode the mile home, exhilarated, at a pace that I, carrying the accumulated bundles, could hardly keep up with.

The market was held three mornings a week—Tuesday, Thursday and Saturday. The other days and all the afternoons, the scene in the Rathausplatz was different. While I was in college I tried to paint the picture:

> "At Pievenick in the market place
> The sun shone down with waning glow,
> Where two cab-horses, face to face,
> Discussed with ponderous nods and slow,
> Long-faded loves, forsaken passions,
> Time's ravages and shortened rations.
> Deserted were the streets; no sound
> Broke on the heavy silence round
> Save the faint plash of waters cool,
> From brazen goose-bills, gaping wide,
> And tongues of drowsy boys, beside
> The wet curb of the shady pool.
> Over the square a lone dog crept,
> Stretched in the fountain's shade, and slept;
> And by the sombre Rathaus wall
> An old fruit-vendor drowsed and drowsed,
> While bees hummed idly in the stall
> And roundabout the green flies browsed.
> The clock on the Rathaus pealed the hour,

And a gargoyle droned from the minster-tower:
'We do not heed your foolish tick
In the market place in Pievenick.' "

Except for the gargoyle and the minster, which are there by poetic license, that is the Göttingen *Rathausplatz* during the 1890's.

– 2 –

Next to the market place, the most attractive physical feature of the town to me was the heavily shaded promenade known as *"Der Wall."* I don't know what imaginative and farsighted *Bürgermeister,* generations and possibly centuries ago, was inspired to transform the town's enduring legacy of the Thirty Years' War, the unsightly rubble of the old city wall, into an element of beauty, a belt around the inner town and a place for meditation and recreation. Nor do I know how long it took men with oxcarts and shovels to cover the stone and mortar deep enough in rich soil to grow trees on it. But there it is, a promenade some thirty feet wide, lined with a double row of linden trees, where pedestrians, raised some twenty feet above the adjoining gardens, may stroll in the shade from the University at the *Weendertor,* past the botanical gardens, to the *Theaterplatz,* with the civic theater and the *Gymnasium,* or from these past the *Volksschule* to the barracks at the *Geismartor.* If their energy holds out, as mine frequently did, they can walk clear round the ancient limits of the town, past the little octagonal house, directly on the *Wall,* in which Bismarck had lived as a student, and from which, booted and spurred, he had stalked imperiously to the lecture hall; and, farther along past the pond where the swans still float placidly under the boughs of silver beeches.

Göttingen's *Wall* is not unique. Nienburg, where Father was born, has a *Wall* as one of its chief features, but I have seen no German city which can come near matching the public pleasance from which the burgher of Göttingen may view its spires and many-angled roofs. When the town, in the middle 1950's, celebrated its one thousandth anniversary, a German poet chanted his own memories of the *Wall*: "The quietness there is a never-ending miracle. You hear the wind in the boughs and, overlooking the Botanical Garden, the chirping of the grasshoppers, but the noise of the city barely reaches it. When the sunset glow has faded in the West, the stars glimmer among the branches and when you look toward the town the church-steeples are silhouetted faintly against the still luminous sky."

It had that kind of breathless magic for me, any time of the day.

CHAPTER THREE

As I look back and re-create in memory the Göttingen that I came to know so well—to know better, indeed, than I ever knew Brooklyn or its eminent neighbor across the East River—faces rise before me, cutting off my view of streets and buildings. There is, first of all, *Frau Bürgermeisterin* Eberhardt, widow of a long-departed burgomaster, who lived in a small flat across the street from the Aunts with a mentally retarded daughter whose obese form was always moving restlessly in the shadows of the room. The old lady was glad of any company, and, God knows, I was grateful at intervals to get away from the tensions of the Aunts' household; so I frequently climbed the stairs to sit down with the warmhearted old widow and consume the chocolates she always had on hand for me. She had Grandma Schwedler's gift of making a boy feel important; she treated me as an equal, and thereby, I think, helped me, by just so much, to grow up.

There was another old lady in Göttingen whom I like to remember. *Tante* Auguste Mensching was a relative on the Günther side, a cousin by marriage of Grandmother's. She lived at the farther end of town in an attractive old house with a garden, just outside the old city wall next the *Geismartor*, the only surviving gate of the old walled town, and opposite the regimental barracks. Grandmother had always rather looked down on this little woman who had presumed to marry into her mother's family. When Father and Mother were in Göttingen in the early eighties, Grandmother took Mother to the housewarming that *Tante* Auguste gave when she moved into her house. Mother told us long after how gracious and appreciative of everything Grandmother had been at the party, and how she sank into a chair when she got home, exclaiming, "Thank God, everything is more beautiful in *my* home!"

Tante Auguste had a daughter, Luischen, a sweet, fluttery creature without much brains but with a warm heart. When the atmosphere at the Aunts' house became too sultry for us, we children went to take refuge with her and her mother. They had a platform under the wide windows looking out on the street and, hour after hour, they would sit there watching the world go by. I cherished them because neither ever pretended to be anything but the kindly, harmless creature that she was, and you could be natural with them. I think the Aunts regarded their unpretentiousness as a lack of appreciation of the obligations of social position.

– 2 –

There were two main social groups in Göttingen, centering on the University and on the regiment garrisoned in the town; but, so far as we were concerned, only the University counted. Our contact with the students was mainly through my brother Fred, who was pursuing his law studies there and frequently brought members of his *Studenten Corps Bremensia* in their little green caps to the house to call on the girls. The elect among them wore narrow ribbons, striped green, red and black, across their chests, signifying that they had emerged from the class of *Fuchs* to that of *Bursche*. That emergence was costly, including as it did long months of practice with the whiplike steel with which they fought their duels, the duel itself with some member of another *Corps*, and the subsequent ordeal of having the wound in the cheek sewn up without anaesthetics on the surgeon's part or the flutter of an eyelash on theirs. The object of the whole performance was to test the student's nerve, on the assumption, if his nerve were sound, his honor and fraternal loyalty could be depended on. It did not always work out that way, as Fred himself learned to his pain.

The duels were forbidden by law but the police habitually looked the other way. Fred let me witness one of the *Mensuren* at an old historic tavern, a mile or two beyond the *Geismartor*. The skill of the fencers and the Spartan disregard of pain were alike evident but the impression that remained with me was one of abhorrence at the cruelty of the ordeal—not the suffering, which must have been bad enough, but the punishment for a boy's inability to control his nervous reactions to the pain. For the boy who thus failed was dropped from the *Corps* and condemned to carry the humiliation with him through life.

The Aunts had friends in all the University faculties, some of them eminent. I remember *Tante* Elsbeth returning from a dinner one night and telling us she had had the distinguished mathematician, Professor Detmold, as her partner at dinner, adding innocently, "and, you know, I wasn't conscious of his great intelligence at all, not at all." She was puzzled when we children burst into a roar.

- 3 -

Among the most frequent guests at the Aunts' house, for Sunday dinner or afternoon coffee, were the Schulenburgs. *Generalmajor* von der Schulenburg was a retired officer of the old Prussian school, tall and lean, with the monocle and the exaggerated, rasping, nasal twang of a musical comedy lieutenant; but he was an affectionate old soul who took a shine to my sisters and liked to warm his old bones at the fire of their unselfconscious gaiety and charm. His wife was an amusing, kindhearted gossip with merry little round eyes set in a ball on a bigger ball, placed on a bigger ball yet, and was always blowing in and out of the house, bubbling with some new tidbit.

Her flutterings in anticipation of her distinguished father's seventy-fifth birthday gave me a glimpse into the tragicomedy of the Germans' passion for titles and decorations. The Kaiser was confidently expected to use the occasion to bestow on the great economist the rank of *Wirklicher Geheimerat*, a title which would raise not only the professor but his wife to the status of *Excellency* and the whole family to the very summit of social distinction. All the great of Göttingen came to offer their congratulations and pay their tribute, but the Emperor's expected emissary did not come, and when the last guest had left the pleasant house on the *Obere Karspüle* there were no newly-tapped Excellencies in it. It was a tragedy of sorts, whose saddest aspect was that sensible people should care so much about so trivial a thing, and that so many of their countrymen were similarly obsessed.

Such things, in fact, mattered enormously in Germany in the 1890's and early 1900's. Certain decorations went almost automatically to officers or public officials when they reached certain grades; first, the Order of the Red Eagle, fourth class, then the fourth class of the Order of the Crown, then the third of the Red Eagle and so on. To be passed over at any point was regarded as a deliberate humiliation. An exceptionally gifted man we knew in Göttingen, indeed, voluntarily terminated a brilliant career in the German army, retiring as brigade-commander, in a huff, because the Kaiser had failed to give him the decoration of a certain grade of the Order of the Red Eagle or the Order of the Crown which the General felt he was ripe for.

The German comic weekly, *Simplicissimus*, published an amusing gag on this hierarchy of honors, introducing a certain mythical *Herr Geheimecommerzienrat* who, the paper reported, boasted the Order of the Red Eagle of the fourth class, rode on the railroad third class, had a reputation for honesty that was second class, and was a dumb ox—a *Rindvieh*—of the first class.

– 4 –

There was one couple that used to visit us at Göttingen who saw the idiocy of the rank-and-honors business with singularly clear eyes and a sense of values that, in its depth of perception, was rare in Germany and, indeed, anywhere.

Mother had met Gertrud von Mauntz at the Paris exhibition in 1869 and, though they did not meet again for over a quarter-century, a lively exchange of letters had deepened their friendship in the interval.

Tante Gertrud, as we children knew her, had a keen mind, a warm heart and a rippling sense of humor that played over everything that her quick eyes rested upon, and none of the false dignity that we children found so oppressive in the Aunts. From the commonplace walk to town she would bring back a dozen capitivating pictures and hilarious stories. One evening, as we were seated for supper, she did not notice that all heads were reverently bowed for the grace that I, as the youngest, was always expected to pronounce. I was about to begin, *Komm, lieber Herr Jesu*, when *Tante* Gertrud burst out: "Today I saw the most exchanting poodle!" All reverence died that instant. *Tante* Gertrud and the poodle had the floor.

Alfred von Mauntz, her husband, with his gray Burnside whiskers, his twinkling eyes and his gentle heart, proved to be one of the notable personalities that illuminated and enriched my boyhood. When I first knew him he could have been only in his early fifties but he had long retired from the army with the brevet-rank of lieutenant colonel. His superiors had noted that the *Herr Major* had disturbing ideas, liberal ideas, and that there were sacred cows that were just cows to him, to whom he might, as soon as not, address a disrespectful "Boo!" The *Herr Major*, that is, did not fit into the ark of Solemn Assumptions commanded by His Imperial Majesty and manned by the crew of the heavily bemedaled and unreflective guardians of the throne. The Major cheerfully agreed that he was in the wrong boat and hurried to climb into another.

When I first knew *Onkel* Mauntz, as we children called him, he was using his freedom to do Shakespeare research, especially in the field of heraldry. This was no amateur's casual hobby. He went at it with the meticulous attention to detail characteristic of German scholarship, struggling after the hidden meanings of English words with all the persistence of an aspirant for a Heidelberg Ph.D. His translations of the Shakespeare sonnets, moreover, had the quality of original poetry. Neither his research nor his translations were given adequate recognition by Shakespearean scholars—partly, I assume, because he was not a member of the union—but he lived by the Goethe dictum—*Die Tat ist alles, Nichts der Ruhm*—the deed is what counts, the recognition is nothing—and was at peace with himself and the world.

The visits of *Tante* Gertrud and her husband were a delight to us children. The keen-witted and aesthetically sensitive pair had one dream—a winter in Italy—which, since they had nothing but a slender pension to live on, they never expected to see fulfilled. In later years, after prosperity came to Father, he helped their dream come true, giving them an eight months' leisurely journey which proved the high point of their lives. I remember *Tante* Gertrud's ebullient letters, full of the beauty, warmth and color of Italy, and of the accumulated tradition of two millennia of history that the sensitive, civilized couple were absorbing and making part of themselves.

I remember, too, how casual and wholly unselfconscious Father was about this imaginative contribution to the lives of two people he cherished.

CHAPTER FOUR

THE people we saw most of in Göttingen were, of course, the Aunts, and there were moments when they filled the foreground so completely that we could see nothing and nobody else.

They were in their middle fifties by this time and, in appearance, a complete contrast to each other. Elsbeth was a compact little bundle of taut wire, thin lips and snapping eyes—the very embodiment of the busy housewife, running the household with a fearful energy that left a wake of sparks whenever she passed. She was Simon Legree himself to the maid-of-all-work, generally a girl in her teens from one of the farmsteads near town. There was one sweet young thing, named Dorette, who was with the Aunts for years, building up a "dot," I take it, against the day of marriage. I remember *Tante* Elsbeth's priceless conclusion to one blistering lecture: "And you ought to go down on your knees in gratitude every night of your life that you have such a good place!"—and poor little Dorette's pathetic whimper, "I do, I do!"

The picture of this stalwart peasant lass going down on her knees every night to thank God for *Tante* Elsbeth was one of the gorgeous hilarities of our Göttingen days.

If *Tante* Elsbeth had the energy and some of the appearance of a ferret, Alma had the stateliness and grand manner of a tragedy queen, entering a drawing room with hands outstretched, and dripping honeyed words. Elsbeth had no intellectual pretensions; so far as I know, she never read anything but the *Göttinger Tageblatt* or the *Hannoverscher Kourier*—and, in these, mainly the romantic serials; but Alma liked to give the impression that she was quite something intellectually, and felt humiliated when she lost at parlor games. Once, when Irma, who could turn circles around *Tante* Alma in mental agility, beat her in a contest of wits, Alma remarked patronizingly, "Well, even a blind hen occasionally finds a grain." Irma, boiling inside, kept her gift of rejoinder for once in abeyance.

My sisters were merciless in their attempts to uncover hidden romances in the Aunts' past. "What opportunities we had, my dears," exclaimed Alma, "if we had wanted to marry! More than once, the issue hung by a thread, a silken thread."

Elsbeth, as always, was more down-to-earth. "Our mother's love affairs kept us so busy, we just had no chance to consider our own."

– 2 –

The Aunts were always putting on a show. When Elsbeth's most intimate friend lay dying in a house that she passed daily on her way to market, Irma, who generally accompanied her, would observe Elsbeth's self-conscious air of melancholy as she looked up at her friend's windows. Finally, one day, they noticed that the windows were wide open. "Now," Elsbeth exclaimed cheerfully, "she *must* be dead! Living, she never *would* open a window!"

Some of the theater the Aunts treated us to was rich in comedy as I look back on it, though it did not seem too funny at the time. But some German verses of mine that I excavated recently from a mass of old family papers indicate that once, at least, I had known comedy when I saw it.

The jingle, written in the manner of Wilhelm Busch, records what I entitled an "Idyll of the Breakfast Hour": As I enter the dining room I ask the Aunts the perfunctory question, How have they slept?—and get the customary litany of aches and pains. Father enters. Alma flutters, and sends Elsbeth to the kitchen to fetch the hot milk; doing it in a peremptory tone, moreover, that she would never have dreamed of using if Father's presence had not inhibited in Elsbeth the instant reaction of the famous Hagedorn temper. Elsbeth does not dare erupt, so she sulks. The temperature of the room rises, the barometer falls. Elsbeth's firm-set lips tell clearly what is going to happen to Alma when she gets her alone. Everyone wishes he were somewhere else. Only Alma, knowing well enough what is coming, nods her head soulfully toward Father, who is wondering what the devil it is all about anyway.

It was typical *Tantentheater*.

-3-

Protocol loomed large in the house on the Weender *Chaussée*. It is focused for me in the commotion I caused when I casually sat down on the sofa during a *Kaffeegesellschaft*. The sofa, I was told in shocked tones, was for ladies; the right-hand seat on the sofa was for the most distinguished lady present. How the Aunts managed, on every occasion, to make the delicate distinctions involved, I don't know; nor how they assuaged the hurt feelings of the ladies who thought they had the right to the high place and failed to get it. But the tragicomedy of the *rechte Sofa Ecke* went on perennially. Akin to it was the flutter that resulted when anyone but the Most Important Person in any party that was leaving the house for a drive into the country took the right-hand back seat in a carriage. That seat was for the chief guest or for Mother. The fact was that Mother did not care where she sat; but the forms had to be observed or the social structure crumbled.

This sense of social grading went even into the quality of the cake and coffee the Aunts served at their gossip parties—*Kaffeeklatsch* was the word, though *Tante* Elsbeth sharply rebuked me when I used it in reference to one of their afternoon gatherings. "We *never* gossip!" she declared. "Their hospitality, with square yards of *Butterkuchen*," Irma wrote me, long afterward, "was renowned every-

126

where, but that they had three sets they invited was known, I think, only to me and one other. The first set had the cake fresh from the baker's; the next had it the following day, when it began to be stale; and the third were allowed to chew at it when it was old and hard; and there was milk instead of cream for the coffee which, itself, had been kept since the first day and 'lengthened,' according to need."

– 4 –

I suppose the trouble between us children and the Aunts was due, in the main, to the fact that their lives, within and without, were circumscribed by formulas which were natural, even hallowed, to them and were not at all natural or hallowed to us children, for all our German upbringing. Father had—to some extent, at least—stepped beyond the narrow world those bounds enclosed, and Mother had never breathed its stale, mediaeval air at all. The world in which the Aunts had their being regarded a stratified society as divine dispensation; princes, counts and barons as not quite ordinary clay; and any person with any title, more worthy of attention than any person with none. With this awe in the Aunts of titles and position went a reverence for anyone having influential connections. They called them *gute Beziehungen,* and the unctuous way the Aunts rolled the term on the tongue, we children, young as we were, found faintly sickening. If I heard the words on their lips once, I must have heard them a hundred times, spoken always in accents of awe.

– 5 –

What irritated us most of all in the Aunts was their determination that not only our minds but our emotions and even our social reactions must conform to their accepted pattern.

I remember one summer morning in the garden—and, as I think about it I seem to catch the faint odor of the ripening apricots on the espalier. Addie, who had spent a year in Lyons working as a kind of gentleman-apprentice in a wholesale textile house, was visiting in Göttingen on his way back to New York, and had been at a dance the night before.

"I am sure he enjoyed himself," *Tante* Elsbeth remarked.

"No," I answered. "I gather that he was bored to death."

"What!" exclaimed Elsbeth, her face flushing with anger. "He said he was bored? Arrogant! A young man going to a party must not be bored!"

I can't imagine that she really meant the kind of iron control over one's capacity for pleasure that she seemed to imply. What she actually was declaring was that a well brought up young man clothed his feelings in acceptable hypocrisies, even to a brother.

– 6 –

The Aunts were at their best in their role as providers. I said that *Tante* Elsbeth ran the household. She did, without dispute. But *Tante* Alma had a large part in the meals which are a glowing memory of our summers in Göttingen.

Those meals were a foretaste of Elysium. Of course, we children did not always get what our elders got—"Dear Hermann," Elsbeth might exclaim to Father, "the pheasants are glorious!" Then, turning quickly to us at the other end of the table, "Children, eat bean salad!"—but generally we all shared on equal terms. Those shoulders of veal, those rich but never too rich gravies, those string beans cooked in milk, those creamed cucumbers, those herring salads, those jellied currant-and-raspberry concoctions we knew as *Rote Grütze!*

The Aunts delighted in our appreciation of their offerings. Father, of course, paid the bills, but the money was the least of what went into the makings of those beautiful meals. Pride in the role of homemaker and provider; the civilized individual's sense of food not as fodder but as a kind of earthy sacrament; the artist's joy of creating and perfecting, which gave dignity and continuing interest to what might otherwise have seemed an unending and finally unendurable chore; a genuine caring for those whom they served; experience, following years of instruction—all those bright intangibles—went into those meals. The memory of them almost makes me ashamed that, in the course of a long and finally affectionate relationship, I have harbored feelings about the Aunts that have sometimes been less than kind.

CHAPTER FIVE

WHAT with the Aunts' cooking, the attractive people we came to know in the town, the friends who came to stay with us, our Göttingen summers were actually anything but the punishment for unimagined sins that the girls and I persuaded ourselves that they were.

Almost every Sunday afternoon that the weather was fair we went on an *Ausflug*. A "flight out" is what the expressive German word says, and a flight out it was, out of the world of pavements, high walls and cramped horizons, into the pleasant open country surrounding the town. Father would send me to Kulp, the liveryman—there were no telephones in Göttingen in those days—to order an open coach, occasionally two coaches, into which we and our guests would pile, I, by preference, riding on the box beside the coachman. The carriages were heavy, the horses were what livery horses generally are; so the drive, seven or eight miles down the macadamized highway to Burg Hardenberg or to Mariaspring, was generally long and hot. But there were compensations at the other end.

The Hardenberg was a ruined castle that had belonged to the counts of Hardenberg for God knows how long. A Count of the name indeed still had a manor house at the foot of the ruin and for all I know may still have it, and it was a romantic experience to me to have him dine with us once in New York, when he was on a visit to the United States—a little like having a lesser Sir Launcelot sit at our table. Most of the outer walls of the castle were down but enough yet stood to give a clear impression of what the whole had been. Indications of the inner walls remained, moreover, giving me the outlines of the rooms; and I never tired of wandering from one to another, letting my imagination re-create their structure, their furnishings, and the life that they had known. There was a little inn at the foot of the castle where we always had coffee, which the inn provided, and *Kaffeekuchen* which we brought ourselves. In the coolness of the late afternoon we would drive back, we young people singing student songs and folk songs as the horses sleepily padded their slow way through the long twilight.

Another romantic ruin was the Plesse, whose two surviving towers —one huge and portly, the other slender and tall—rose out of a dense forest to overlook the countryside. Archaeologically, the Plesse was less interesting than the Hardenberg, since, except for the two towers, its destruction had been complete, but it was an experience to climb the winding stair in one of the towers from which, you knew, the Counts von Plesse had watched for the approach of their enemies or of some cavalcade escorting wagons of potential loot. There were tables and benches in what, I suppose, had been the castle's inner court, and coffee was served there.

After coffee, we invariably went on foot down the long wooded slope to Göttingen's most enchanting *Ausflugsort*, Mariaspring, while the carriage took the long way round with anyone who preferred it. Walking through those woods was more than a half hour's painless exercise. I learned early that, to a German, any woods were a kind of temple. One of the most moving of German songs asks the question:

> "Wer hat dich, du schöner Wald,
> Aufgebaut so hoch da droben?"

and answers it with the high solemnity of an anthem. If in the cool of the evening the God of the English walks in gardens, the God of the Germans walks in the woods. I had the sense that the green-coated foresters were a kind of priesthood whose duty it was to keep the temple ready at all times to receive the deity. Walking down from the Plesse to Mariaspring you were hushed by the sense of a Presence.

– 2 –

There was nothing hushed about Mariaspring. There, of a Sunday afternoon, or a Wednesday, the sweet young things of Göttingen, the *Backfische* with their long braids wound round their heads, were wont to dance with the *Corps* students. At long tables next to the dance platform sat the students, by *Corps*—the *Bremenser* in their green caps, the *Borussen*—young aristocrats, most of them—in blue, and the others each in their color; and on the terraces, climbing the hillside in the mottled sunlight and shade, the fathers and mothers of the girls with their younger children—professors and their families, in the main—sat at stone tables consuming vast amounts of coffee and *Kaffeekuchen*. An orchestra played waltzes, polkas and mazurkas, not too badly, punctuated at intervals by the pop of an air gun in a shooting gallery near-by. The young people trotted coyly forward and back and swung round, or whirled in the traditional German waltz that knows no relief of reversing; but dizziness seemed never to overcome them—only the heat. Then they would retire from the platform, flushed and out of breath, the girl on the young man's arm, to be restored properly to the bosom of her family.

Sometimes we took the excursion in reverse, taking our coffee and cake at Mariaspring, walking up the green slope to the Plesse in the soft summer twilight and picking up the carriage there. Whichever way we did it, the orchestra in the greenwood, the colorful, whirling figures on the platform, the family groups on the successive terraces, were a picture whose colors remain vivid after half a century, and an experience which, in a period of speed and noise and violent appetites, speaks to me still of the simple and satisfying pleasures of a civilized society.

There were two country inns on the eastern side of the town that we used to drive to occasionally, in the villages of Bremke and Eichenkrug; both, alas, now in East German hands and, for the time at least, beyond revisiting. Bremke, I remember chiefly because it was in the inn there once, as we were starting to go home after our coffee, that Father caught *Tante* Alma slipping the lumps from the sugar bowl into her reticule. Alma flushed as she explained that Father had paid for the sugar, so why not take it along? Father was firm. "I think," he said, "we can afford to buy our own sugar." To one brought up like *Tante* Alma, on the sanctity of the individual *pfennig*, this was heresy, but if your brother had been corrupted by American ways, what could you do but acquiesce?

Eichenkrug I remember for wholly different reasons. While the family were chatting around the inn table I liked to wander up through the beechwoods to the ruins of two castles, known as *Die Gleichen*. The castles, on neighboring hills, had, according to tradition, belonged to feuding brothers, who had fought each other until nothing or next to nothing remained of either castle, or, I suspect, either family. The ruins themselves were almost obliterated, suggesting only faintly a wall here, a battlement there, lost in the conquering forest. The very indefiniteness of the remains of what had been both human habitations and strongholds of security, stimulated my imagination, but not so much as the forest itself. A German beech forest is like no other forest anywhere: the sturdy, majestic and yet graceful trunks, the smooth bark, the sunlight filtering through the leaves, the dusky aisles, clean of underbrush, stretching in all directions into a green infinity.

Wandering alone in those woods, those summer afternoons, year after year, remote from my solid, practical American world, German romanticism took hold of me. In those forest depths, German dwarfs and fairies were inextricably mingled with knights in armor and princesses in trouble, to make an iridescent, unreal world into which

I sank as into a mound of perfumed, silken cushions. It was more than my native land that I lost contact with. Those summers I lost my contact with reality, and it was years, even decades, before I fully recovered it.

– 4 –

There was, remote from Göttingen, a wholly different German countryside, which, for other reasons no less romantic, bound me to my German heritage. It was an estate of about three thousand acres of level farmland and forest, fringed with pine barrens and sandy heath where the north wind blows in the salt air of the Baltic; and included a little thatch-roofed village called Wahlendow, which gave the estate its name. The manor house—designated the *Schloss*, though it made no pretensions to palatial splendor—was surrounded, like comparable British country houses, by attractively landscaped parkland whose farther edges, as we sat at coffee on the veranda in the late afternoon, deer would shyly invade. The estate belonged to a friend of Father's boyhood in Nienburg, Harry Gebhard—from whom I got one of the two middle names that fill my closet with their bare, unwanted bones—a bearded, robust outdoor man, and, in my contacts with him, good-natured and kindly. He had acquired his property by marrying a singularly unattractive woman whose charm for him had obviously been her wealth. He managed the estate with industry and competence, but gave as little attention to his wife as he felt he decently could. The thought of her haunts me even now, and takes the edge off the happy memories that I associate with the spacious, comfortable manor house and with "*Onkel*" Gebhard himself. A neglected wife, an unloved mother, without respect or authority in the house her wealth had purchased, she seemed to do nothing but move restlessly out of one shadow into another, a pathetic, irrelevant, premature ghost.

The Gebhards had an adopted daughter, of an age with their own daughter, Grete. Ruby was fourteen when I first went to Wahlen-

134

dow, and all tomboy. Even three years after that, when I saw her again, the tomboy was still strong in her, though now she was a tall, muscular girl, with the black hair, blue eyes and bright coloring of her beautiful Irish mother, and a competence and selflessness which were her inheritance from her German father.

For beneath the Irish deviltry and gaiety was a core of Teutonic strength and responsibility—which made Ruby, even at seventeen, the actual mainstay of the troubled, inharmonious household, as well as a kind of "lady of the lamp" to the villagers, whom she nursed when they were ill, or comforted when death knocked at the door.

We were just two school children on vacation, that summer. We rode horseback over the wide heath, with my riding, Ruby pointing out, something less than standard on any self-respecting estate. We went rabbit-shooting, with Ruby designating me as a "lifesaving station" for the rabbits; when any came my way, they were safe. We raced on bicycles down the forest paths and went head first over the handlebars on the soft turf when our pedals tangled; and, altogether, acted the teenagers that we were. But the fellowship that we found would, sixty years later, still be a welcome, warming element in our lives.

By the end of my visit to Wahlendow, Ruby had become the most compelling of those friends, in Göttingen and elsewhere, who were a cherished part of my German world; as I was part of the German earth, the German *Geist*. Each of these friends was a vine, growing up out of the German soil and fastening itself about me. If one could imagine a Laocoön with vines instead of serpents coiling about his limbs, the picture would have been true of me.

– 5 –

German friends, German food, German *Gemütlichkeit*; German cultivation, German music, German simplicity of living; German romanticism speaking to me in German woods and German ruins and enchanting Mariasprings! I might easily have become a diluted German or, worse, a man of two countries, who did not know in which he belonged, and really belonged to neither.

It was Mother who saved me from either fate, and kept me integrated; Mother, pronouncing to Father, one day, the only words resembling an ultimatum that I can remember her ever uttering. They were these: "I want one of my sons to be an American."

~ Part Four ~

CHAPTER ONE

MOTHER's ultimatum—if that is what it was—was no reflection on my brother Addie who, after his five years' absence, had resumed his place in the American scene. What she meant, moreover, when she said she wanted one American son was something deeper than conformity to the outward American pattern. When, in her early girlhood, the word America had entered her consciousness, it came in a radiance of a dream to which a man might gladly give his life. The dream had come true in the form of a home, free of the menace of Authority, in a land where the spirit had elbowroom, and the vision, infinite horizons. She was seeing me in relation to her father's love of freedom, his part in a revolution that had enlisted many of the noblest minds in Europe, his flight from the agents of reaction, his battle, in his adopted country, for Abraham Lincoln and the cause of the slaves. The dream, the aspiration, the struggle, were symbolized for her in the word America. What she meant, when she said that she wanted me to be an American, was that she wanted me to be possessed by the American Idea.

She must have recognized what mountains stood in the way of such a consummation. The most powerful pressures that bore upon me during my adolescence seemed to doom me to that hyphenated state that was neither American nor German but was accepted as natural and indeed praiseworthy by the men and women of German background. The German language which was the language of our home wherever, in Brooklyn or New York, that home happened to be, the customs of the home, the German church in which I was confirmed to German Lutheranism, the German boys who were my closest friends, the German food I ate, the German maids who cooked or served it, the guests who sat at our table and stood around the piano singing German songs, our frequent summer sojourns in Germany, where we settled into the life of a German community and were as much a part of it as any German, had, by the time I was sixteen, made me German in all the deeper areas of tradition, character and personality.

– 2 –

Father accepted Mother's ultimatum with surprising docility. Perhaps he wasn't too sure he had acted wisely in sending my brothers to Grandmother Hagedorn for their education. More likely, he too wanted one of his sons to be an American. Not that Adolf wasn't; but in him, as in me, there was division, not of conviction but of feeling; and the air of New York's textile center and his service in the National Guard's famous Seventh Regiment was taking care of that.

Besides, the year was 1898. Under the influence of the war spirit that was in the air that spring, Father—for the first time, I think—was feeling the stirrings of patriotism for the country of his adoption. I remember him, one morning early, running up the stairs from the breakfast table, with the *New York Herald* in his hand, his face flushed with elation as he shouted the news of Dewey's victory at Manila. No less vividly I remember his anger when letters came from the Aunts reflecting the general German feeling about the war— you could count on the Aunts to echo the accepted "line"—the hope and expectation of Spanish victory, the scorn and even contempt of America. He set his sisters straight, and with vigor, which was balm to Addie, the girls and me.

Father's newly upsurging ardor for America, however, was merely a contributing factor in the situation which now unfolded. He happened to be as ready for drastic action in my case as was Mother, though for different reasons. My health was something less than robust; obviously, I needed more outdoor life than was possible at the Brooklyn Polytechnic Institute that I had been attending. Word had reached us that one of the Achelis boys was going to an American boarding school, a rather startling move, outside the German-American tradition. The principal of "Poly Prep" agreed that The Hill School in Pottstown, Pennsylvania, might, indeed, be the place for me.

– 3 –

Alike to the boys and the faculty at The Hill, I must have seemed a funny-looking youth with my sugar-bowl ears, the nervous twitch that was the survival of the St. Vitus dance that had plagued my early adolescence, and the diffident manner of a stranger from another world. Except for young Fritz Achelis—and he was far less German in mind and spirit than I—the boys at The Hill all had wholly American backgrounds, talking a common language of quips and banter that I understood only vaguely and could no more talk than I could talk Arabic. I am sure they did not mean to make me feel an outsider, but that was what I was, and it was no help when one of the boys discovered the slight suggestion of a puff at the shoulders of my bath wrapper, indicating that it had been originally intended for a woman's shoulders. It was, in fact, a hand-me-down from Mother who, after buying all the clothing, linen, towels and such that the school regulations required, went thrifty, being sure that no one would ever guess.

I made an initial mistake. When I registered and was asked to give my full name, I responded with Teutonic literalness: Hermann Ludwig Gebhard Hagedorn. The boys seized upon it, gleefully. I can still hear my brilliant classmate, W. Russell Bowie, later one of the chief ornaments of the Episcopal Church in the United States, bellowing the nine syllables down the hall, and his puckish roommate taking up the chant with special attention to the gutturals. I never knew when my name—all of it—would not come beating on my ear. I got so tired of it that I never after revealed it to anyone in college,

141

or, in fact, to my own children until they were in their twenties. I was Hermann Hagedorn, no more, and that was that.

But, outsider as I was, I became, for an instant that winter, the object of what seemed to me such flattering attention that I felt I could smile at the mockers of my "Dutchiness." By vote of the school, I was elected president of the Reading Room Association. I was enormously set up. Here I was only a Fifth Former and a "new boy" at that, in a school of two hundred, elected to so responsible a post. It was a great honor, I said to myself, with true Teutonic solemnity.

It was not long before I recognized how beautifully I had been made the goat. There *was* no Reading Room Association. There was a reading room, sure enough, and the "president" of the mythical Association was supposed to see that the magazines were kept in order. So what I had been elected to, with the connivance, no doubt, of some member of the faculty who recognized the use that might be made of this new boy's unhumorous conscientiousness, was the honor of clearing up other boys' disorder. I am glad that, when the truth dawned, I had the grace to grin at myself and my pomposity and gratefully remember the incident as a first halting step into a new world.

It was not necessarily a better world than the world I had been brought up in, but it was different; it was the world, moreover, in which I would live my life, and it was essential that I understand it, come to terms with it and make it my own.

– 4 –

Two men and a woman at The Hill built a bridge from the land to which the ties of blood and sentiment bound me to the land to which by birth I owed allegiance.

John Meigs, the headmaster, was in his late forties when I came to The Hill, a stocky, foursquare man with a broad forehead, wide-set eyes, and nostrils so flat and wide that when, after his death, a bust of him was made for the chapel, it had to be of white marble rather than bronze to avoid the inference that he had been a Negro. Here was no mild-mannered and bookish school principal, no sharp-featured disciplinarian, fit to rule a school and not much else. In that stocky figure under the canonical, flat-topped derby hat was Power, as I knew it in my father and would know it again, long after, in Theodore Roosevelt; the power of that "MacGregor," whose seat, wherever it may be, is the head of the table. Power radiated from John Meigs as he sat at his desk in "The Study" that was the nerve center of the School and its judgment seat; power was in his heavy tread down the center aisle of the schoolroom that was chapel and auditorium and general study hall rolled into one; power was in the words he spoke to us boys with passionate conviction at morning and evening prayers, and, behind the words, in the hunger that we might all become the kind of men he longed to have us be. Back of the power, indeed, was the passion—it is not too strong a word—to build men. He had a gift for finding boys who needed what The Hill had to give and had qualities that he felt the School itself needed; boys of physical stamina and spiritual purpose whom he picked out of the shadow somewhere, and set down in the midst of his school for what their underprivileged but eager lives could give the privileged but less integrated. Some of these "scholarship boys" became memorable leaders in the School and subsequently at college, but the failures—and there were such—never deterred John Meigs in his search for the penniless boy who might give fresh insights to boys who had money and perhaps brains, but little else.

John Meigs had been a professor at Lafayette College and "Professor" ("Prof," when he wasn't around) he was still to the faculty and the boys, though he was the last remove from the professorial type. He was, in fact, a high-caliber executive who might have held his own in competition with any of the great industrial tycoons of his time, with depths of faith, compassion and aspiration which none of the Fricks or Hills, the Carnegies or Harrimans revealed. He knew by name every one of his two hundred boys and made each one feel important to his headmaster and to the School. Yet, sympathetic, even tender, as he might be, Prof could be hard, even brutal. The hot temper beneath the disciplined exterior could flare up when he believed you had lied to him or betrayed his trust in other ways (and, occasionally, for no discernible reason); but, if you played fair by him and the School, he gave you responsibilities that helped you grow. His laughter was as robust as his anger.

What I remember about him most vividly, however, is his voice at prayers, booming out certain passages from Paul's letters to the men and women he was trying to hold in the faith; and doing it with an intensity of conviction and appeal that, so far as I was concerned, cut through all the barriers that adolescence casts up against moral instruction. I can hear him now reading the passages about putting on the "whole armour of God" that we might be able to "withstand in the evil day, and having done all, to stand," and that other passage about "whatsoever things are honest, whatsoever things are just . . . pure . . . lovely . . . of good report . . . if there be any virtue . . . any praise, think on these things." Prof did not seem to be reading words written eighteen hundred and more years before. He was emitting flames out of his own impassioned heart. Even sixty years later, Prof's love and power give the words the immediacy of a personal plea, and something more; as, behind John Meigs, I feel again the dynamic Jew of Tarsus, and behind him, looming overwhelmingly, One greater than he.

I didn't know it until long afterward, but what Prof did by these readings and by the burning words of prayer that followed was to awaken in me a recognition of the need of working at this business of becoming a man, which is the first step toward the achievement of becoming a free man. What he did, in effect, was to lay in me the only dependable foundations for citizenship in a republic.

Twenty years after I left The Hill, I tried to capture and fix the significance of a life lived so vigorously and effectively in a setting relatively so obscure:

> "I hear him laughing down the hall somewhere
> To think that anyone should call him dead
> Or talk as though the best of him had fled

To some blue haven of the upper air.
Make no mistake. Joyous, and strong to bear
   Burdens, he walks these halls, high-spirited,
    With you and me in his great heart and head.
We may not see his face; but he is there.
And he will still be there when you and I
   Climb feebly the long slope and turn to view
    Our gaudier grandeur and our noisier fame,
And see a desert; while afar his cry
   Shakes into manhood boys he never knew
    And kindles hearts that never heard his name."

– 5 –

As headmaster, Prof had a magnificent partner in his wife, Marion. "Mrs. John," as she was known, was an incandescent personality as great in faith as her husband, and with a capacity for creative love that permanently changed the direction of many lives. She is clear in my memory, sitting, in cream-colored tulle, at the organ in the big schoolroom, playing hymns at Evening Prayers; or, after the service, walking down the aisle between the desks, at Prof's side, looking into the faces of the boys nearest her with tender, humorous eyes; or, in the Gym, Saturday nights, gaily playing waltzes and two-steps while we boys danced together until, at nine-thirty, we sang "Auld Lang Syne," with Mrs. John's clear soprano rising above the uncertain tenors and baritones and basses of the boys. I never asked myself, so far as I can remember, whether Mrs. John were beautiful, yet the picture I retain of her with the dark, questioning eyes under the curling chestnut hair, and the loving, somewhat quizzical smile as she welcomed you to the Sky Parlor on the top floor of the headmaster's wing, has a radiance that makes any question of physical beauty irrelevant.

To me, as I look back, Mrs. John is the symbol of that vision that was the essence of The Hill's greatness in the days that she and Prof were the School's directing spirits—the hunger that God might be the center of the life of the School and the center of the life of every boy in it. Her vision took into its concern every member of the wide-flung Hill family and, beyond them, the world whose character their lives would help determine. I can see now what I could not see then, that Mrs. John was of the lineage of the Old Testament prophets. Like them, she had a nation on her heart. Like them, too, she knew that the nation could be redeemed only by the "remnant" that had God at their lives' center.

Together, Prof and Mrs. John conducted the School in the Thomas Arnold tradition, with the building of body, brain and spirit joined to make a whole man. The School stood high in athletics as in scholarship, and higher yet in that area in which there are no grades or entrance examinations, no scores or championship records to set in brass letters on the schoolroom wall; only the new line, overnight, of a boy's lips that spells maturity and the light in a boy's eyes that means purpose. That area she shared on equal terms with Prof, though she presided over it and did it with a determination as dedicated and persistent as Prof's in the fields that were peculiarly his.

Mrs. John had the passion for souls of all great Christian spirits—and no one who knew her could question that she was one of the noblest of her generation, if not among the best known. There were those who charged that, in her eagerness to save boys from the pitfalls that lay in wait for them, she drove one or another to a pitch of emotional intensity that was unwholesome and brought disastrous reactions. I never experienced anything of the sort. She sent for me, now and then, when she thought she saw a slackness in me that required challenge, but she never gave me moral or emotional indigestion.

Of these interviews in the Sky Parlor I recall the deep-toned earnestness of her voice, one minute, and the low rippling laugh the next; the quoting, perhaps, of some favorite line of hers from Browning, a reference to Jacob Riis and *How the Other Half Lives*, which had just awakened thousands to conditions they had not imagined; her wistful query, "What are *you* going to do, Hermann, to make the world better for your having lived in it?"—and the sense of a caring that would be satisfied with nothing short of the highest in her boys, not as individuals only but as members of a world society. It was essential to be decent, to be honest, to be unselfish, to be kind, but it was not enough. You must do something with your life.

> "We are not here to dream, to drift,
> We have hard work to do, and loads to lift."

The memory of those Sky Parlor sessions brings back the simple verses, spoken with a trusting yet quizzical smile on Mrs. John's lips and an appeal in her eyes that cut a groove in my mind which the events and labors, the successes and failures of more than a half century have been unable to erase. Father and Mother had given me moral standards, but Mrs. John woke my social conscience.

> "Not with swords, not with guns,
> Mother of boys, you arm your sons.
> East and west, south and north,
> With a word in their ears, you send them forth;
> With a word you gird their souls
> For storms and starry goals,
> And send them over the lands
> With a torch, a torch in their hands."

I am sure there were men and women in Germany who might have widened and deepened my conviction of useful living as Prof and Mrs. John widened and deepened them. It happens that it was in America that I encountered them, and it was to America that, unconsciously, they bound me.

CHAPTER TWO

THE third of the trio at The Hill who helped me to find myself as an American was the extraordinary person who was the head coach and athletic instructor at the School. Michael F. Sweeney held the world's championship in the high jump, but, large as that fact loomed among professional athletes, what counted more at The Hill were the winning teams he was turning out, year after year, in football, baseball and track. More important still was his gift for combining inspiration, the strictest discipline, a personal knowledge of the needs, it seemed, of every boy in the School, and unaffected concern and caring for him.

I had no contact with Mike Sweeney until my second year at the School. I was the least athletic of boys but he had his eye on me, and had come to the conclusion that my flabby body was merely an expression of an inner condition that needed looking after. Had I ever done any running? "You haven't the strength for the sprints," he pointed out, "but you've got long legs. We'll try you out for the mile."

Thereafter, Mr. Sweeney set me jogging, round and round, on the narrow board track back of the Sixth Form building, teaching me how to use my legs and my arms, teaching me how to breathe. I became conscious of a new interest in life. Spring came, the quarter-mile cinder track dried out, Mr. Sweeney tried me out on a slow mile, and gave me elementary tests in timing myself.

Working regularly with the track squad, I became conscious of fellowship with boys who, being athletes, had always seemed to me to belong to another world. Then, one day, as I went past the bulletin board in the Archway on my way to dinner, my heart skipped a beat as I saw my name in the list of boys selected to eat at the track training table. A day or two later there was another list: the team picked to take part in the Princeton Interscholastics; and, by all things wonderful, my name was on it! I bought a new track shirt with the narrow blue-and-gray ribbon of The Hill colors sewn diagonally across it, and could have felt scarcely more exalted if it had been the sash of the Order of the Garter.

After the romance, the reality; after the thrill, the line-up on the Princeton track with the muscular bodies to right and left of boys who had grown up in the hard competition of sports, and I, a six-months' skinny neophyte; the sickening pace of the fourth quarter, the sense of all strength spent, one boy after another passing me; then, staggering over the line, seventh, and making my way, blindly, nauseated, to the dressing room; and Mr. Sweeney bending over me, saying, "It's all right. You'll learn to use what you've got. You'll do better next time."

– 2 –

The fact was, I didn't. The meet was with a Philadelphia high school, on our home grounds. I was on the point of winning, spurted too soon, and came in fourth.

I felt humiliated. It had not been my body that had proved inadequate, but my intelligence. Mike was sympathetic, but explicit. You ran a race, it seemed, as much with your brains as with your legs. During the ten days that intervened before the Triangular Meet with Lawrenceville School and St. Paul's (of Garden City, Long Island) that was to be the culminating event of the season, Mike coached us milers more, I seem to recall, on the mental factors in a race than the physical.

He had studied the records of the milers on the other teams and had developed his strategy accordingly. Lawrenceville, it appeared, had a plodder who couldn't spurt but was deadly on the long pull. "It'll be their strategy to send one or two third-string men off at a killing pace, the first quarter, in the hope of wearing you out before the race is half over. Don't take the bait. Go your own pace: 75 seconds for the first quarter, no matter what the others do." He timed us again and again till we knew to the second how fast we were going. At the final session, before the meet, speaking of the corks that runners carry for the culminating moments of exertion, he uttered a bit of simple wisdom which, with the years, took on universal significance for me: "Don't press on the corks until you have to."

– 3 –

The day of the Triangular Meet was one of those clear, warm, windless May days when heaven and earth and man seem to sit down together under a tree and bask in mutual appreciation. We fed the visiting teams at our training table, and I remember a little sinking of my stomach as a Lawrenceville boy counted up the score by which his school expected to win the trophy, beginning with the mile run. But I remember, too, my own unspoken "You don't say!"

On my way to the locker room below the athletic field, I encountered Russ Bowie who was to be the announcer. He struck a pose. "Mile run," he announced. "Won by Hermann" . . . Pause . . . "Ludwig" . . . Pause . . . "Gebhard" . . . Pause . . . "Hagedorn. Time: Nine minutes, fifty-nine and four-fifths seconds."

I grinned. The hour was past when anyone could get a rise out of me on the score of those Teutonic syllables.

I knew that the boys, lined up along the straightaway—Prof in his flat-topped derby among them; of course, with Mrs. John—were not too happy as we milers took our places for the start. The mile run was the first event, and The Hill milers were second-rate, or worse. The School's chances even for second or third place were slim, and for winning the race so slight as to be outside the reckoning even of the most sanguine. It looked dismally as though The Hill would be starting the meet with a defeat so humiliating that it might have a devastating effect on the team's morale.

I don't remember any special agitation as we milers from the three schools waited on the line for the crack of the pistol. What I do remember is the leap forward of the expendable Lawrenceville runners, setting a pace, as Mike Sweeney had predicted, that would put them and anyone who tried to keep up with them out of the race by the end of the half mile. One of the St. Paul's boys took the bait, but we Hill boys had been forewarned. I knew that, no matter what time any other boy ran that first quarter in, I had to run it in 75 seconds, no more and no less. That was the figure I had been trained to do; slow enough, even by school standards, humiliatingly slow in comparison with what college runners did, but a pace I knew I could maintain, and I had learned to maintain it.

As I went by the starting-post, at the end of the first quarter, Sweeney was there, a stop watch in his hand. "Seventy-five!" he called. "Good boy!"

The expendables dropped out early in the second quarter. The rest of us stayed bunched. "Two thirty!" Sweeney called, as I passed the post the second time. "You're all right!"

The bunch began to open up as we entered the third quarter, with the top Lawrenceville boy pushing ahead, and a couple of the other runners dropping back. At the beginning of the fourth quarter there were three of us together, seven or eight yards back of the leader. To my surprise I wasn't half as tired as I had expected to be at that point. I didn't increase my pace; the two who were bunched with me must have fallen back; for suddenly I realized that there was no one between me and the Lawrenceville runner. I remember the thrill as I told myself that I was going to get second place, which meant that I would get my "H." But another thought followed instantly: "Second? Why not first?"

We were two-thirds around the oval by this time, with less than 150 yards to go. I put on a little speed and started to close in on the Lawrenceville, man, a yard, two yards, three. Then I went into high gear.

151

A roar went up from the crowd on the home stretch. Two hundred boys were shouting my name. My name! Of all things wonderful! But Mike Sweeney wasn't cheering. "He's done it again," he was muttering to his neighbor at the finish line. I had spurted too soon; I would peter out before I could reach the tape.

Happily, I knew nothing at the time of his dismay. I had my eyes fixed on the Lawrenceville runner's head. So long as it was bent forward, Mike had told me, I would know he still had fight in him. If his head fell back, he was done. The cheers were continuous now. "Hagedorn, Hagedorn, Hagedorn!" I scarcely heard them, I was so busy watching my opponent's head. As we tore into the straightaway, it suddenly flopped back. A second later I was up with him; another second, I had passed him.

On the turf at my left I was conscious of a huge creature in a bathrobe, jumping up and down, cursing, in language I had never heard before on that field, as he urged the Lawrenceville boy forward. I found out afterward that he was John De Witt, the captain of the Lawrenceville team, later to win national fame in football at Princeton. He gave me the final shot in the spirit that I needed. I plunged into the tape, the winner, and fell into Mike Sweeney's arms. "Good boy, good boy!" The words were such music as Drake heard on the *Golden Hynde* when his Queen tapped his shoulder with a sword, saying, "Rise, Sir Francis!" Through a haze of happy exhaustion I heard the cheers from two-hundred-odd throats, giving the School "three-times-three" with "Hagedorn!" at the end of it.

A minute later, as I made my way on air to the locker room, I heard Russ Bowie's voice in the distance, announcing the mile run: "Won by Hagedorn, *The Hill*; second, Davis, Lawrenceville; third, Buttolph, *The Hill*. Time: four minutes fifty-four and two-fifths seconds."

The time was pretty bad even by prep-school standards; The Hill record at that time was 4 minutes, 40 seconds. But the mile was, as I said, the first event of the meet, and the wholly unexpected victory gave the team the lift it needed. We won by an overwhelming score. It was all schoolboy stuff, of course, and my triumph was a schoolboy triumph. But it did something to me that went 'way beyond the hour of acclaim. It gave me a sense of achievement; it gave me assurance, courage, a kind of dumb faith that somehow I could pull the best out of the worst. Again and again, in the years that followed, when achievement of any sort seemed to elude me, and hope of any real success in the field of work I had chosen seemed impossibly remote, I found myself saying, "You did it once. You will do it again." How deep into the fabric of my life the experience went can best be judged by the fact that every year, for forty-odd years, I felt impelled, on the 26th of May, to send Mike Sweeney a message of remembrance; and, since his death, no 26th of May has come and gone without a grateful thought of that greathearted Irishman, that comprehending and creative spirit.

– 4 –

None of my family witnessed my triumph, such as it was, or, three weeks later, my graduation. They were, as usual, in Germany.

In retrospect, their absence underscores the deeper drama—unperceived at the time and recognized only long after—that lay behind the emotions, the tensions and the exultant culmination of that mile race.

That day I gained my first firm foothold on the American shore.

Winning the respect of my fellows in the field of athletics—the only area in which it could be securely won in the boy-world (the race was a lively item in Hill legendry, for years thereafter)—integrated me in the School in my own mind and in the minds of my schoolmates. I belonged. Within the limits of the community that was The Hill, I was part of the American social fabric.

CHAPTER THREE

WHILE, at The Hill, I was gaining my first firm foothold in that America which is an orientation of the spirit rather than a specified area of land and water, rivers, mountains and plains, a different drama was moving, deceptively, toward the canonical ending of American success-fiction.

Father was making money. The long struggle to make ends meet that had darkened the eighties and early nineties had ended. Father could afford to take long vacations; he learned, in fact, that he could not afford not to take them; the longer his vacations, the more money he made. In May or early June, each year, he climbed the gangplank of one of the North German Lloyd liners he invariably traveled on— the *Lahn*, the *Kaiser Wilhelm der Grosse* or the *Kronprinzessin Cecilie*—watched the American shores recede, sniffed the sharp sea air, and for three, four, five, and finally for six months every year, was a gentleman of leisure, reveling in the comfort of the house he had built for his sisters, nearer the center of the town, or strolling through the woods from the Plesse to Mariaspring with relish and relaxing tensions.

On the Exchange, his friends dutifully bought and sold, sweating through summers remote by four decades from air conditioning, packed themselves into the elevated trains at the end of the day, or sank exhausted on the plush seats of sooty suburban trains; but Father strolled along the Weender *Strasse* or called on *Oberstleutnant* This or *Geheimemedizinalrat Professor Doktor* That and chatted about the "peace-loving" Kaiser or the Boxer Rebellion in China or the glories of *Siebzig, einundsiebzig* (1870–1871), living in a world as alien to cotton futures or the boll weevil as Tierra del Fuego.

At midday, when his Exchange colleagues would be rushing across the street to Schultz's basement restaurant for a bite of lunch and rushing back to the Floor, Father would sit down at the head of the table on the Aunts' "glass veranda" and consume saddle of veal that melted in his mouth, with string beans, cooked in milk, compote and salad, and, for dessert, *Tante* Elsbeth's incomparable raspberry-and-currant concoction. After dinner he might sit at his desk in the sitting room, catching up on his correspondence, until, in the middle of the afternoon, the call came for coffee in the *Kegellaube*, with *Butterkuchen* and a game of the swing-bowling that he loved, and was good at.

Now and again, he would take us all, including the Aunts—always, damn it, we growled, including the Aunts—to Baden-Baden or some other watering place where Fred, who was on the lower rungs of the Prussian administrative system, might join us for his vacation and, for two or three weeks, be a member of the family again. Father would sip the waters (wherever we went they tasted like tepid bouillon, flavored with slightly decayed eggs) and stroll about the *Kurgarten*, hobnobbing with retired Excellencies, mostly generals, or some prosperous *Geheimecommerzienrat*, while the open-air orchestra played the *Wilhelm Tell* overture or some gay bit of Offenbach.

Father would return to New York in the fall with a capacity to appraise the realities of the market for raw cotton and for textiles that few of his exhausted friends who had been on the spot all summer could even approximate. He began to make really big money (as money went in the cotton business) when he started to spend half of every year in Germany.

– 2 –

This had its obvious advantages for all of us. We lived well; we had a waitress and an "upstairs girl" in addition to the cook. Father had always been generous, even in the gray, lean years. Now, with a mounting fortune, he was lavish. He gave Mother and the girls elaborate wardrobes, and I shudder a little as I recall how heedlessly my sisters used to exhibit their closetsful of expensive dresses to some cousin less fortunate than they, for whom a single new dress was an event. The girls' clothes were, of course, to modern taste, a fright, but to the girls—and to me—they were the last word in splendor. I can still feel the texture of the foulard of those balloon sleeves that I stuffed into the sleeves of their cloaks like the proper young man in the social world that I was trained and proud to be.

Father gave none of us children large allowances, but he never failed us when our exchequers were low and we had a reasonably good case. Elsie, impulsively generous herself, with no money sense at all, was always broke; Irma, long-headed and farseeing, always had a reserve. Father seemed to take a special delight in helping us out of a hole. His joy in giving, indeed, was one of the most attractive expressions of his loving nature. His generosity to his friends in Germany, now that he was making money, was continuous and unfailing. There must have been a half-dozen couples—the delightful von Mauntzes, of course, among them—who every year at Christmas received a barrel of Newtown pippins, and a case of American canned fruit, the peak of luxury to Germans. His generosity to me gave me three months' roaming through Italy, one year, and two months in Egypt and Sicily, another; each journey, by myself, learning to take care of myself, making friends on my own; each journey a widening of my horizons, a deepening of my perspective.

– 3 –

Only fifty-odd years later have I come to recognize how graciously, after years of repression, Father released me—to a point. He had inherited none of his mother's demonic possessiveness. Mother made no effort, either, to hold me in her shadow. She knew that the Hill had become a second home to me; she knew of my devotion to Mrs.

John; but I never saw in her the slightest suggestion of any jealousy. Both Father and Mother wanted me to be open to the influence of creative and invigorating personalities. That was all. The fear that one or the other of these personalities might loom so large in my life as to overshadow the influence of either Father or Mother seems never to have given them the slightest concern.

– 4 –

As a mark of our newly achieved prosperity, we joined the Exodus of the Snooty from Brooklyn to Manhattan, Father renting a four-story-and-basement house on West 88th Street, just in from the Park. He rented it, I said. Even after thirty-five years in America he apparently never even considered purchasing a house. A house that you owned tied you to the land on which it stood, and he must remain foot-free. Who could tell, some day he might want to return to "the old homeland"—*die alte Heimat.*

With the house we acquired the owner's black butler. I remember the solemn family conference at which Father raised the question whether it were right to plunge to the tune of the fifty dollars a month that Thomas would cost us. Since none of us had the remotest idea what Father was making, and he took no step to enlighten us, our opinion wasn't worth much, but Thomas became a cherished fixture, the perfect family factotum.

Father spread himself in other ways, subscribing to orchestra seats at the Metropolitan Opera House for every Saturday afternoon in the season, and arranging with a livery stable for a victoria, two lively bays and a coachman, to be at Mother's orders for shopping or afternoon calls.

– 5 –

I have before me, as I write, a three-quarter-length photograph of Father, made by Falk, the most perceptive, stylish—and expensive—

camera-portraitist of the period. Father is leaning with one arm on the back of a leather-covered armchair, suggestive both of power and opulence. His other hand rests lightly on his hip, revealing the satin lining of his long frock coat. A slender watch chain crosses his waistcoat; a pearl stickpin is in his tie. There is mastery in the pose, in the clear, untroubled eyes, the strong, broad nose, the firm chin, the white cheek whiskers, the generous, assured, faintly smiling lips. This man has "arrived" and has no question that he will maintain the heights he has charged—and won. He is master of his fate and captain of his soul.

If any intrusive specter was lurking in the back of the studio, the camera failed to catch it.

– 6 –

Silks, satins; a butler; a carriage with a coachman in livery; pride, a sense of achievement, the assurance of a serene future—all this, or most of it, was on the credit side of Father's six-month vacations in Germany. The account on the debit side was less obvious; and, at that time, none of us had learned the art—difficult, sometimes, even for bankers—of accurately reading balance sheets.

We did not realize that we were trying to live in two countries at once, one foot in America, the other in Germany. I suffered less from this transatlantic straddle than Mother and the girls, since I was at Harvard by that time, where vacations were three months long, and no longer, and where my roots were going deep. For Mother the strain of the semiannual upheaval must have been severe, the closing and reopening of the house, the packing of innumerable trunks. (I have one of the trunks still, marked "Mrs. H.H. No. 22"!) The girls, I am sure, suffered deeper strains, living with one set of friends for six months and having to pick up old threads—not always too successfully—or seek new friends, the next six.

On both sides of the ocean their friends were, in the main, German. Of all the young men who came to our house on 88th Street, during those prosperous, relaxed, happy years, I can think of few who were not German. "Father managed to direct our sympathies in one certain line," Irma remembered long after. "He was terribly intolerant with others we liked."

The Americans who came to our house, indeed, felt strange there. Father would never think of going to bed Sunday evening before the last young man was gone. Ten o'clock, he felt, was closing time, and he started winding the clocks at that hour, or offered his daughters' callers "a cigar to smoke on the way home." It wasn't that he distrusted his daughters. According to his traditions it just wasn't proper for a girl to be entertaining young men after her parents had retired.

Father, devoted to the girls, was inclined, moreover, to look with mistrust on any young man who fluttered around them, but especially on the Americans. He understood the background of the Germans and knew what he had to do if he wanted to know more about any of them. With the Americans it was different. This stalwart, handsome young man from Texas, for instance . . . who was he? Who were his father and mother? What was his background? He had the commonest of American names. Suppose he became a serious suitor of Elsie, whom he was calling on? How, Father asked himself, could he permit a daughter of his to marry anyone with so undistinctive and colorless a name? So the Texan was cold-shouldered and edged out. Thirty years later, when Elsie, bearing an aristocratic Bavarian name, was surviving only by virtue of the paying guests she had in her house, the Texan, rich, powerful and respected, was counted among the great of the land.

– 7 –

Father knew his America too superficially to recognize such possibilities. He beamed, on the other hand, on the young German baron who came to the house two or three times a week to call on Irma. I don't blame him. We all loved "Sunny Jim," as we nicknamed him. He had all the gifts and graces of the cultured and traveled scion of an ancient line, a wide knowledge of men and books, of art and music, bubbling gaiety, and, on occasion, a gravity and a wistful tenderness which, together, made a personality which I for one found irresistible. Irma found him irresistible too. They sparked to each other, each calling out the wit and the charm of the other. The baron wasn't handsome. His face was heavy and had the dark color of a man accustomed to drink heavy wines, not necessarily ever to excess, but too often.

His story was as romantic as any serial in Grandmother Schwedler's beloved *New Yorker Revue*. Up to the day he had left Germany, a few weeks before he first came to our house, he had been the aide-de-camp and close personal friend of a ruling grand duke of the Empire. The grand duke had a daughter. Whether the baron fell in love with the daughter and she with him or whether the daughter was enamored with the baron without response from him, I never knew. However it was, her father and Sunny Jim agreed that the younger man must leave not only the grand duchy but Germany itself. There was no row; the sovereign and his aide remained friends and, a year or two later, the grand duke came to America to visit his former aide. His daughter, subsequently, and not too happily, married one of the Kaiser's sons.

Grandmother Schwedler, who knew the world, however remote from it she might at any time be living, regarded the baron with disapproval. "*Ein Lebemann*," she commented curtly. "A man about town."

Perhaps. But my abiding affection for him denies it.

Irma came to love him with all the intensity of her Günther heritage. He loved her, I am sure. Why he did not ask her to marry him I don't know. The relationship dragged on, year after year, tearing Irma almost to pieces. Whether or not there was a bond of loyalty to the princess which he could not bring himself to cut, I never learned.

Grandmother declared that he kept the relationship going for the meals and the wine it brought him. I am inclined to think that, this time, the otherwise clear-sighted old lady was unduly cynical.

The baron's devotion survived twenty years of separation, reaching out to Irma finally, in a mad, despairing appeal, to which there was, for Irma, only one possible answer. But that is a story which lies beyond the limits of this volume.

CHAPTER FOUR

Our family was almost as German when it was in New York as when it was in Germany. In affection, I was wholly a part of it. I was devoted to Father and Mother and the girls; and I felt a quite particular affection for my brother Adolf, so genuinely big-brotherly. I liked the young Germans, moreover, who came and went; and I was fond of the elderly German couples who were Father's and Mother's contemporaries and came periodically to the dinners that Father and Mother loved to give, and gave, in fact, with exceptional zest and grace. But I had found moorings that were not the family's moorings. I began to beg off on the annual transplantings.

At twenty-two, I was becoming restive as the dependent son of even so greathearted and generous a father as mine. In the process of becoming an American, I was naturally seeing the world in terms different from the terms in which he saw it. More than the differing points of view of the elder and the younger generation divided us. Father's roots were set deep in one world, mine were reaching down deeper and deeper in another. His world seemed to me the world of the past; the world of kings and aristocracies, of immemorial social customs and traditions; of titles, caste, position; mine, a world of new social, political and economic explorations; of effort to find new answers to old problems. His world to me was a dying world, with the future lying not with the Bismarcks and the Kaisers, with German might and German dominance, but with the free spirit, the spirit most compellingly revealed in Abraham Lincoln and seeking fulfillment under the inspiration of his life.

Once more, in the family story, the spirit of Lincoln was confronting the spirit of Father's idol, the man of blood and iron.

Clear as all this appears to me now, it was vague and unformed then. All that I saw distinctly was that, deeply as I loved Father, I felt freer and more myself when an ocean lay between us.

So I came to know New Hampshire, and on the farm of my Harvard teacher and friend, George Pierce Baker, learned to feel the awe he felt of lofty and serene Mt. Chocorua. With other Harvard friends I came to know the rocky shores and inland waters of Maine, the silent wilderness of Moosehead Lake, with Mt. Katahdin blue in the distance, and the forest trails of Mt. Desert. I canoed on Lake George, and had a memorable experience when I met a great American, the veteran of the 1848 revolution in Germany and of the Civil War in the United States, the venerable Carl Schurz. That passing touch with a man who refused to let his heart's allegiance be hyphenated, had its part in making me an American.

For weeks at a time I was in Quogue, on Long Island's south shore, where lovely Dorothy Oakley was my companion in the churning surf, and my unwitting and persuasive teacher of Americanism.

– 2 –

I doubt if, in the early years of the century, there was a boy in Germany or America more fortunate than I in his girl friends. In looks, personality and temperament, my German friend Ruby and my American friend Dorothy were sharply contrasted: the one, dark, angular and bubbling with deviltry; the other, fair-haired, graceful and self-contained, paddling her lone canoe on a lake of poetry and music. Yet, dramatically different as they outwardly were, in all the deeper matters of spirit and character they were alike; both honest to the last fiber of their strong, energetic and resilient bodies; both rich in faith that was less a refuge than an instrument of intelligent and effective living; both outgoing in love that meant action; both alert to the responsibilities of the daily routine and of the challenge of the national need; both with a clear sense of first things first, and with the humor that is the essence of any sense of values; both courageous in danger and brave in sorrow, with the capacity to pick up the broken pieces of life and, by a miracle of their indomitable spirits, mend them so the crystal vessel might show no cracks.

– 3 –

Dorothy came from a long line of Hudson River and Westchester County stalwarts—English, Dutch, French or Welsh in origin—and was a part of the traditional American pattern by virtue of a grandfather who had been a farm boy, and had run away to the big city and made good. When I came to know him, Cyrus J. Lawrence, her mother's father, was a successful banker and the country's most eminent collector of Barye bronzes and Mary Cassatt paintings. Her mother's mother was the daughter of Richard March Hoe, the inventor of the rotary printing press which had made modern journalism possible, and one of the mid-nineteenth century's ablest industrialists. Both the Oakley and the Lawrence line linked her to the saga of American self-reliance and enterprise, the saga of freedom and the passion to keep the torch alight.

Dorothy thus proved to be American not only by blood. There was a fire in her heart for her country that kindled her mind and her spirit whenever she spoke of it. She was the only person, my own age, that I remember, who helped me see what America meant.

She proved to be unusual in other ways: at sixteen, when I first met her, a clear-headed, clearhearted young woman who mingled gaily with her contemporaries but had hidden recesses to which she withdrew when she failed to find response on deeper levels. Her thinking went into metaphysical sea depths in which mine could give out only helpless bubbles, but we met happily on what was to me the surer beach of an earthly ocean, coming into fellowship where the Atlantic, shooting its white spears up the sand, did much of the talking. I have a picture of Dorothy sitting on the upjutting

164

timbers of an ancient wreck, looking out over the tumbling breakers, a white sunbonnet on her head, a light scarf blowing in the wind, and the mystery of the sea reflected in her eyes.

A dozen years after, I recalled to her these afternoons on the beach:

> "I wonder, had you wept or had you smiled,
>   Could you have read the book of things to be,
>   Those summer dusks we sat beside the sea,
> And, like the children that we were, beguiled
> Our wiser sense to think that we but whiled
>   An hour away in casual company?
>   Could you have known what now is memory,
> I wonder had you wept or had you smiled? . . ."

A half century later, I still wonder.*

– 4 –

What I remember most vividly about Dorothy, when I first knew her, is the purity of mind and purpose shining out of her clear blue eyes. She seemed to live in a kind of rain-washed June air, and made me think of Joan of Arc.

There was actually, deep down, more than a little of Joan in her. Even at sixteen, it happened, the fires of religious intolerance had singed her. Her mother, after years of chronic illness, had been healed in Christian Science, actually raised, in fact, from what two highly respected physicians had declared to be death. Her consequent, possibly overzealous acceptance of this "strange cult," as it was called, had scandalized the sedate Hudson River community in which the Oakleys were living, and she had been denounced from a Protestant pulpit as a "pernicious influence." Because of her mother's heterodoxy Dorothy herself had been refused admission to an exceptional

* He needn't. I had the chance to marry a hard-headed businessman who would have given me greater ease in material living; but Hermann had understanding of the intangibles. We have had rugged times, occasionally, but never a dull moment. I recommend the intangibles. D.O.H.

private girls' school in the town and had been forced to travel to New York for such classes as she could attend, three times a week, at a school there. (Even old-line Americans seem, in the 1890's, to have had Father's doubts of the public schools.) Carefully directed trips through Europe gave her the cultural depth her intermittent schooling could not give.

Out of the experience Dorothy had derived no sense of grievance or martyrdom, only a painful diffidence, a sense of being somehow outside the pale; so that, when I came along and proved to be without antagonism toward her religious beliefs, I took on shape and color in her eyes which had little to do with any merits of mine as a person. What I, on my part, saw was a girl who dared to be herself, though every door closed against her, resolved to hold tenaciously to the faith that had given her back her mother, and to make that faith effective in her own life. As in Browning's Evelyn Hope, so in Dorothy, "spirit, fire and dew" were mingled to make a girl whom a boy, however self-centered and immature, would want to remember on either side of a great ocean.

– 5 –

Sometime toward the end of my sophomore year, German and American habits of mind and custom came into conflict to produce a major crisis in my relations with Father.

Even before I entered Harvard—the day before, in fact—Dorothy and I had come to an understanding regarding our feelings for each other. Her family knew of it, but not mine. By German tradition, student engagements were strictly taboo, signifying an irresponsibility that was, from a social standpoint, even worse than failure to win promotion in school. No self-respecting young man was supposed to ask a girl to marry him until he had achieved a substantial position in business or a profession. On the surface that was sound enough, but the result was that few German men married before they were in their early thirties and, then, girls ten or more years younger than themselves. Involved in the custom was the position of the husband as the master of the house, with the wife often as the wholly subservient and obedient mate. Not infrequently, a husband actually regarded his wife as merely the eldest of his children, addressed her as *mein Kind*, and treated her as a child with no mind of her own and no claims as an individual.

Against this deeply ingrained German view of marriage stood the American ideal of a partnership of two young people, generally about the same age, and frequently very young indeed, starting from the bottom together, and working their way up together.

Knowing how Father felt about student engagements, I nursed the hope that Dorothy and I might keep secret our commitment to each other until after I had my degree. Of course it didn't work. Dorothy's family could not, naturally enough, understand why I should be unwilling to tell my family about the engagement, and became restive and suspicious. I, on my part, trained to fear equally my Father in heaven and my father on earth, could not bring myself either to face the commotion that my transgression of this ancient taboo would stir up, or to try to explain to the Oakleys a situation which, I knew, was nonsense from the American point of view.

I am sure I must have cut a shabby figure in the eyes of Dorothy and her family, but I cut an even shabbier one in my own; and, finally, sat down at my desk in Cambridge and wrote Father the terrible truth. The following Friday, when the last of the week's lectures was over, I took the train to New York to face the drums and the brass.

It was near midnight when I arrived. Our generally happy home was like a house where someone lay dead. The girls, hearing me come up the stairs, opened the door of their room a crack to give me a solemn, sympathetic welcome, such as a condemned criminal might expect. Mother was loving as always, but solemn too. Father had gone to bed, too upset to talk, that night.

No one had any objections to Dorothy. The family knew her and liked her. Their dismay was directed wholly at me—my irresponsibility, my adolescent disregard of what was "fitting" in a man of probity and self-respect. If I had hit Dorothy over the head and carried her to Cambridge, the gloom could scarcely have been deeper.

Curiously, I have no memory of what happened when the actual avalanche hit me. It must have happened at breakfast next morning. There must have been words, hot words, on Father's part, but I seem to remember only the grief in his eyes.

Before I returned to Cambridge, we had arrived at a compromise. The family would acknowledge the engagement on condition that it remain secret until I graduated. The Oakleys had no objections.

A few weeks later, to my horror, I heard that Father had solemnly called on Dorothy's father and mother to tell them what he proposed to do for Dorothy and me in the way of a financial settlement and to ask what he could expect the Oakleys to do. After almost forty years in America, he knew as little of American ways as that.

– 6 –

The painful struggle about the engagement made me realize more sharply than ever that I wanted to be on my own. I went to see the man generally regarded as the most perceptive of the mentors of youth at Harvard, my teacher in English composition and already my friend, Dean LeBaron Russell Briggs. What possibilities were there at Harvard for me to work my way through the remaining two years of my college course?

I remember the quizzical look in his blue eyes and the kindly lines in the pink granite of his face, as he invited me to spend the following weekend with him, to talk it all over at his summer home near Plymouth. Sitting with him on his porch, looking over the stark landscape of scrub pine, or driving with him in his buckboard, listening to quaint stories of his Cape Cod neighbors, I came to see aspects of New England that were not in the history books. I learned too—surprisingly in that place and from this lean, weather-beaten Yankee —that independence and self-reliance might, in certain circumstances, not be the indispensable steppingstones to manhood that I thought they were. "When you go apple-picking," the Dean said, "it's no virtue to reject the use of a ladder just to prove that you can climb a tree. The point is the number of apples you pick."

He frowned and looked unhappy, squirming in his chair, as he always did when he was about to say something which might sound preachy. "Your father is giving you a head start on a lot of young men," he said. "I don't think I would reject the head start if I were you." His face wrinkled in a wry smile. "Just consider it an obligation to go further than you might go, without it."

The course that the Dean suggested might, I recognized, not be as dramatic as a declaration of independence, but it made sense, and might be no less exacting.

The whole serio-comic episode contributed to my growth as an American.

CHAPTER FIVE

IF THE Hill helped me to win an American bridgehead and Dorothy fortified it, Harvard consolidated it and made it permanent. Harvard, in retrospect, is a succession of almost daily impacts, extraordinarily illuminating to a youth brought up to regard himself, in the presence of age or authority, as a respectful nobody; and America, except in the area of invention, industry and finance, an undeveloped intellectual and aesthetic wilderness.

Harvard, as I look back, is George Herbert Palmer presenting the Greek philosophers, one by one, with the urbanity of a host introducing distinguished guests recently arrived from Athens. It is, day after day, confronting the enigmatic smile and impenetrable *café au lait* eyes of George Santayana expounding Plato in an unimpeded and seemingly casual flow of such language as I had never imagined any man could improvise. It is being one of a Sunday evening gathering at Charles Eliot Norton's, noting the weight of erudition on those bent shoulders and the gleam in those never satiated eyes. It is watching President Eliot striding, erect and austere, across the Yard; and Josiah Royce, with his deceptively infantile face, making his way dreamily under the elms to the neo-Gothic library. It is reading Milton under the direction of that warmhearted Scot, William Allan Neilson. It is wincing at the Kittredge thunders and following them into the deepest sanctuaries of Shakespeare.

Harvard to me is seeing Dean Briggs leaning against the doorframe of a lecture room on the top floor of University Hall, rubbing his spine up and down as a cat might rub against a man's leg, while with his shy, winning smile, he elucidated the art of English versification. It is Barrett Wendell, in accents more Oxonian than Oxford, talking to me, a half-baked sophomore, as though I were of his own age and eminence. It is Nathaniel Southgate Shaler, looking like some Elizabethan sea rover, teaching geology and writing five connected, five-act dramas on the great Elizabeth, just to prove that Darwin was wrong when he said that a lifetime in science spoiled a man's taste for poetry.

Harvard to me is consuming beer and pretzels at midnight while George Pierce Baker thought through with his eager "Dozen" what the American drama needed to grow out of its pinafores and short pants. Harvard to me is Raphael Pumpelly, as an undergraduate, climbing the "roof of the world" in northern India, and another upper classman knocking on the gates of the forbidden city of Khiva in Turkestan, crying, "Open! It is I, Langdon Warner!"—and seeing the gates open. Harvard is meeting Theodore Roosevelt in the office of the *Harvard Advocate*, not as President of the United States but as a fellow *Advocate*-man, though he happened to have served twenty-seven years ahead of the board of which I was a member and had gone quite a way in the intervening period. Harvard, to me, finally, is the enduring daily of the savage, occasionally obscene and invariably penetrating red-ink comments of an undergraduate, two years my junior in age and two years my senior in college *—the attractive, gifted and doomed Swinburne Hale—determined to make a writer out of the friend he cherished; and learning to take his merciless criticism, and, in the end, to be grateful for it to a degree that I am grateful for scarcely anything else that Harvard gave me.

Harvard is all these things to me. To experience them was to experience three centuries of New England in four years—the aspirations, the discipline, the freedom; the respect for the individual, the urge to aspire and to venture; the challenge to think, without any encouragement to believe that thinking was ever going to be anything but the

* There was a three-year interval for me between my graduation from the Hill and my entering Harvard.

"tough" process that George Meredith, as Baker frequently reminded me, declared it to be; the pursuit of excellence and the impatience of all my mentors with anything short of it.

I have no doubt that other young men have had similar experiences at Oxford or Heidelberg, or Upsala or the Sorbonne. It happened that I had them at Harvard and subconsciously identified them with the American tradition. Beating, day after day, upon my mind and spirit, they helped make me an American.

– 2 –

Since Harvard was wholly rooted in America, conceived for the purpose of validating, maintaining and developing the dream that was America, even as early as the mid-1630's, and since I was, heart, mind and spirit, a part of Harvard, I began to think of my country not as something I had acquired by right of birth, or chosen by a process of education, decision and resolution, but as a possession that had been immemorially mine. German as I was in blood, language and tradition, I found myself singing,

> "Land where my fathers died,
> Land of the Pilgrims' pride,"

with a conviction—and no recognition of the facts could argue me out of it—that my forebears actually had died as Americans on American soil and had shared such pride as the Pilgrims may have had in the pine barrens they sweated over to get a living. The "embattled farmers" of Lexington and Concord were in my ancestry, and my own great-great-grandfathers had been "ragged Continentals" at Valley Forge. The tradition I recognized as my own was not the German tradition I had been brought up on, the tradition of Martin Luther, of Goethe, Schiller and Heine, of Frederick the Great, Bismarck and the Hohenzollern dynasty, but the tradition of Washington, Jefferson and Franklin, of Boone, Lincoln, Longfellow, Whitman and Emerson.

It sounds ridiculous. I can't explain it. But it is so.

172

CHAPTER SIX

WHEN Mother laid down her "ultimatum" about my becoming an American, Father saw the implications no more clearly, I am sure, than he had seen the implications of his desperate and cruel action in sending the elder boys to his mother. He must have had plenty of imagination to make the money he made in cotton but he never seemed to focus it on his family relations. Annoying as such myopia was in our day-to-day family life, it became devastating when his self-will went into operation on a big scale.

– 2 –

As Father approached his sixtieth year and the fortieth anniversary of his coming to America, his thoughts turned toward retirement. He had made a comfortable fortune and could maintain his hyphenated family amply on the income from his investments. He enjoyed the routine of life he had worked out—six months of business, followed by a six-month vacation—but he had known too many able men whose judgment had faltered with advancing years to think that he could keep up his pleasant routine indefinitely. If he stayed in business too long might he not run the risk of losing all he had made? Was it not wiser to retire while his powers were at their peak?

Retire? Where to? He could not visualize himself sitting around the 88th Street house, reading the memoirs of the generals of the Franco-Prussian War, which, with an occasional novel of the more substantial sort, had for years been the literature of his leisure hours.

He might, of course, buy a place in the suburbs, and, like one of his Exchange friends, raise roses. But he didn't care about roses, except in vases; and he didn't think much of the suburbs, associating them with overcrowded trains filled with soot and coal gas. The widespread recognition of Florida or California as the Ultima Thule of the retired was still decades below the horizon. Anyway, Father had claustrophobia and shrank from any journey involving sleeping cars.

So far as I know, no place in America entered his mind when he thought of retirement. When he withdrew from the Exchange, there was only one place to withdraw to, and one kind of living to pursue —the pleasant, leisurely living of his German vacations, among companionable people of background, cultivation and position, people with plenty of time, people who liked and respected him as a man who had achieved. He thought of *Geheimrat* This, *General* That, *His Excellency* the Other, able and interesting men all, who also had achieved.

He thought of his American friends, too, I am sure, and knew he would miss them. What he did not think of, so far as I have ever been able to discover, was the possibility that he might owe something to the country that had welcomed him as a young man, given him an opportunity to make a living and, at last, a fortune, and thrown about him and his family the protection and the splendor of the institutions of free government.

He had made his money out of the American soil. Could he, in decency and honor, grab it and go?

So far as I know, the question never occurred to him. Yet he was a man of sensitive perceptions in all his other relationships, a man to whom sentiment was immensely important, and, where his native land was concerned, compelling beyond all reason. It is all an enigma to me, the enigma that, I suppose, most blind spots are.

– 3 –

I was relishing an American summer in 1905, so I wasn't with the family when Father's dream of returning to Germany to live, which had simmered in the back of his mind for forty years, started actively cooking, and I don't know how much of it he shared with Mother. My brother Fred, I am sure, abetted him. Fred, who was advancing brilliantly in the Prussian administrative service, had never ceased to long for the home he had missed so desperately during his boyhood's long and lonely exile. He saw a hope at last of having the parental roof within reach and, I am sure, encouraged Father's daydreams. So Father's ghastly, earlier mistake served to fix and seal the later, even deadlier folly.

Father did not really need much encouragement. The man who, two years before, had been the spearhead of the sensational battle to keep Daniel J. Sully from cornering the cotton market, acclaimed as the Exchange's "Iron Chancellor," was as irrational as a seventeen-year-old, when sentiment took possession of him. There was no family conference on the proposed transplanting of the family and all its possessions, such as there had been on the issue of hiring black Thomas for fifty dollars a month; no real discussion even that I remember.

Without warning to any of us, at a dinner marking the fortieth anniversary of Father's arrival in America, he took the fateful, decisive step. Without premeditation, I am sure; perhaps, under the emotional impact of the celebration, Father closed the speech which was the evening's culmination with the announcement of his decision to retire to Germany to live.

Dorothy's mother, who was present, noted the look of dazed dismay on Mother's face and subsequently reported that Mother, later that evening, had confided to her that Father's speech had given her her first intimation of his determination to transplant himself, his home, his wife and their two daughters, to his native land. I have never been able to quite believe that Mrs. Oakley heard or, at least, interpreted aright what must have been whispered words, for I could not conceive of Father, who was generally tenderness itself with his family, as ever being so insensitive, abrupt and highhanded. Mother must have known of Father's determination. What happened, I suspect, is that, hearing Father make his announcement, possibly unexpected at that time, and make it there, in the house where, after the long, lean years, we had all been so happy, she had suddenly been overcome by the finality of his decision, suddenly, perhaps, recognized the tragedy that it portended.

– 4 –

When, a few months later, Father was back in Germany for his customary vacation, he started casting his eyes about for the house at the rainbow's end. To rent, as he had always rented, in Brooklyn and New York? No, indeed. To buy. On his native soil he had no fear of being chained to the land. This was where he wanted to be and would always, he was certain, want to remain. For he would be home, home after the long exile. His thoughts turned to the Rhine. Was the Rhine not the river of German romance, the symbol of German defiance to the ancient enemy, France? There proved to be a house with some twenty acres of parkland, vineyard and garden for sale, near the picturesque little village of Niederwalluf and opposite, a mile or two downriver, from Mayence. Fred looked it over and approved. Father, Mother, the girls and I (I was with the family that summer) visited it, and agreed it was wonderful. Fred put through the deal.

Why the girls and I approved so lightly a purchase that implied the uprooting and transfer of our home from America to Germany, I can explain only on the ground that we had to such a degree been encouraged to believe that Father knew best, and had, in fact, been so definitely discouraged from thinking for ourselves that, in relation to Father, the critical faculty simply did not function.

In the shadows thrown by the brightness of Father's success, I see, again, Nemesis bestirring herself. If we three had been permitted as children to develop opinions of our own and to speak out, how much Father—and we all—might have been spared!

None of us children, except perhaps Fred, had any personal interest in this fantastic venture in sentimentalism. Dorothy and I had, of course, no intention whatever of going to Germany to live;

176

and the girls, German as they were in many of their attitudes, were basically American, and had never really been happy in Germany.

Like the fisherman in Heine's "Lorelei," we fell under the spell of the Rhine, the house, surrounded with magnificent trees, the long promenade parallel to the slow-moving river, the rose garden, the vine-clad, ancient-appearing stone water tower, the vineyard sloping down to the river, the hidden arbor, hung with wisteria, over the river's edge, the boats passing upriver and down, the woods and meadows of the farther shore, the sense of legendry and history all about us. Whether Mother ever fell under the spell which overcame the rest of us, I never knew. As always, she said little, accepting with her habitual patience what she knew—or at least believed—she could do nothing about.

Addie, in New York, successful cotton broker that he was, practical-minded in his integrity and in his freedom from the blandishments of the romantic imagination, was living with his attractive wife Edith, half German and half of the Old South, in prosaic New Jersey, beyond the circle of the Lorelei's enchantment, and was the only one of us children who saw the folly of the uprooting that Father was so happily anticipating. But his protests—vigorously seconded by his wife—went unheeded.

Addie's father-in-law, father's old friend, Otto Arens, robust and forthright, did his best, in his own blunt way, to save Father from himself, "*Hermann, sei doch kein Kamel!*" Freely translated, what he said was, "My God, don't be an ass!"

– 5 –

When Father returned to Germany, the following spring, it was not to his customary leisure but to the exacting if enticing labor of conferring with architects and dealing with contractors. The house he had bought was too small to suit the expansive mood that his decision to return to the Fatherland had generated. He wanted a mansion worthy of the place in the world that he had made for himself. So the house was to be enlarged by two wings, and the whole interior to be rebuilt to provide a magnificent staircase with carved rail supports, impressive living rooms with views over the Rhine, a great dining room, looking north and west and south, and, to balance it on the eastern end of the house, a spacious billiard room, like nothing we had ever had or dreamed of wanting before. Upstairs, beside extensive master bedrooms and guest rooms, there was to be a suite for the girls, a suite for Auntie, and a suite for Fred and me. There were to be—and the neighboring towns crackled with comments on it, when the word got around—six bathrooms. In New York, two had been a scarcely imagined consummation.

CHAPTER SEVEN

W HILE Father was building his house on the Rhine, wholly unexpected and breath-taking things were happening to me on my side of the Atlantic. For nine years, consciously and unconsciously, I had moved toward this mystical shape, this dream, this compelling reality that is America. In June, 1907, incredibly, America ran to meet me.

By sheer luck, the poem I wrote for the graduation of my class at Harvard in June, 1907, went clear across the country, and set tongues wagging, prematurely, about a new birth of poetry in America. The public interest was due, in part, to the rhythmic hoofbeats of a "troop of the guard" riding to the relief of humanity beleaguered, and even more to the catchy refrain:

> "On to the walls, on to the walls,
> on to the walls, and over."

But mainly responsible for the excitement that the poem stirred up was the circumstance that, when I delivered the lines in Sanders Theatre, Harvard's academic auditorium, a friend and clubmate of mine, John Reynolds, who happened to be the Harvard correspondent of the Boston *Herald*, was sitting on the platform next to Dr. Francis Greenwood Peabody, Dean of the Divinity School, who had given the invocation. When the bearded cleric exclaimed impetuously, "That's the best class poem I ever heard!" Jack sensed a story.

What followed was fairly dizzying. CLASS DAY POET LEAPS TO FAME was the two-column *Herald* headline. Every Boston paper published the 107-line poem in full, several following it with interviews with me and news stories about me. The *Post* included the poem in the series of "One Hundred and One Gems of New England Poetry" it was publishing. The staid *Transcript* even commented on it, editorially: "In as yet a somewhat more restricted sphere, the Harvard class day poet of this year has repeated the experience of Lord Byron who awoke one morning and found himself famous. Efforts of this kind have rarely survived the hour of their delivery . . . but the public is still discussing Hermann Hagedorn's poem, and the question is going around: 'Are we at last to have a revival of real poetry in this country?'"

The *Traveller* took up the theme. Was the fact that I was of German extraction a significant factor? The *Globe* noted that the query of the British ambassador, James Bryce, "Where are your American poets?" had, in one case, at least, found an answer.

The interest spread to New York, where the *Sun* gave a column and a half to the poem and a reprint of one of the Boston stories. *Town and Country* gave the poem two pages; *Harper's Weekly*, an editorial. A St. Louis paper published the poem; but how much farther west it went I can only guess from the letters I received in the years that followed, from people who had cut the poem from their local papers, recited it in school public-speaking contests, or pasted it in their scrapbooks.

– 2 –

After fifty years, I find myself thinking that people must, indeed, have been thirsty for something to stir their pulses, to have acclaimed, as they did, the thin fare I gave them. Even my picture of the charging troopers fails to bear objective scrutiny. How young men were supposed to charge walls, and surmount them, on horseback, I don't know, but, happily, no one at the time raised the question. "More metre than matter" was, years after, the comment of a friendly critic in the *Outlook*. Apart from the attractive picture of youth in full gallop, riding on a quest, the poem was, in fact, vague and woolly, as a young man's aspirations are likely to be; but, ringing through the verbiage, was a challenge to the spirit to rescue mankind from the domination of scientific intellectualism, that was valid then, and is valid still:

"An anxious generation sends us forth . . .
From west and east, from south and north,
Earth's children, weary-eyed from too much light,
Cry from their dream-forsaken vales of pain,
'Give us our gods, give us our gods again!'
A lofty and relentless century
Has pierced the very inmost halls of faith;
And left no shelter whither man may flee
From the cold storms of night and lovelessness and death.
Old gods have fallen and the new must rise!
Out of the dust of doubt and broken creeds,
The sons of those who cast men's idols low
Must build up for a hungry people's needs
New gods, new hopes, new strength to toil and grow . . ."

I don't believe that the acclaim, those June days, did me any harm; nor, in the long run, any good. What remained in my mind, after I came down to earth, was the sense that something I had said had apparently given a "lift" to a great many people, and that these people were expecting me to give them the same kind of lift again. I don't know if I recalled Grandmother Schwedler's conception of the poet as prophet, but it seemed to me that there was nothing I wanted so much as, now and again, to speak to the highest in my countrymen, and, by God's grace, to speak for them.

It was a very romantic idea, but, though the currents of modern poetry have since flowed in wholly different channels, it has been incorrigibly tenacious.

CHAPTER EIGHT

FATHER did not see me graduate. He was in Germany, supervising the completion of the house. It was not a happy experience. Sometime, that spring, the shadowy figure which had begun to stir in the recesses of Father's mind when the question of my brother Fred's future had first arisen, twenty years before, attached herself to him as his permanent companion.

The enlarging of the villa on the Rhine into the thirty-room *Protzenkasten,* as the Germans call the houses that rich men build as symbols of their success, cost Father three times what he expected, and twice what his fortune, substantial as it was, should have indicated to him that he might, in prudence, spend. The construction, moreover, taught him more of the petty meannesses of Germans-on-the-make than he had ever imagined could be. He realized with a jolt that he was operating in a different dimension from that in which he had lived and worked, the preceding forty years. He recalled the broad-gauge attitudes of American businessmen. They could drive a sharp bargain and, if you didn't watch out, some might rook you; but they were never petty; they would not cap a bill for $180,000, as his German contractors did, with a charge for the two-cent stamp that bore it to your door.

Being a resident, Father found, was different, moreover, from being an occasional visitor and honored guest. Some of the Excellencies palled on closer acquaintance or showed their true colors by touching him for a loan, trying to inveigle him into buying valuables of theirs that he had no interest in, or otherwise indicating a desire to tap his bank account. What was worse, Father began to recognize that, in the eyes of the people who ate his dinners and drank his wines, he was no longer the distinguished foreigner; he was just another retired German merchant who did not even have the *Commerzienrat* title that any second-rate industrialist or banker got sooner or later, merely by keeping out of jail. Father thought more and more about his Cotton Exchange friends, and the easy informality of his relations with them, in contrast to the bowings and scrapings of his relations with his newer, German friends. He began to be homesick for America as he had not, for the last ten years in America, been homesick for Germany.

His children, even his children, seemed to go back on him. Almost before the house was completed, Fred, Irma and I, for each of whom Father had provided such spacious quarters, were either married or engaged.

Nor was that all. Grandmother Schwedler had, in her shrewd realism, recognized from the start the folly of this return to the Fatherland; but she had fallen in with it because she had no choice, returning with the rest of the family to a country that meant nothing to her except a stupid lack of basic conveniences. Philosopher that she was, she established herself and Venie in a little apartment in a neighboring village, building her own little world about her, with her Goethe pictures and books, the little ebony cabinet with the bust of Wagner, and the engraving of Doré's "La Paix." When it was all completed, she lay down and died, as any tree, transplanted too late, would die.

Her death, coming without warning, on top of his disappointments and disillusionments, shocked and bewildered Father. What had he done that everything should be so different from what he had hoped for, that everything should go so wrong?

His body uttered the agonies of his dismay as his proud lips never would. His skin broke out in eczema that plagued him night and day. The mansion on the Rhine that was to have been the frame of the successful man of affairs playing the gracious host for distinguished friends (and no one could play it better) became a hospital in which Mother and my sisters went back and forth, perpetually and helplessly, around a once strong and proud man, reduced to pitiful impotence and outbursts of frenzy. Numerous *Professor Doktors* and *Geheimeräte* solemnly plastered him with salves, but to no avail. Their medicines could not penetrate to the sick heart and the tormented spirit.

CHAPTER NINE

WHILE Father, in Germany, was suffering torments of conscience, dismay and disillusionment, inextricably mingled, Dorothy and I were delightedly discovering phases of American life that we had read about but never expected to experience. Neither of us ever having been west of Buffalo, we decided, when we married, that June of 1908, to go to Colorado on our honeymoon.

I don't remember which of us first had the happy thought, but neither of us was averse to following such inspirations if they seemed to us to have merit. We had both been brought up in a sheltered atmosphere—Dorothy in the suburbs, I in the city; and we wanted to "rough it." Besides, we both had the feeling that we needed to know something of our country, and Colorado seemed a good place to begin.

We picked Manitou Springs as our base, but it didn't satisfy us. Manitou—today a horror of cheap souvenir shops, filling stations and "tourist homes"—was at that time an unpretentious collection of country boardinghouses, tucked picturesquely in a fold of the mountains that are a great wall west of Colorado Springs; but it was too close to civilization to satisfy our romantic notion of the West. We wanted to experience the wilds; we wanted to stay at a ranch.

There were no "dude ranches" in Colorado in those days, but the parents of a classmate to whom we paid our respects recalled that a certain couple named Patterson, "up in the White River country," had been known to keep boarders. "Pat's" was the place for us to go.

We had never heard of the White River and had no idea where it was. I assume that our friends told us it was not exactly around the corner; but in the excitement of anticipation the fact did not penetrate. We got to Pat's, sure enough, but it took us three days—sixteen hours by rail on a transcontinental limited, ten hours by stagecoach, eight hours by one buckboard and a final two by another!

I don't remember how we communicated with Pat to find out if he could have us, unless it was by telephone, though poles and wires were still rare in the Rockies; but somehow we communicated with him and got word from him to come.

The journey, by itself, proved worth the effort, quite apart from the rewards we found on our arrival; for, in the course of those three days we stepped out of the ordered and sedate America we had grown up in, the America of balloon sleeves, high collars and top hats, into the frontier America of the 1880's. On the first lap, by rail to Glenwood Springs, my Harvard "Institute of 1770" hatband brought us the acquaintance of a lean youth who looked like an Indian and proved to be Shaun Kelly, Harvard senior, and roommate of President Roosevelt's son Ted. Our acquaintance ripened quickly, due more to my bride's beauty and charm than to any attractions of my own. When, after two days at the Springs, Shaun took the stage for the first seventy miles of the hundred-mile journey to his ranch near Steamboat Springs, Dorothy and I had promised him that, after a month at Pat's, we would visit him for the final ten days of our Western adventure.

The second lap of our journey was brief, taking us in two hours by train from Glenwood to Rifle, where we were to spend the night and take the stagecoach, the following morning, for Meeker, the scene of a famous massacre by the Indians, some thirty years before. There was no station where the conductor dropped us off, an hour after midnight, and no sign of a town; only darkness and, overhead, a canopy of stars. I had wired to the only hotel in Rifle for a room, and expected, I suppose, in my innocence, that we would be met by the kind of hotel bus, familiar in eastern summer resorts. We were met by nothing and nobody. Finally, in the black distance, we became aware of a light, swung gently to and fro, a light that, as it drew near, revealed a boy pushing a wheelbarrow. The barrow was for our baggage.

Our room in the hotel was located behind the bar where, in the light of a smoking kerosene lamp, a group of hunters and trappers stood before an open fire—June is chilly, in those parts—consuming "forty-mile red-eye." I don't know whether we or the handsome frontiersmen were more abashed at the unexpected encounter. I was nothing to astonish a Colorado mountaineer, being just another tenderfoot, but Dorothy with her curly blond hair, and the rosy cheeks that set off her deep blue eyes, was a sight such as Rifle was not granted often, by day or by night. The men showed her a respect akin to awe. Dorothy's gaze actually was as wide with wonder as the hunters'. She had never seen a bar, or breathed air in which smoke and the fumes of alcohol were so thickly mingled. The mixture followed us into our bedroom.

The four-horse stagecoach we climbed into next morning was of the Concord type, subsequently made familiar by Western horse operas; with the inside seats facing each other, the driver's seat level with the coach roof, and the baggage strapped on behind. There were only two passengers in the stagecoach besides Dorothy and myself: a wide-bosomed Negro woman on the way to some ranch, "up-country," as cook, and a rough, burly, heavily moustached character who appeared to be some sort of judge. The cook, when lunch-time came, broke off, with her big fingers, for each of us, a "hunk" of the juicy blueberry pie she had brought. The judge made himself less agreeable, regaling us with tales of manslaughter and hangings which to us cotton-wool babes-in-the-woods lost none of their grisly quality by the casual manner of his narration. I must have been more tough-fibered than Dorothy, for when, at a stage station where we changed horses, the judge to her relief, joined the driver up front, I followed, hoping—not vainly—for more.

We stepped straight into the West of romantic fiction that day. The road could be called such only by courtesy. It was actually a series of parallel ruts cut deep in the gumbo-mud and only recently dried out. The coach was carrying U.S. mail and had a schedule that had no mercy on passengers. We lurched in and out of the ruts, pitching from side to side in our seats, never certain that, at the next lurch, the coach might not topple over. Now Dorothy was in the colored cook's lap and now the cook in Dorothy's. I don't know how I clung to my perch at the far left of the driver's seat.

We clattered in a cloud of dust into Meeker at five in the afternoon. It proved to be a pleasant little town with a tree-shaded Main Street and a two-story hotel which might have seemed at home anywhere in New England.

We resumed our journey, next morning, in the two-horse buckboard of the rural delivery mail carrier, who deposited us, after a six-hour drive, at the "town" of Buford. The "town" was actually the post office and nothing else; and the post office was a two-room cabin, set in a grove of cottonwoods, remote, by miles, from any other human habitation. Buford, in fact, was geographically an elusive conception. When there was a Republican administration it was on the north fork of the White River; when there was a Democratic administration it was on the south fork. The appointee who held the cigar box that held the stamps set the location of the "town." That year it was a woman. Postal service in Buford was sketchy. I wanted a postcard. The postmistress was not in sight but up from the river came her husband, a fishing rod on his shoulder. He inspected the cigar box and looked blank. "Say, Mrs. Bartlett," he called to the rear of the cabin, "whar d'ye keep them postal cards?"

"Pat," a good-natured, slouchy frontiersman, met us at Buford and, in another buckboard, drove us the final miles of our three-day journey in search of the wilderness.

– 2 –

Pat's place was as primitive as any romantic Easterner might desire. I never knew how many acres he owned or if he owned any at all at the time we were there, or merely squatted. It was an unpeopled land of woods and waters, peaks and valleys and mirroring lakes, of icy streams and pines and shimmering aspens, eight thousand feet above sea level where houses were five miles apart and the nearest settlement was thirty miles away.

Owner or squatter, Pat wasn't much of a ranchman. He had a few straggly cows, two or three scraggly horses and a few chickens, scraggly too; but the only activity in which he engaged with any degree of interest was the pursuit of what he euphemistically called "mountain veal." He engaged in it, we noted, mostly in the early morning before the rest of the world was astir, or on occasions when he had seen the game warden pass up the road on the way to Trappers Lake; and he scouted carefully before he descended to the ranch with the deer across his saddle. I became aware of his strategy once when he took me along.

Mrs. Patterson was stocky, with a face like a potato, and was obviously the boss of the ranch. She was a devout Seventh-day Adventist, and demonstrated it by resting so ostentatiously every Saturday that we nearly starved, and by working, Sundays, from the uprising of the sun to the setting thereof, as though she were thereby proving the validity of her creed. She "bedded" Dorothy and me, as the phrase went, in the gable of the two-story log cabin. The bare room had one astonishing and disconcerting feature: its walls and slanting ceiling were papered with issues of the Denver *Post*. Black headlines and illustrated Sunday horror stories were the last things we saw at night and the first things we woke up to in the morning.

Using newspapers as wallpaper, we agreed, was not a bad idea but we balked at the pattern. Didn't Pat have a tent? He did. We heard coyotes howling at night, not too remotely, and now and then a mountain lion. Bears were a possibility as midnight callers. One night a heavy animal did, indeed, shake the rail to which the tent was lashed, but it turned out, next morning, to have been a stray horse. Any four-footed invader was a possibility, I suppose, but we were united in our conviction that anything was better than those illustrated horrors on the wall.

Pat liked us and we liked him, but Mrs. Pat was a stern moralist and, we gathered, suspected that we were a pair of runaway teen-agers on a very reprehensible lark. Dorothy was twenty-five but she looked sixteen, and I, a year older, could have passed for eighteen. So Mrs. Pat was standoffish, and clearly a reluctant provider, hoping, perhaps, to make us seek a lodging elsewhere; perhaps at Marvine Lodge on the way to Trappers Lake, a favorite gathering place for fishermen.

But, the first Sunday evening that we were at the ranch, Dorothy came upon a cheap little organ in a back room, and casually started playing the hymns she had played when she was the organist of a little church in Englewood, New Jersey. Mrs. Pat's tense features relaxed and the shadow lifted. From that moment, Dorothy was acceptable to those devout and close-set eyes. Anyone who played hymns must be virtuous. There was a marked improvement in the food and shortly we even had desserts.

We didn't discover America at Pat's ranch but we discovered a way of life that was typical for vast areas of our country that we had known nothing about. We rode, we fished, we called at neighboring ranches, we knew June as it might have been on the day of Creation; we saw the aspens twinkle like water in a mountain brook; we caught our breath at the magic of an evergreen sparkling with icicles in the morning sun once when Pat had left the hose playing on it all night; we listened to the silence under the stars, broken only by the sighing of the night wind in the pines or the occasional bark or bellow of some wild creature in the distance; we learned about the stern justice and wild humor of men on the frontier, and about the loneli-ness of women.

– 3 –

Unexpectedly one morning a horseman, leading two ponies, came clattering down the steep hillside back of the ranch. It was our friend, Shaun Kelly, coming to take us to his own ranch. We hur-riedly packed our trunk—yes, we had brought a trunk!—and made arrangements to have it go by buckboard to Meeker and thence by express to Glenwood Springs. The few essentials we required for our visit to Shaun's we stowed in two flour bags that Mrs. Pat dug up. Then, with Dorothy's curls tied back with a shoestring, we were off with Shaun for the ranch he called "Cabincourt."

The twenty-five-mile ride carried us back into history a hundred and fifty years. Virginians crossing the Alleghenies into Kentucky in the 1750's and sixties knew such a wilderness. There was no road and the trail along which Shaun led us was shortly no more. The compass in Shaun's hand was our guide as we rode through tangles of fallen timber and brush that all but dragged us from our saddles. Now and again we emerged from the forest into lovely "parks" where deer had clipped the lush grass, so we seemed to be riding over carefully tended lawns. For miles we rode through glades of pine and aspen, along sloping meadows, bright with wildflowers, down steep declivities and across rushing streams where you could do nothing except trust to the instinct and the surefootedness of your pony; and then again into all but impenetrable tangles of virgin forest. That day we learned the meaning of the word "wilderness."

At Shaun's we learned about homesteading. He and his father had taken out a homestead claim, and Shaun worked, every morning, clearing his brush-covered acres. Two or three times while we were with him he gave us his own personal rodeo, perching us on the top rail of his circular corral while he broke in some wild pony.

– 4 –

The method of our return to civilization dramatized the passing of the Wild West's era of the horse, the dawning of the era of the automobile. We arranged by telephone to have the only car in the region meet us at the northern terminus of the road that led to Meeker, and thence to the railroad at Rifle. Escorted by Shaun we started on the twenty miles of cattle trail to where the car was waiting. Suddenly, from somewhere, a herd of long-horned steers drove

past us on the trail. We had no time and, in fact, no space to seek
security by the trailside. The herd came thundering upon us and, in
an instant, we were in a bellowing sea of dust and horns and steaming
breath. Huge, hot bodies pressed against our knees on both sides,
threatening to crush us. Happily, our horses kept their nerve, and
Dorothy and I were so enthralled by the experience that our imagi-
nations had no chance to present the obvious possibility of our
horses bucking, and throwing us under the hoofs of the herd. The
fact was that they were so intent on where they were going that they
soon left us behind.

Waiting for us at our destination was an Overland car, so antique
as even to antedate gears. It was, in fact, belt-driven. On the rutted
road to Meeker that morning the belt broke. The driver asked me,
Would I mind loaning him my belt? I did, not without reluctance,
for reasons that are obvious. The belt did the job and was returned
to me at Meeker, happily intact.

– 5 –

Dorothy and I were finishing a sketchy meal at a "two-bit" Chinese
restaurant, in preparation for the drive to Rifle, that afternoon, when
a boy tapped me on the shoulder. "The sheriff wants to see you,"
he said.

I blinked my astonishment. "Me?" I asked. "What sheriff? And
what does he want to see *me* for?"

"He's over to the hotel," the boy answered, "an' he wants to see
you." And with that cryptic statement he turned and was gone.

I had never been wanted by a sheriff before. I went to the hotel,
not in trepidation but puzzled.

In the lobby I confronted a sawed-off, thickset man with a face
tougher than hickory, and a bright badge indicating his office. "I'm
told you want to see me?"

"I'm Al Ellison," he said, in the tone of a man who assumes that
no one could be so ignorant as not to know all that the name

implied. "I'm told you've hired Jake Dimond's car to take you an' your lady to Rifle?"

Now what is criminal about that? I asked myself.

"You see, it's this way," went on the sheriff. "There's a couple of horse thieves broke out of the jail here last night."

Horse thieves. Shades of the Wild West! I pricked up my ears.

"Got out by the stovepipe hole." I tried to visualize the proceeding and gave it up. "They goes on a drunk an' then tellyphones me where I kin get 'em back."

Here was a new twist to the cops and robbers game. "That was considerate of them," I commented.

"Considerate, yo'r aunt!" ejaculated the sheriff. "They knows well enough, in this kind o' country we got here, they'd starve to death or get pumped full o' lead. But I ain't takin' no chances. No one can't break out of the Glenwood jail."

I assumed that he spoke with authority and offered no comment.

There was room in the car I had hired, he pointed out. "Would your lady object if we come along?"

Dorothy was sitting in one of the round-backed chairs that lined the walls of the lobby, watching us with fascinated interest. I gave her the picture. She reacted as I expected: it would be a lark.

The sheriff joined us. "You'll be all right, ma'am," he assured her. "I followed them boys nine hundred miles to Gallup, New Mexico, an' never laid an iron on 'em. I says, 'Boys, yo' know me. Yo' know I never wings a man, I lays him out.' An' they come along, right an' proper, like we was goin' up the aisle in church."

Dorothy was suitably impressed.

"Let me show yo' something." The sheriff led us to a framed picture hanging next to the registration desk: a photograph of four dead men in a row. "Them's the men what tried to rob the bank." A note of scorn was in his voice. "Them eastern crooks think they can pull something on the hicks. Well, I learned 'em. They can't pull them things here. Not so long as Al Ellison's sheriff."

193

The four dead men did not serve to reassure Dorothy, but on her face, I noted, amusement mitigated the horror.

"Them horse thieves," the sheriff assured her, "they won't peep." She was willing to take his word for it.

We picked up the horse thieves, handcuffed together, at the ten-by-ten strong box that was the jail, the sheriff leading them out to the car and making the introductions. Dorothy and I, remembering the stories of horse-rustling we had read, and of corpses swinging from cottonwood trees, expected to see ruffians whose desperate character would be written on their faces. Actually the thieves looked like any law-abiding ranch hand or nester and considerably more trustworthy than the sheriff. One, whom the sheriff addressed as Pete, was in his middle forties; the other, who was addressed as Burt, was perhaps half that age, an attractive and, I surmised, essentially good boy who had got into bad company.

The seats of the car were arranged as in the stagecoach we had made the journey in from Rifle, with the back seats facing each other. Dorothy sat next to the driver. Back to back to them sat the horse thieves, still linked by the handcuffs, and, facing them on the back seat, the sheriff and I.

The thieves were thoroughly relaxed, showing no signs of their "binge" of the night before. A herd of horses on the road through which the car passed excited their professional interest, evoking comments on the merits of this or that animal which indicated that arrest and the prospect of a prison term had not dampened their enthusiasm for horseflesh or disciplined their itching fingers.

The elder of the thieves pulled out a pocket flask, took a long swig and offered the bottle to his partner, to the sheriff and to me. "Forty-mile red-eye" had no appeal now for the youngster, Burt, but the sheriff took it. The bottle passed back and forth between Pete and the sheriff and was soon empty.

The sheriff thereupon brought out a flask of his own. Now a problem arose. The empty flask had a long, coiled lemon peel in it to absorb some of the rawness of the frontier "cat-gut." The full flask lacked such mitigating balm. The problem was how to transfer the lemon peel out of the flask that had no whisky into the flask that had whisky but no lemon peel. The sheriff and his charges tried their jackknives and got nowhere, they begged a hairpin of Dorothy and did no better. They tried a piece of copper wire that the driver fished from somewhere. No luck. Finally, the sheriff had the brilliant thought of pouring the whisky out of the flask that had the whisky but no lemon peel into the flask that had the lemon peel but no whisky, and, as a reward poured half the contents down his own gullet before offering it to the elder of the thieves.

The sheriff shortly showed the effects. "I followed these boys nine hundred miles to Gallup, New Mexico, I did"—his voice was getting a little thick—"an' I never laid a iron on 'em. I says, 'Boys, yo' know me. Yo' know I never wings a man, I lays him out.' Ain't it the truth, boys?"

"It sure is, Al," the thieves agreed.

The sheriff took another swig. "I don't blame you boys for stealin' hosses," he said. "I done that myself. I blame yo' for gettin' caught."

"Whar'd you lift 'em?" asked Burt, with the interest of one professional in the experience of another.

"Never yo' mind whar' I lifted 'em," said Al. "I ain't tellin'." Then, again, he was repeating his now familiar pattern: "Nine hundred miles . . . Gallup, New Mexico . . . an' never laid an' iron on 'em. . . . This feller Pete thar," he went on, speaking as though his prisoners were in another county, "he's a tough one. Ought to swing. Would ha' swung, ten years ago. The country ain't what it was! But the kid here, he got into a game he oughter stayed out of." I cast a sidelong glance at the boy who was flushing but trying to appear unconcerned.

"Burt's mother, she come to me," the sheriff went on, "and tried to get me to let him go. I'm sort o' soft-hearted, I am, an' she cried so, I'd ha' let him go if 'twarn't that Election was comin' along this November. I couldn't be havin' the Democrats sayin' I was soft on hoss thieves. An' the country needs me for another term."

"Oh, I dunno, Al," said Pete, grinning.

"Nor I neither," echoed Burt. "I sure don't."

Peter was carrying his liquor better than the sheriff. Burt was wholly sober. Both, turning now and again to call Dorothy's attention to some unusual feature in the landscape, were gravely courteous, invariably addressing her as "ma'am." Dorothy (she told me later) never had an instant's fear of them. She wasn't so sure about the sheriff.

The sheriff belched. "I don't think yo're appreciatin' yo'r blessings," he said in hurt tones. "I mighta shot yo' both when I caught yo' in Gallup, New Mexico. Or strung ye up. But I didn't, an' I don't know why. I never even lays an iron on yo'. I says, 'Boys, yo' know me. Yo' know I never wings a man, I lays him out!'"

We heard that story, at intervals, all afternoon each time more maudlin than before, more ruffled at the edges.

We had reached the top of the long hill that slopes sharply to Rifle and the railroad, and the sun was dipping to the horizon, when suddenly Pete who had turned to peer between Dorothy and the driver, clutched the driver's arm. "Stop!" he ordered. I caught my breath and saw the sheriff's hand fall on his gun.

The driver stopped the car. Coming up the road I noted a riderless horse and, some distance behind, its rider, walking to relieve the horse of his weight on the long climb.

Pete leaned toward the sheriff. "Al," he said, with a grin, "thar's something in them saddlebags. Shall I get it?"

"No," said Al. "I'll get it."

As the horse came even with the car, the sheriff climbed out and took hold of the bridle. Then, out of one bulging saddlebag he drew a wicker-bound demijohn of whisky, took a long pull, passed it to Pete and offered it to the rest of us, not forgetting Dorothy. Thereupon, he took another pull, longer than the first, and put the demijohn back in the place he had taken it from. The car resumed it's way. As we passed the dismounted man on the slope, the sheriff gave him an elaborate salute.

In the hotel at Rifle that evening the driver, the sheriff, the horse thieves, Dorothy and I had supper together.

– 6 –

Our Colorado experience taught us that New York is not all of America, and New England is not all of it, and that the nation and the people we are all a part of are something greater than any section of them, however rich in money, power, prestige or tradition it may be. We began to apprehend not only the physical breadth of America, unrolling hour after hour and day after day, as the train bore us eastward, but, in terms of the spirit, also its height and its depth.

CHAPTER TEN

ONE month after Dorothy and I had our ham and eggs with Al Ellison and his horse thieves we were at Father's villa on the Rhine, sitting down to a different sort of meal. It began with caviar and ran on through eleven other courses—I have the elaborate printed menu before me—turtle soup, lobster, rack of veal, *paté de fois gras*, Roman punch, partridges, artichokes, dessert, cheese and fruit; each course accompanied by its own rare vintage of Rhine wine or French claret, ending, where it all began, with champagne—Roederer *Carte Blanche*. Accompanying the food and the wines was music from an orchestra, down the hall, playing the Mendelssohn and Wagner wedding marches, an overture of Mozart, a waltz of Johann Strauss, a Hungarian dance of Brahms and, topping it all off, a Sousa march that, as a climax to Mendelssohn & Co., sounded unbearably crude and hollow. I winced at the thought that, to most of the guests, these brassy rhythms were America.

The occasion was the banquet following the wedding of my sister and cherished comrade, Irma, to a massive pillar of a man named Bensen, whose markedly masculine frame and features belied fantastically the name "Willy" by which he was generally known. Irma had always said she would never marry a German. She had also said she would never marry a doctor or a navy man. Such resolves are dangerous. She married all three. Bensen was a German naval staff surgeon, attached to the yacht *Hohernzollern* on which the Emperor liked to cruise, summers, along the Norwegian coast and, occasionally, winters, in the Mediterranean.

The dinner, interspersed with speeches, lasted four hours, though the tedium of sitting was relieved from time to time when the father of the groom proposed a toast to the bride's family or the father of the bride proposed a toast to the groom's, and other people toasted yet others. Then everyone would get up, sing *Hoch sollen sie leben!* —and walk around, clinking glasses with everyone else. Since there were fifty guests present, that represented some twenty-five hundred clinks to a speech. The scene had more than a little sparkle, with the women in bright gowns and all the diamonds they could raise, and various army or navy officers in dress uniforms, dripping with decorations.

It was all familiar to me, but to Dorothy it was alien and depressing. She did not like champagne or, in fact, any wine, and was shortly the only one in the room who was coldly sober, always a depressing experience. She did not speak German, moreover, and none of the effusively polite officers at our end of the table bothered to fetch up from his subconscious any remnants of English that he might have retained from his school days. One old gentleman, a cousin of Father's, did, indeed, come up with a laborious English sentence but the result did not seem to make Dorothy feel any more at ease; for what he said was—and how proud of himself he looked as he said it!—"Young lady, you are no longer a virgin!" I suppose it would have made quite a commotion if she had slapped the old boy's face; but he had it coming to him.

– 2 –

This second half of our honeymoon—six weeks in the mansion on the Rhine—brought the first half into sharp relief. We told the story of our Colorado adventures, of course, with Al Ellison and the horse thieves as a climax. Mother loved them but Father missed the point and was shocked. "My dear boy," he remonstrated, "how could you bring your lovely bride into such an environment, among such barbarous men!"

"But they weren't barbarous!" Dorothy explained. "I didn't trust the sheriff but the thieves were so respectful, even deferential, that I would have felt safer alone with either of them than I would have felt with most of the men I have met in New York ballrooms."

Father shook his head. "You are a child," he said. "You are both children. You do not know the realities of life."

It seemed to us that there were realities which Father did not know. He had never been near the frontier, or even, so far as I knew, read about it. He knew no more of its habits, customs and codes than a babe in the womb knows of crab apples.

"Women are rare on the frontier," Dorothy explained, "and that gives them a kind of security they don't have elsewhere. Let me tell you a story that the mail carrier told us on the drive in the buckboard from Meeker to Buford. There was a mail route through the mountains near-by where the carrier was continuously held up by bandits and robbed."

"You know," I interrupted, "protecting the United States mails is considered basic, a matter of the actual capacity of the government to protect itself and maintain its authority and self-respect."

Dorothy took up the tale again. "The Post Office Department tried everything, short of calling out the cavalry. Nothing worked, until someone who knew the West had the idea of giving the route to a woman. They gave it, in fact, to a girl of eighteen, unarmed. After that there was no more trouble." *

"My dear child," Father said incredulously, and, not wanting obviously to tell his new daughter-in-law that she had been fed fairy tales, changed the subject. "But that herd of cattle you were caught in!" he exclaimed. "You might have been trampled to death."

"We didn't try to buck them. We flowed with them; so we were safe."

* A newspaper clipping among my papers, with a Colorado date line, confirms the story.

200

He shook his head, in deepening bewilderment; and sadness, too. I think he felt that he no longer knew me.

– 3 –

We did not enjoy the house that Father had built under the curious illusion that all his children would ever be around him. As a monument to success the house was all that Father could have dreamed. As a home it was too big, too lacking in intimacy, too unlike the unpretentious, cozy houses we had known and loved. The furniture that had been adequate and even rather splendid in the 88th Street house seemed insignificant in these palatial rooms, and Father added expensive new tables and sofas and chairs that had no overtones of memory for any of us, and were as impersonal as furniture in a warehouse.

After the simple life at the ranch, the luxury was fun, for a while. The nice, friendly, obsequious servants, six of them, were warm in their interest and tireless in their service; but the tall, lean housekeeper who directed them was an alien innovation in our household. Outside, of course, were the gardeners. I never did know how many of them there were. I suppose, in coin of the realm, the flock of them cost less than black Thomas, the cook, and the waitress-chambermaid we had had in New York, and I'm afraid that the bent old crone who weeded the flower beds got no more than her bare living; but the very numbers gave me, during those six weeks at Niederwalluf— God help me!—a sense of superiority which I remember with shame. I wasn't crude about it but I was conscious that I was the son of the manor, and accepted, as my due, the servility that was shown me. Dorothy was unimpressed by the splendor, such as it was, having, one generation back of her wealthy grandparents, the Westchester village where every housewife did her own work, and a hired girl—if, for a season, you had one—was a member of the family. I am grateful that the democracy of the Hoes, the Lawrences, the Gilberts and the Meads, who sleep in the South Salem graveyard, is in the blood stream of my daughters and my grandchildren.

201

The thrill of luxury and lordliness faded quickly in the tension that possessed the spacious mansion. There had, as I have indicated, always been tension when Father was around, double tension when he was out of order physically in any way. He had never felt any obligation to minimize such disturbances as being purely personal matters which it was an imposition to communicate to others, except in emergencies. In the past, they had been little aches, little pains, frequently half imagined. Now the suffering was real. There was no exaggerating the severity of the eczema or the torture he endured.

The tension that Father unwittingly created was deepened by the presence of his sisters. The Aunts, who had come for the wedding, stayed on, without urging, convinced that their *geliebte Bruder* needed them in his illness, needed them more than ever. Elsbeth, with her sharp features and quick movements, nosed into everything. Alma, sculpturesque and dramatic, floated about Father, officiously, paying his bills and taking over other financial matters he had to deal with, renewing his compresses, bringing him shawls and blankets when he sat for an hour on the upper veranda. Aggressively indispensable, only they two, the Aunts seemed to say, really knew what Father needed. Mother could scarcely get near him; one sister or the other was always at his side. I am sure that Father would have preferred Mother near, but he was as fearful of hurting their feelings as the rest of us were of hurting his. He was susceptible to adoration, moreover, and Mother was never given to gush. She watched the comedy and did not think it very funny, and felt her anger rise; and bit her lips, and said nothing.

The tension that possessed the house was due in the main to Father and the Aunts, but to something else besides. The thirty-room mansion, the whole place, in fact, with all its beauty, its luxuriance of roses and perfectly kept lawns, its orchards, its vineyards, sloping to the Rhine, was alien to all of us. It was ours, inasmuch as Father had paid for it—and how!—but we did not possess it, not really. It was an illogical and unnatural phenomenon in our lives, expressing nothing in our history as a family, or in any of us as individuals, not even Father's sentimental hope some day to return to his *Vaterland*. He had never dreamed of this kind of *Protzenkasten*. The thing had crept up on him, as it were, under the subtle persuasions of the architects, making him feel that this was the sort of place he ought to want and should have as a suitable frame.

Being alien to the nature of all of us, the effect not of growth but of a violent dislocation, the house had on it what an earlier generation would have called a "curse," and we, less dramatically, would call a "jinx." It just wasn't right, it wasn't in the flow of things, it wasn't what people who have a personal relation to Deity call "guided." A line written three thousand years ago tells the story: "Unless the Lord build the house, they labor in vain that build it." The Lord wasn't called in when Father called in the architects, and if, unsummoned, He had spoken to Father in the night watches—and I strongly suspect that He did—Father hadn't listened.

– 4 –

September gave way to October. The Aunts stayed. Then, one day, when it appeared that the tragi-comedy could go on no longer and they would have to go, they had an idea. The doctor who came periodically from Stuttgart to consult with Father's local physician had a sanatorium in one of the southern city's attractive suburbs. What could be better than for Father to go to the sanatorium where the bearded *Herr Geheimemedizinalrat Doktor* could visit him daily? And in order to make sure that their "beloved brother" got everything he required, they, the Aunts, would go with him.

Mother, startled at the brazenness of their determination to take possession, waited for Father to say that, if he had to go, it was Mother he wanted to have with him. He did not say it. Mother bit back the tears, and the anger, and watched them go with dry eyes and a lacerated heart.

She hoped, from day to day, that Father would send for her. He was too miserable to write, so the Aunts wrote for him, telling, not obtrusively, but unfailingly, how they were doing for him, responding to his every even unspoken wish, mitigating his misery as only sisterly devotion could.

To Mother, longing for Father, homesick, I am sure, for America, lonely, overwrought, feeling it all as the final straw of forty years of acquiescence and adaptation to these sentimental and possessive women, every word was a stab.

Dorothy, climbing the broad stairs from the first floor one day, came on Mother, seated on a step, halfway up, in tears and a state of collapse. "I can't stand it any longer," she whispered as Dorothy crouched beside her and drew her into her arms. "I can't stand it any longer."

It was so unlike Mother to make a scene of any kind, or to weep under any circumstances, that we recognized that we were facing something pretty serious. Elsie, whose compassionate, selfless nature concealed a temper that Grandmother Hagedorn herself might have envied, was ready to go and blow up the sanatorium, Aunts, Father and all. But we settled for a better idea. We sent for Fred.

Ever since his first return to the family, after his years of exile as a boy, there had been a close bond between Fred and Mother. Each took pride in the other's realism, integrity and freedom from sham; each recognized the other's dependability and sound judgment. Transfusing the admiration was devoted love, as undemonstrative as it was deep.

Fred saw the situation at once and knew what to do. He wrote *Tante* Alma with affection but with a firmness and clarity that could be depended on to penetrate the thickest epidermis: She and *Tante* Elsbeth had thrust themselves between Father and Mother. Mother was suffering under it and something must be done. At once. Fred had a way with the Aunts and he could say such things without causing permanent wounds. He knew them through and through— the bad with the good, the sentimentalism with the genuine kindliness, the malice with the dramatics, the sham with the devotion; and was fond of them, and they knew it. His letter would hurt but they would blame themselves, not Fred.

The response was immediate and tearful. They were returning to Göttingen at once. A letter from Father next day begged Mother to join him.

– 5 –

They had ten happy weeks together. Father was winning his way back to health, and was devoted and charming and gay. His heart, when he listened to it, and when his pride or his sentimentalism or hypersensitivity didn't get in the way, was always right. Mother expanded in the radiance of a love which had never really failed her, only been submerged in the self-absorption of Father's physical suffering. They took leisurely strolls together by day, and, in the late autumn evenings, sat beside the round walnut table with its bright embroidered cover, reading under the kerosene lamp. They were renewing their youth, alone together as they had not been alone, for so long a period, since the first year of their marriage, free of responsibilities and tensions, forgetting the big house, forgetting the happy home they had had in New York, forgetting everything except each other.

No rancor of Mother's toward her husband's sisters clouded the serenity of those weeks together. I have before me, as I write, the letters she wrote the Aunts during that period and, remembering her resentment, a month or two earlier, at their intrusion between her and Father, I am amazed at the letters' warmth and intimacy, their artless pleasure in communication, their assumption of complete understanding, the solicitude for Elsbeth's and Alma's welfare, the appreciation of the letters they wrote and the gifts they sent to add to her comfort and Father's. It was not that she was fashioning pleasant phrases to cover her true feelings. She had never acted a part and she would never have dreamed of trying so to go against her nature. The affection of these letters to the women who had plagued her by their possessiveness all her married life and, a few weeks before, had driven her to the edge of a nervous breakdown, was wholly sincere. It was not in her to nourish an abiding grievance.

205

Resentment could not live in the atmosphere of her heart. She not only forgave; apparently she forgot.

By Christmas, Father was almost completely well. "We have reason," Mother wrote the Aunts, "to look with full assurance to the future."

One evening Father peered up from the book he was reading and was startled at the faraway stare in Mother's clear blue eyes. She had had a stroke. Two weeks later she was dead.

CHAPTER ELEVEN

Nemesis!

Father knew it was no longer he who possessed the house, but the shadowy figure that seemed, always, almost within sight or sound or touch.

Even while Mother was alive, Father had thought of rectifying what he had come to see was a tragic mistake and was prepared to swallow his pride, pack up the family belongings again and return to the land which had given him opportunity and happiness. But, without Mother, he could not face the ordeal. Anyway, though he offered the house for sale, nobody would buy (it was exactly fifty years before anybody did buy it, at a price one-twentieth of its original cost in dollar value). He remained in it with Elsie, the last of the children he had planned it for, until she too married and left him, alone save for Mother's perennially sprightly and beloved sister Venie; remained to meet there the ultimate tragedy of his divided life.

I don't know whether he ever faced the height and the depth of the fatal blunder he had committed. But, in his grief for Mother, it invaded his dreams. It would seem to him that she was with him, yet aloof, and made him conscious of wrongs against her which must forever keep them apart. The same dream recurred at intervals and cast a pall over the succeeding days.

Father returned to New York for a visit in the fall of 1910, his first since he had so lightly sailed away from America three short years before. He had torn up his life by the roots, torn up the lives of his wife and daughters, his wife's mother and sister; he had scooped up forty years of memories and associations as a child scoops up a handful of jacks; packed a lifetime's accumulation of furniture, books and pictures in a procession of moving vans and, at sixty, set out to shape himself a new life.

His wife and her mother were dead; he himself had suffered a devastating disillusionment and a nerve-racking illness. The home he had sought to establish in his beloved Fatherland was a mockery, the girls flown out of the nest, with homes of their own; his sons too were married, and away. He could not fail to be aware that the house he had built as a symbol of his success as a businessman was a monument to his failure as a man of judgment and foresight.

These painful realities were inevitably in his mind as he trod American soil again. From the first moment he found everything different from what it had been. It would be. He was living in a Fifth Avenue hotel instead of the modest brownstone front on West Eighty-Eighth Street. The Cotton Exchange, where, for forty years he had drunk the wine of struggle and daring and failure and success, was just a noisy place where other men battled and lost or won. He was a visitor where he had been the "Iron Chancellor," who helped make the big wheels turn. His friends were cordial, but busy, of course, as in the old days he had been busy, and his talks with them were of inconsequential things. In a sense, he was already a ghost in that high-ceilinged place of bustle and shouting, in which his vision, his judgment and his fighting force had made Exchange history. I don't know if he ever mustered the courage to return to West 88th Street to look up at No. 32, where we had had our home, with Mother as its guiding spirit. I doubt it.

Father told none of us—not Adolf or myself, or our wives—what this return meant to him in desolation, heartache and bitter self-reproach. But I remember the strain of the visit, the sense that he was shutting himself off from all of us. The familiar tenderness was there, on the surface; the generosity was there, as of old; but there seemed no way of reaching through them to his lonely, troubled heart.

– 3 –

I feel a chill in my spine as I regard, from a perspective of half a century, the unfolding of the process of retribution in Father's life. This Nemesis, hovering always in the shadows near him, whip in hand, is no spiteful goddess, jealous of his happiness and success. She is the child of law; she is herself law: cause and effect, sowing and reaping, the tree and its fruit. Without passion, inexorably, she moves through her inevitable sequences. Only one who has not felt her lash can withhold pity from this good man on whose anguished back the Shadow was about to rain her sharpest blows.

~Part Five~

CHAPTER ONE

DOROTHY and I were living with our two children in Greenfield Hill, back of Fairfield, Connecticut, when, in the summer of 1914, ultimatums began exploding across the peaceful European fields. Breathlessly we watched the record unfold; and forty-odd years after, in the histories, it is not very different from the contemporary press accounts: the ruthlessness of the demands of Austria-Hungary on Serbia, the recklessness of the German Kaiser's refusal to lay a restraining hand on his ally; Germany mobilizing, France mobilizing, Russia mobilizing; the Kaiser on his palace balcony cynically proclaiming the reverse of what the day-by-day record reveals: "Envious people everywhere are compelling us to our just defense." German armies crashing into Belgium.

For a few days, Britain, her Cabinet sharply divided, held aloof.

It was a warm, cloudless Sunday morning—the date was August 3rd —when my neighbor, George P. Brett, the shrewd and able head of the Macmillan publishing house, himself English-born, rode over on horseback, from his farm, two miles away, to see me.

I happened to be outdoors when he rode up. "What is Britain going to do?" he asked, asking the question, indeed, less of me than of his own dismay and dread.

I don't know out of what depths I drew my instant answer, but I have never questioned its validity. "She'll have to go in. She can't afford not to."

It was more than Harvard and The Hill, more than my marriage and the six years I had lived apart from my German family, that had established in me a capacity to weigh the day's news with mental, if not yet wholly emotional, objectivity.

Three years before, I had been given glimpses of the Kaiser, the German military machine and the German national mood which had prepared my mind to some degree to evaluate the events as they unfolded. In the course of a summer with Father in Niederwalluf, Dorothy and I had spent a week with Irma and her husband at the great German naval base at Kiel. As staff surgeon on the imperial yacht *Hohenzollern*, my brother-in-law, Willy Bensen, had the chance to see the Kaiser at close range. From Willy's cautious utterances and Irma's sardonic comments, we derived a picture of the Kaiser and his entourage which was something less than reassuring.

They saw him as a brilliant man of astonishing contrasts, alert to every turn in international affairs, realistic enough to see that he must break the aristocracy's monopoly of the command posts in the navy, and courageous enough to outrage his aristocratic officers by placing a commoner—they called him a *bourgeois Schwein*—at their head; yet surrounding himself with young nobles whose chief function was to play the part of king's jesters and accept whatever indignities he might, in a jocose mood, choose to subject them to. The Kaiser's taste for mediaeval pomp appeared insatiable, and, in certain aspects, he was straight out of Gilbert and Sullivan. "When he sneezes all the officers have to salute, and civilians have to take off their hats." Hungry as the Kaiser was to win the hearts of his people, he failed because, as Bensen put it, "he never allows himself to forget that he is Emperor. He never asks a personal question, always keeps to safe subjects—" subjects, that is, that would not imply that there might be a common human denominator between the Emperor and the person with whom he was conversing.

The picture Bensen gave us of this variously gifted man, inclined to be kindly, but vain, volatile and unpredictable, was supplemented by vignettes of the Empress, bringing a discussion of general interest again and again to an appalled silence by the injection of some irrelevant Bible quotation; and of the snooty Crown Princess—"when she walks on deck all you can see is her nostrils"—making the officers on the yacht do humilitating antics for her pleasure.

Any illusions which I might have retained regarding those Hohenzollerns who had looked down upon me in my childhood from the walls of our successive homes, evaporated in the realism of Bensen's close-ups. If this were monarchy, I was glad I lived under a republic, for all its political shenanigans. If this monarch, furthermore, were the determining voice in German foreign policy, I would want to weigh his actions in the light of what I had learned.

During our visit at Kiel, Dorothy and I got a look at German armed might, for the harbor was filled with battleships, the wharves lined with torpedo boats and the streets teeming with men in uniform. At Kiel, too, we came face to face with the arrogance of the German officer-mind.

Through my brother-in-law we were invited to tea on one of the German battleships. We were courteously received; but the fact that we were Americans appeared to inhibit none of the officers who entertained us from commenting scornfully on the American fleet, in the harbor on a courtesy visit. Perhaps they thought of me as a German—the language, those days, ran trippingly off my tongue—and counted on my being sympathetic; but Dorothy was unmistakeably American. It seemed, indeed, because she *was* an American, that they went out of their way to lead her to a porthole and point out to her derisively what seemed to them the absurdities of American naval construction and American naval pretensions.

By no flicker of an eyelash did Dorothy indicate that the German Navy's conception of international relations on the person-to-person level seemed to her something less than persuasive.

We were at Niederwalluf, in the big house on the Rhine, when all that we had seen and heard at Kiel suddenly became a matter of close, personal concern. Without warning, the Kaiser sent a gunboat to the port of Agadir in southern Morocco, ostensibly to protect

German commercial interests, but actually to undertake a daring cast into France's cloudy, colonial waters in central Africa. The gunboat's name was *Panther* and "the *Panther*'s leap," was instantly a matter of feverish concern in every European chancellery. How would France react? Was this the moment all Europe had been dreading? Had the mercurial Kaiser gone off, half-cocked, once too often? Was this "The Day" that his officers had been lifting their glasses to in German messrooms and officers' casinos? Or would the situation once more be smoothed out?

Our house at Neiderwalluf throbbed with excitement. My brother Fred was an officer in the reserve; Willy Bensen and Elsie's attractive husband, Captain von Poschinger, were in active service.

The Aunts, who were visiting Father, were aflutter, and clearly thrilled.

"Good Lord!" I said to *Tante* Elsbeth. "Why can't you Germans get together with the French and, once and for all, clear up this insanity between you?"

The old girl's eyes snapped. "You don't understand. The French are our natural enemies!" And what you did with enemies, I gathered, was to smash them.

Knowing *Tante* Elsbeth, and the habit of her mind to think only what everybody else was thinking, I had the chilling sense that her foolish words were significant.

– 3 –

With these experiences in my memory, I was inclined to believe what the accounts in the press indicated, that the Kaiser and his generals were out for conquest; and, for all Europe, it was *sauve qui peut*.

My family in Germany, I found shortly, were seeing the tragic picture in quite other colors.

"A frightful catastrophe has come upon us, my children," Father wrote Addie and me, late in August (writing, of course, as was customary with him, in German). "Three great powers, impelled by envy and hate, have declared war against us. Oh, children, what we have gone through defies description! We were as though paralyzed, and it still seems like a frightful dream. My whole inner being is shaken, and only by an effort can I grasp the terrible truth of it and realize that hostile powers have waylaid us, and want to annihilate us. Our noble Kaiser, who, for twenty-six years, preserved the peace of Europe, struggled to the last minute to prevent the war."

Was it possible, I asked myself, that Father knew nothing of Austria's brutal ultimatum, of the Kaiser's proud refusal to hold back his reckless ally? Obviously, he had access to no newspapers except the German, repeating daily the single theme that he passed on to us: "We have been basely betrayed. Long ago everything was prepared by our foes for the assault upon us at this time."

Indignation against "the outrageous web of lies our enemies are spreading over the world" boiled over in every letter. "I am so unhappy over what they are saying about us in America," Father wrote. "How you must have suffered under the infamous, lying reports, dictated by hate, greed, envy, jealousy! Our enemies work against us in the press, day and night, bribe the newspapers in the neutral countries, make their lie-factories operate overtime."

Each member of the family wrote me, all saying the same thing in different words: Germany was the innocent lamb, attacked by ravenous wolves who envied her her green pastures, and anyone who intimated the contrary was inconceivably mendacious. It was when Elsie's gallant husband, "Lutz" von Poschinger, wrote me the same story from the front in France that I recognized that I was being systematically worked upon.

The poet Schiller has a line in one of his plays to the effect that "you catch the purpose and your hackles rise." (*Man merkt die Absicht und man wird verstimmt.*) Well, mine rose, though I recognized my correspondents' sincerity. But when my beloved Irma, with her hitherto dependable intelligence, solemnly joined the propaganda chorus, I felt a pang that seemed to gather into itself all the grief of the family division.

The early weeks of the war were to me a nightmare of inconceivable happenings. Nothing in the easygoing world in which I had come to maturity had prepared me to believe in the possibility, in that fourteenth year of the twentieth century, of such violence and destruction, such callous inhumanity, as every day summoned me anew to face. All I had heard or read of war had dealt with armies clashing on battlefields, with civilians generally at a safe distance and protected under international codes of war. I knew, of course, about the sack of cities in the Thirty Years' War, but that belonged to the evil past, out of which, I had assumed, as most of my contemporaries had assumed, mankind had emerged. War had been "hell," by its very nature, not "hell" by deliberation, planned in advance and ordered; not "hell" with a purpose.

But here in Belgium was "hell"—they called it "frightfulness"—proclaimed as military policy; cities destroyed, regardless of the civilian population; cathedrals, precious libraries, whole villages, wantonly given to the torch, and, picked at random, hundreds of burghers shot in reprisal for some sniper's bullet from some leaf-shrouded attic window. The stories were no product of overheated minds, no "scurrilous lies," as my family insisted, and, I know, believed. Germany herself, through her commanding officers, proclaimed them, plastered them on the walls of public buildings, to warn and to deter.

The deliberate atomizing of age-old social organisms appalled me. Some verses I wrote, early in the war, reflect, better than any memories I might now set down, the dismay, bewilderment and horror that not only myself but millions of my countrymen felt at the revelation of demonic forces in the world we had assumed had long been exorcised. I present them not as poetry but as documentation.

> "What cries, what crashes in the street?
> What riotous madness in the square?
> Oh, frightened heart and flying feet,
> Weeping mother of babes, be fleet!
> Flee like the doe, flee like the hare!

The terrible hunter is out to slay.
  War, the hunter, with flaming gun!
  His blighting shadow is over the sun.
  To cover, to cover, ye hunted, run!
  Mother and maiden, babe and nun.
Out of the house and the streets, and away! . . .

This way, that way, this way, for flight!
  All that the years have laid on your heart,
Through toil and passion and dear delight,
  Crowd on your market-cart.
And out, out, out of the terrible town,
  Out, from the smoke and the crying,
Out from the dear walls, crashing down
  Over the living, the dying. . . .

Out, with your cart-load of despair,
  Out, with your shards of faith!
Out, with your old dame in her chair,
  Moaning, and crying for death.
Out, out out! And whither? Who cares?
  Life is ended. Death is come.
Vain are your lifted hands, and your prayers.
  God is fallen, God is dumb.
And we, we! We are dead. And the roads
  Where the neighbors go with their carts
Are the roads of the ghosts in hell, and the loads
  They push are their broken hearts."

CHAPTER TWO

MEANWHILE, through every letter from the family, rang the exultation at the German victories.

Our family poet, *Tante* Alma, waxed lyrical: "Our armies sweep forward in a mighty rhythm, victory after victory, such as world history has never known." Elsbeth sings: "In the East as in the West, our victories are simply dazzling." Father takes up the chant, "Our armies are pushing forward mightily, everywhere victorious."

No one in the family, apparently, had had any intimation of a battle on the Marne, or the Allied victory that had blocked the Germans' crucial, initial thrust; nor of the setbacks both the Austrians and the Germans had suffered under the pressure of Russian armies in the East. For the family, it was victories and nothing but victories.

"Our hearts are full of gratitude to our just God who is defending our holy cause," Father writes. "Never have we felt the blessing of God as now. We are all aglow with the heroic deeds of our glorious armies and those of our allies!"

– 2 –

The German legions, sweeping through Belgium in that first series of victories that were so thrilling to Father and the Aunts, did something to me, and, I am sure, to millions of others in America and Europe—wherever the authentic story could be told—that was more terrible than any of the reported atrocities.

They uncovered the face of Death.

They made Death a guest at every breakfast table, staring at us through the pages of the morning paper. They uncovered the horror of life which had always been there, under the surface, but had been kept hidden from us for generations by our escapist cult of the "nice," the pleasant, the agreeable, what we liked to call the "constructive" elements of life. Obliterate the symbols of death, avoid mention of death, as you avoid mention of cancer, prostitution and other aspects of the intolerable.

For me, as undoubtedly for millions of others across the United States in those August days, my horror of the realities that lay under the surface of the "pleasant" was transferred to the agents of this uncovering. We thought we were recoiling from the "frightfulness" that the Germans were proclaiming as a legitimate instrument of war. We were. But, on deeper levels, what we were recoiling from was the frightfulness of life itself, which the Germans happened to be the first, in two centuries or more, to fling into our faces. It was characteristic of them that they should do it with their familiar and incomparable thoroughness.

– 3 –

Father himself was too old to be active in the war effort and sought refuge in his children from the turmoil in his heart. His sons-in-law and daughters-in-law seemed as dear to him as any of his own, and he wrote periodically to all ten of us—in America, at the front, or back of the lines in Germany—long letters, infinitely touching in their tender caring. Remote geographically though all of us were from him, he brought us close, in his love, entered into our lives, gave thought to our problems, felt concern for our needs, rejoiced in our children, took pride in our successes, such as they were.

Unconsciously, and by no action of ours, I think we helped him survive. Pouring out his devotion, sharing his anxieties with us, his passion for his country, his dread of her downfall and his faith in her triumph, he derived new strength of body and spirit from each hour's absorption in us. In this ultimate ordeal of his life, the very tenderness of his heart, that made him vulnerable to every contact with the evil times, seemed to sustain him.

-4-

It was inconceivable to Father that Addie or I in America might have any view of the life and death struggle other than his own. "Do everything you can to spread the truth about the war," he wrote me.

In case I might have forgotten what that "truth" was, he stated it again, point by point: "We were shamefully attacked. Everything had been prepared by our foes, years in advance, everything settled, signed and sealed. Britain is responsible for the whole thing; her envy, mistrust and jealousy were the cause. We had prospered too much."

Father's "truth" found me, in November, as unconvinced as I had been in August, when the Kaiser, in his war speech from the palace balcony, had set the official "line." None of Father's repeated asseverations of Britain's guilt had served to shake the conviction I had come to, that Germany, using Austria as her catspaw, had started the war. But, assured as I was that the facts on which I based my judgment were far nearer the realities than those that Father was so sure were "the truth," I got scant comfort from my certainty. For my emotions stood out against my reason. Soberly gratified though I might be at every German setback, every German victory set my Teutonic heart beating a little faster. Ambivalence is the word for it, and it made for tension and a feeling of guilt whether it were the heart or the reason that, for the moment, prevailed.

My beloved Addie, eight years my senior, whose brotherly counsel I had always found sound and had generally followed, was seeing the picture in other terms than mine. He was not, like Father, deluding himself with the idea of a long-term, calculated assault on Germany by the Entente powers, or sharing the fantastic notion that the American press was actually in British pay. He was convinced, however, that American financial interests, economically linked to Britain, were affecting American opinion and public policy, and that I myself was unduly influenced in my thinking by what I read in the papers. On almost every issue that arose between the Allied and the German point of view, Addie was inclined to lean toward the German, and I toward that of the Allies. The ever-sharpening tension between us was kept from the breaking point only by the genuine, stubborn affection we had for each other.

As I look back to those dark days, I feel ashamed that I never gave my brother credit for his courage in maintaining, throughout the period of American neutrality, a point of view, shared indeed, by millions of Americans in the Middle West and Far West but sharply out of key with the opinions of most of his friends and associates in business and in social life in the East. It required no courage on my part to take the position I took. I was flowing with the tide. I was everybody's "fair-haired boy," who was linked by blood, tradition and kin to Germany, yet took the Allied side. But Addie stood almost alone, subject to malicious tongues and lifted eyebrows; and he stood fast.

– 5 –

So, as the months passed, the crop which Father and his beautiful, imperious mother had sown, almost thirty years before, was falling to the scythe. Brothers in conflict, Addie at odds with the world in which he moved, I myself at odds with myself. Father, too, was divided in his heart, remembering his "beloved old America," where he had been so "unspeakably happy. . . . I loved America, and I can only say that I am grieved beyond measure, sometimes to the point of tears, that America has taken so hostile an attitude toward us."

His love was sincere, but it had never been deep. He had been a loyal and conscientious American citizen, but the ideals of freedom, democracy and the individual citizen's responsibility to the general good had never taken hold of him as they had taken hold of Grandfather Schwedler, for instance, or Carl Schurz or countless other Americans of German birth who had contributed richly to American life.

He had, in reality, never become an American at all. He had remained a transplanted German, and he forswore his American allegiance, that first winter of the war, without a quaver, so far as I could note, and became a German subject again. "I have never been prouder of Germany than I am now," he wrote. Much as I regretted his giving up his American citizenship, I had to admit that there was something magnificent in the gesture with which he resumed his status as a German. For, with his allegiance, he transferred to Germany all his American securities except a sum he conveyed to Adolf to cover the allowance he had pledged to me; transferred it in order to purchase German war loans.

Even his German bankers were shocked at such sacrificial faith, begging him not to put all his eggs in one basket, precious as that basket might be to him, and to them. He would not listen. For forty years on the Cotton Exchange, Father had practiced the fine art of "hedging," but, in the most momentous investment of his life, he refused to hedge, though his whole future was at stake. Germany would win the war, he was sure; and, if she didn't, what would anything matter? Father was not one to do anything by halves.

– 6 –

About the time that Father turned his back on America, I was turning mine, definitively, on Germany.

Not wanting to add unnecessarily to Father's burden of grief, I had been careful in my letters not to let him see how deeply I had come to differ from him on the war; but, sensitive as he was, he divined it. Instead of being angry with me, as I might have expected, he was tenderly sympathetic. "I see from your letters, my boy, the struggle you are going through to determine what seems to you right and true. Your natural inclinations must obviously be with us Germans. Your father is German, your mother was German-born, your blood is German." On the other hand, I had clearly "fallen all too much" under the influence of the British and French, reading American newspapers which were practically all under Britain's orders, directly bribed or misled by a decade of Britain's anti-German agitation. He seemed to fear that Dorothy, American as she was by birth and heritage, might be influencing me against Germany. "Help Dorothy to see what the Germans have achieved and what a marvelous nation Germany is."

He blew up only once, when I told him that one of the reasons for American hostility to Germany was the fear that, if Germany were victorious she would ultimately seek to expand in the Western world.

"How can intelligent people believe such rubbish?" he replied. "Only a bought press would publish such egregious nonsense. We Germans want nothing except to live in peace!"

He believed what he said, I know, with all his passionate spirit. It never apparently occurred to him that there might be voices around the "peace-loving" Kaiser, and, indeed, within him, that wanted power, ever-widening power, and were determined to get it at any cost.

To him, the Kaiser was the tender, loving father-of-his-people depicted on the sentimental picture-postals he sent me; kneeling in prayer before the altar, visiting the wounded; the stainless leader of a stainless Fatherland.

"Have faith in the German cause," he pleaded. "It is true, sound and right, and, believe me, the eyes of the blinded will yet be opened. The British have hypnotized the world, and there is no counteracting what they have done. The Americans will not let themselves be persuaded. But our victory will convince them!"

I can't believe that Father realized what he was saying, which was, of course, that might makes right. But that idea was precisely what the British propaganda, which Father so resented, was telling the world that Germany stood for, precisely the reason why an ever-increasing segment of the American public was saying that Germany must be defeated.

Tenderly, earnestly, in letter after letter, he sought to bind me to the German cause. "Have faith in the German character," he pleaded. The Germans were not like the British, whose "lying" reports screamed to heaven, and the worse things went with them, the blacker the lies. "We speak the truth. Our reports from the front are the truth, and nothing but the truth. Every word issued by our Supreme Army Command or our government is purest truth!!!" *

-7-

I am sure that Father believed exactly what he said. With childlike simplicity, he was identifying the moral standards of all Germans, even those of the government and its imperial master, with his own personal standards of character and conduct, his own integrity, his own single-minded and selfless devotion to the Fatherland. He himself spoke the truth, and nothing but the truth; therefore the government did. He himself wanted only to live in peace; therefore every German, and the government itself, wanted it.

There was something touching in his identification of the national character and purpose with his own. It was also naïve to a degree that would be reprehensible in a boy or girl of fifteen. A grown man has no right to be so naïve. The naïveté was nothing accidental, moreover; it was no mere personal idiosyncrasy. It was, in fact, a direct result of centuries of papa-knows-best government, deliberately planned and persistently fostered in Prussia and, indeed, in all the German states. How, in Father, the tradition had survived forty years of American living, is a mystery, but his letters are sufficient evidence that it did.

The phrase, "government by experts," has an alluring sound. The actuality, in Germany, had, on the surface, worked superbly. It made for honest and exceptionally efficient government and for a loyal, orderly, industrious, dutiful people, trained to think only what Authority wanted them to think, to obey unquestioningly, and to leave government to the men who made it the central business of their lives. It would work so long as a reasonably beneficent Authority could maintain the papa-knows-best myth. If ever that myth were punctured, what would a politically immature people do when they

* The exclamation points are his.

226

were suddenly thrust into a crisis in which personal responsibility, initiative, sound judgment and the capacity to act were required? And, if the Authority ever ceased to be beneficent and became something else, then what?

Father's childlike acceptance of the infallibility of Authority reveals him to me as a symbol of that political leukemia which twice brought his beloved Fatherland to the point of death.

CHAPTER THREE

MEANWHILE on my side of the Atlantic, I was watching with deepening dismay what seemed to me the ineptitude of the Wilson administration's handling of the submarine crisis.

Not since the decade preceding the Civil War had the American public mind been more confused than in the early years of the First World War. The horror of the fighting itself, the orgy of profiteering, following the Allies' purchase of arms and munitions, the resounding messages of the President to the German government and his scuttling retreats, the fear of the politicians of saying anything about the war that might lose them votes, in case the political picture were different tomorrow from what it was today; the glorification by the German-Americans of everything German and their clamor against everything American; all these brought a Babel through which chirped the chatter of the sentimentalists, assured that a wand could wave away any menacing demon and "get the boys out of the trenches by Christmas." *Safety First* became the day's popular slogan.

Through the sound and the fury of conflicting voices, one voice came as a fresh wind: Theodore Roosevelt's. What he said was simple and clear, and he said it in words which anybody could understand and which meant exactly what people understood them to mean. Safety first? No! Duty first! Prepare! Be strong! Make your heart ready for sacrifice.

As for the German-Americans: Be loyal. No fifty-fifty allegiance here. America is no polyglot boardinghouse. "But if you *are* loyal, you are as good an American as any other."

He was strident, at times, extreme in his language and unfair occasionally in his judgments; but his forthrightness and his passionate devotion to his country were exhilarating. He seemed to know, moreover, where he was going, to be afraid of nothing and nobody, and to be willing to risk, if necessary, whatever political future he might yet have.

I had met Mr. Roosevelt casually when he visited Harvard. I actually met him to talk to, for the first time, at Sagamore Hill, when he let his friend, Lawrence F. Abbott, publisher of the *Outlook*, bring me out one balmy Sunday in May, 1916.

It was a stirring moment when "the Colonel"—all America's "Colonel," those days—strode down the steps into the Trophy Room where Mrs. Roosevelt, in simple white muslin, had gathered her four or five guests. I remember the warmth that seemed to go out from that vigorous body and the way he thrust his head forward to let his one good eye peer with absorbed interest into every new face.

I sat at his left at dinner and he regaled me with yarns of his ranching days. Noting my name, he asked me about my family background. I told him of Grandfather Schwedler and his meeting with Lincoln after the 1860 election, of Father's return to his Fatherland, and my own position on the issues between America and Germany. He was obviously interested, and ran after my departing taxi to ask me to come again, a week or two later, and to bring my wife.

– 3 –

As Germany intensified her submarine campaign and the protests of the American government began to bear in them the menace of action, Father was appalled. "What frightful anxiety I have suffered over America, and am suffering still," he wrote me, in March, 1916. The following January he was still hoping that Congress might be "sufficiently informed" of Germany's military and naval strength "not to plunge America into the war." But what could the American people do with Britain cracking the whip?

<h2 style="text-align:center">– 4 –</h2>

One hot July day, thirty years before, I had watched Father, accompanied by my sisters, walking across Berkeley Place to take our brothers to a steamer bound for Germany and his mother's home. Here, now, was the pay-off. "My thoughts go out to you and Ell, in particular sympathy, these days," I wrote Irma when the United States broke off diplomatic relations with Germany. "Of course, you are heart and soul for Germany, but that doesn't make it any easier for you to see this break between Germany and America. I am, of course, as completely for America, as is only natural. It is a tragic matter all round. God only knows what will come of it."

The letter never reached her. It was returned to me, a few weeks later, stamped: "Mail service suspended to country addressed."

CHAPTER FOUR

Seldom in American history, has the instant effect of decisive presidential leadership been more dramatically shown than in the reaction of the public to President Wilson's call to the nation to accept the state of war which the German government, in folly which was half desperation, had thrust upon us.

"To make the world safe for democracy!"

In the course of the Phi Beta Kappa poem which Harvard invited me to deliver, that June, I gave the picture of this transformed America as I saw it:

> "Who would have thought a month of Spring
>   Could work so deep a change?
> Who would have thought a dream could sting
> The dead to new life, quivering,
> And shake dull hearts with echoing
>   Of music new and strange? . . .
>
> Who would have thought that April days
>   Could work such conjury?
> Up from the crowded towns ablaze,
> Up from the green hills, like a haze
> Slow-rising to some magic lay's
>   Unearthly harmony—

231

Walls and resplendent spires
        Have risen, and stand!
A place of faint, far choirs
And chimes and candle-fires,
A month of new desires
        Has made a noisy land.
A place of prayer and search,
        A house of God, a church!

Lo, how the spires ascend!
        Lo, how the arches rise!
Lo, how the pinnacles pierce the clouds
        To melt their glow with the sky's! . . .
What roof strains to the stars
        Over hill, over plain?
What Gothic glory covers you both,
        California, Maine?
The valleys feel a sacred stir
        In every leaf and clod;
And from every mountain, every hill,
        The pillars loom up to God.

Who said, 'It is a booth where doves are sold?'
        Who said, 'It is a money-changers' cave?'
Silence to such forever, and behold! . . .
It is a vast cathedral . . . wall and spire,
To house a nation's purified desire!
A church! Where in hushed fervor stand
        The children of contending races,
Forgetting feud and fatherland—
        A hundred million lifted faces. . . ."

Some of that was wishful thinking; but the sense of a great lift,
a great hope, and a glorious challenge, was in men's hearts. And the
President, with his glowing words, had put it there.

I did not have to look about for "war work." I had it. I was running
the Vigilantes, an organization of writers whose aim was to bring the
issues confronting the nation clearly before the public through articles, poems and stories syndicated to newspapers all over the country.
We had cherished the dream of awakening the public, especially in
the schools and colleges, to the need of education for citizenship, but
America's participation in the war had narrowed our original purpose.
The war held our whole attention, its causes, its aims, the uncertain
German-Americans, the pro-German periodicals of the prewar period
converted to a poisonous pseudo patriotism; racial prejudice, class
antagonism; all the foes of our own household, open and covert; all
the forces working against national unity.

Before the war was three months old, four hundred writers aligned
with us were fighting the German propaganda in America by bringing
to the presentation of pedestrian themes the touch of the imagination
which gave them wings. Editors all over the country recognized it, and
printed what we sent. By the end of the war fifteen thousand newspapers were publishing our material.

A pro-German periodical, in the course of an attack on the Vigilantes, took a sideswipe at me as a "renegade German-American."
The term itself was absurd. A renegade German I could not be since
I had never been a German. A renegade American I certainly was
not, for if I were, the periodical in question would be praising me.
Was it possible that there were people in the United States who
regarded German-Americanism as a definite entity?

To my astonishment, I found that my father's old friends, in what
my sisters and I had always called, not too respectfully, "the German
crowd," took the renegade idea seriously. I began to hear from them
and, when I met any of them downtown, they told me sharply what
they thought of me. For me to do what I was doing—that is, utilizing

the talent and the machinery of the Vigilantes to call attention to the insidious nature of the German propaganda, was treason to my German heritage and a disgrace to my father's name.

An old friend of the family stated the case against me with no malice but with deep conviction. He himself was entirely loyal to America, in a negative fashion, and he expected me to be loyal. I should buy Liberty Bonds, of course. If I were drafted, I must, of course, serve. (It happened that I was well over draft age, and he knew it.) But voluntary, open and active espousal of the American cause, No; by all that was absolute, No. Any other course was disloyal to my father and to the rest of the family now living in Germany and, in one way or another, fighting for Germany.

I could not accept his well meant plea, or the pleas of other family friends who were sincerely concerned for me personally and for my family's good name. In any such crisis as the nation was confronting, family ties, I pointed out, could not be allowed to interfere with the individual's freedom of action, or fetter his hands, brain or spirit.

The very heart of the American experiment in free government was involved. As no other nation in the world, America depended for the unity of her people, even for her existence, on the speedy amalgamation of the aliens who came from the four corners of the earth to claim her welcome. The melting pot had done its work; and it had done it because, by and large, the men and women who had claimed the liberty and the opportunity that America offered had recognized and sought to fulfill the dream that motivated her—the dream of a people united on the basis not of soil, tradition, blood, race or ethnic solidarity, but of an idea, the idea of freedom for the individual to fashion his own life, and, in cooperation with others, a new society, freer and politically more disciplined than any the world had known. To let sentiment, even the sentiment of family love, paralyze the capacity for action, even the willingness to act—at a moment in history when that idea, that dream were in deadly peril—would, in my eyes, be a betrayal of everything that the words "America" and "American" implied.

This, or something like it, was my answer to my father's friends.

The attitude of these people, these basically honest, loyal people, made me aware, for the first time, of the depth and scope of the problem that the divided hearts of the German-Americans presented. The great majority, I was certain, were normally for America first, last and always, having no sympathy for the German government and no more than the normal sentiment, shading off into indifference, of any naturalized American for the country of his birth. But the Wilson administration had given them no leadership. America's voice, during the years of her neutrality, had been ambiguous, tortured and self-questioning. The German voices, speaking to the German-Americans, had, on the other hand, been clear, definite and assured: Germany had been flagrantly attacked by Britain, Russia, France and Belgium, for no reason except jealousy, envy and general malice. Britain controlled the American press, so the news America was getting was false. Germany was winning the war and would show this British "vassal," America, who was master. Germany was the greatest nation in the world; republics were hopelessly corrupt and inefficient, democracy was a delusion, and so forth and so on, straight from the shoulder, and beyond debate.

Millions of the German-Americans, hearing the two voices—one timid, hesitant and uncertain; the other, masterful, clear-cut and assured—followed the leadership that seemed to them to know where it was going and that definitely intended getting there.

I determined to do what I could to show these misguided people where, I believed, their hearts' home really was, and where, I knew, their true destiny lay. I would frame an appeal to them to stand forth and say where they stood.

– 5 –

> "Lord, in this day of battle,
>   Lord, in this night of fears,
> Keep open, oh, keep open
>   My eyes, my ears.

Not blindly, not in hatred,
Lord, let me do my part.
Keep, open, oh, keep open
My mind, my heart."

While I was writing my appeal to the German-Americans, there were those who were wondering where I myself stood. A Greenfield Hill neighbor wrote the New York *Herald* that I had better be watched. I had a German name, my water tower "commanded" the arms factories in Bridgeport—six miles away—and "queer-looking people"—poets frequently qualify as such—were seen coming and going at my place. The *Herald* sent the letter to the editor of the Bridgeport *Post*, George C. Waldo, who happened to be a friend of mine, so that particular dart fell to the ground.

I mentioned the incident to Colonel Roosevelt as a prime bit of "comic relief" in the days' dark drama. He took it more seriously than I did, and reacted characteristically. He was due to speak in Bridgeport, shortly after, and instantly accepted my invitation to drop in for tea on the way. Dorothy and I invited four Greenfield Hill neighbors to meet him—the flint-faced farmer living next to us; the local carpenter, a gentle, rural philosopher; the reticent, black-moustached mail carrier and his father, the local "Mr. Republican," a magnificent curmudgeon with a bristly beard.

Our Yankee friends were, one and all, admirers of the Colonel, but had no awe of greatness. The Colonel, on his part, recognized them as his kind, and their lively give-and-take was as man to man, in complete equality.

When the Colonel was about to depart, he turned to the pink-faced, sleek, too-well-groomed boss of Bridgeport, John T. King, who had come with him, and said in a voice that all in the room could hear: "John, I want you to know that Hermann Hagedorn is a friend of mine and if there is ever anything that you can do for him, I want you to do it."

His words did what he expected. I had no more trouble in Green-field Hill and when we held war rallies in the old Congregational Church I was asked to preside.

CHAPTER FIVE

I WAS seeing a good deal of Mr. Roosevelt, that first summer of the war. He was deeply concerned about the German-Americans, sharing my conviction that the great majority were loyal, but suspicious of the belated conversion of the German-language press to the American cause. He asked me to luncheon at the Harvard Club occasionally with other men of German background, to get such advice regarding the German-American issue as he thought we might be able to give.

"Gentlemen," he would say, his voice rising into the falsetto, "you may think that you have come here to have a good time, but, for your sins, you're going to listen to a speech of mine." Thereupon, he would draw a manuscript from his pocket and read an address he had been asked to deliver at some predominately German-American college in Ohio or at some Liberty Loan meeting in St. Louis.

It was a challenging experience to me, with my German training of awe for my elders and betters, to criticize the thought or expression of a former President of the United States, notably this particular one.

"Good Lord, Colonel," I remarked after the first of these luncheons, "who am I to criticize any speech of yours?"

"I wouldn't ask for your criticism if I didn't want it," he replied. "John Hay was perfectly useless to me in discussing policy, when I was President, because he always agreed with me. Now, Elihu Root! That was something else. He fought me every inch of the way. And, together, we got somewhere."

I gathered that I wouldn't be invited again if I failed to say what I believed.

The comments of the guests, including my own, were frequently sweeping, and I was amazed to note the humility with which the Colonel made the cuts or emendations we suggested. I remember his wry comment, as he thrust the manuscript back into his pocket at the conclusion of one of these sessions: "My *poor* baby! I don't *recognize* it any more."

– 2 –

It was after one such luncheon that the Colonel drew me into the high-ceilinged living room of the Club. The Harper publishing house was bringing out a series of biographies of notable Americans, written specifically for boys, and wanted one written about himself. Would he help the writer, whoever he might be, to get fresh material? "I told them I would," the Colonel went on, "provided you did the book."

"I? But, Colonel . . . !"

So far as I knew, Mr. Roosevelt had read nothing of mine except a little book called *You Are the Hope of the World*, an appeal to boys and girls to prepare themselves for effective citizenship. I knew he had read that, because he had spoken of it in a Fourth of July address that year; but that would have given him no hint of any potentialities I might have for writing biography. Perhaps the possibility of having a man of German stock writing about him appealed to his sense of the dramatic, since most German-Americans regarded him as their bitter enemy. Possibly he surmised that my position with my German name and background might not be too easy, and wanted to help.

When I had caught my breath I told him how deeply his suggestion stirred me; but I had had no experience in biographical writing; I couldn't possibly do such a book.

"Of course you can do it," he ejaculated, his teeth clicking through his friendliest smile. "I am sure of it."

When the Colonel was sure of anything, you were not inclined to debate the question further. But still I demurred; not out of coyness —on the contrary, out of a kind of terror. Who was I to write a biography, even for boys, of this half-mythical creature—as he appeared to me—who, for seven and a half years, had stood astride the world? My negative was reluctant but I intended it to be final.

The Colonel accepted it only conditionally. Before I decided definitely, I should see Hitchcock, the Harper's editor. "If, after talking it over with him, you still feel you can't do it, why, that's different. But see him first."

I found Ripley Hitchcock at his summer home in Woodstock, New York, a tall, spare man with kindly, humorous eyes. The afternoon I spent with him and his gifted wife set a new course for my life.

– 3 –

The Colonel kept the promise he had made Harper's and gave me generous letters of introduction to friends of his youth and political associates of the later years. "Tell him everything, good, bad and indifferent. Don't spare me in the least bit. Give him the very worst side you can think of, and the best side of me that is truthful. . . ." *

Besides the letters, he gave me ample opportunities to pump him regarding his past, whether it were at the Harvard Club, at Sagamore Hill, or in the New York office of the Kansas City *Star*, for which he was writing three articles a week. He was not easy to pin down to any routine of question and answer, as eminent attorneys opposing him in two libel suits had found to their despair. If I gave him the slightest provocation, he jumped from his own past to what clearly interested him far more—the troubled present. I got very little from him, in fact, by direct questioning. I got a great deal by just being with him and seeing him in action; more, indeed, than I could ever have drawn out of him by the most penetrating questions. Perhaps he knew it would work out that way, and arranged things so it should.

I saw him in relaxed moods at the luncheon table when he was the friendliest of hosts and the fascinating narrator of personal experi-

* T.R. to W. W. Sewall, Oct. 8, 1917. *Collected Letters*, Vol. VIII, p. 1244.

ence; I saw him in moments of bitter resentment and fury, and moments of tenderest feeling; I saw him with Mrs. Roosevelt—which is a story in itself; I saw him alone, and I saw him in the presence of thousands, pounding home his challenge; I saw him in defeat and frustration, and I saw him in a final moment of triumph. I was with him when he thought he was dying and already saw the jackals approaching the dead lion. I was with him on a day that to him was even more tragic. By grace of his generous friendship I came to know him as he lived and breathed. Face to face with him, in laughter, in anger and in sorrow, I saw how great a man he was, how lovable and how magnificent a human being.

Through him I learned what no books could have taught me, what it means, in courage, vision, devotion and practical sense to be the kind of American that Mother had wanted me to be.

CHAPTER SIX

In Germany, meanwhile, the activities of mine which had so enraged some of the family's old New York friends, as well as other pro-Germans, were receiving occasional scurrilous attention. The Cologne *Gazette* paid me the compliment of declaring me a *Schweinehund*, a mythical animal supposed to combine the most reprehensible characteristics of bitch and swine. Another paper labeled me a *Schmutzfink*, a creature wallowing in the mire for sheer delight in filth.

Someone apparently sent my brother Fred, now Under Secretary of State in the ministry of Food Supply in Berlin, the reference to my "unholy activities," as the Cologne paper described them, for he wrote me—and how the letter got through the American lines I have no idea—that if I had any feeling at all for Father I should stop at once what I was doing. So far, he wrote, he had managed to keep the press reports about me from Father's eyes. If ever Father found out about them, he said, it would put an unbearable burden on his unhappy spirit.

– 2 –

It was only forty years later, when I read Father's letters to Irma during these war years, that I realized how the war had been wearing him down. The triumphant sweep of Germany's armies through central Europe, culminating in the conquest of Roumania, provided enough victories to allay the thirst of any patriotic German, but, for Father, the former elation had been dulled by iteration.

The big house, moreover, had become a prison. The government had commandeered his cars and his horses: he no longer could walk the mile to the railroad station, so the occasional trips to Wiesbaden which had brought him male companionship in the earlier years of the war, were no longer possible. The house itself seemed, day by day, vaster and emptier, lonelier and chillier. The government was rationing fuel and had no pity on you just because your house was bigger than your actual needs required. Food, too, was rationed, and he would not have dreamed of asking any concession from Fred who was himself doing most of the rationing. Father's sense of rectitude and obedience to regulations, moreover, would not let him cultivate the black market; but Auntie and Elsie, who, with her children, was staying with Father, more femininely practical, and disturbed by the way he was losing weight, pocketed whatever scruples they may have had, and cultivated an amiable bootlegger. In a large Chinese vase in the icy dining room, they secreted the occasional leg of lamb, snatched and paid for in the dark at a side door.

Day after day, Father moved like an unhappy shadow through the corridors of the big house, looking backward in sorrow, looking forward in dread, and aching with longing for his children. Would he ever see them again?

His recurrent dream about Mother tormented him. "For two nights, the whole night long," he wrote Irma, in May, 1918, "I dreamed of our beloved Motherling, and could have wept, the days following. And it was again as it has been at other times. I dreamed that I had not been good to her and she would have nothing to do with me."

Nemesis, Nemesis!

CHAPTER SEVEN

I DON'T believe that Father would have been as distressed as Fred imagined if he had known the form that my "unholy activities" had taken. The appeal to the confused and double-minded among the German-Americans that I had set out to write had grown into a little book, whose challenge was epitomized in its title, *Where Do You Stand?* To my delight, it brought almost immediately a break in the lines of that "German crowd" in New York that had been so sure I was a traitor to all they held most dear. Addie, who himself thoroughly approved of my "appeal" and had actually, I suspect, felt more acutely than I the abuse poured on me by the German irreconcilables in New York, jubilantly brought me reports of one family after another in our acquaintance reading the book and finding it "a real comfort." I was, they declared, "decidedly on the right track."

The book traveled fast and I began to get letters from German-Americans in other parts of the country, including many editors of German-language newspapers and periodicals who admitted that the way I pointed out to them was the way they wanted to go. They knew that America was their home, and they actually wanted no other; knew, too, that they had been running on the wrong track, and wanted to get back on the main line. But they were not to be won by the persuasion of the sledge hammer, or drawn into the American community with the lasso. With so many emotions, memories, urges, longings involved, I knew what caring and tact would be needed to bring these people back into the American fold.

I enlisted the interest of German-American leaders in New York and in the West in the possibility of an organization that should testify to the American people the single-minded loyalty of the Americans of German origin to the United States and her free institutions. Here, it happened, we crossed wires with a government-sponsored society, The Friends of German Democracy, which had been created by the federal government's propaganda arm, the Committee on Public Information.

So far as my associates and myself were concerned, any effort to develop among German-Americans an interest in German democracy was beside the point. Let the Germans have any form of government they wanted. Our aim was simply to make German-Americans into straight Americans, looking forward, not back.

We determined to organize what we called a "National Patriotic Council of Loyal Americans of German Origin." Influential support was promised us in Washington by such men as Franklin K. Lane, Secretary of the Interior, and Senator Henry Cabot Lodge. The principal German-language papers across the country agreed to back us, and leading papers in New York City indicated that we might count on them. What, in our political inexperience, we failed to reckon with was the possibility that the Committee on Public Information might not look kindly on our effort to supplant its own German-American "baby," the Friends of German Democracy.

It seemed a far-reaching piece of good fortune when, on the recommendation of Frances Kellor, special adviser on race relations, the federal Commissioner of Education, P. C. Claxton, invited me to serve as a dollar-a-year "racial adviser on Americans of German origin."

My job was to promote "mutual understanding and unity" between the German-Americans and their fellow citizens, to develop "an understanding of American ideals, principles and action" among them, and "to stimulate the understanding and prosecution of the war."

I rounded up the German-American leaders in New York—in the main newspaper publishers, editors, or presidents of social, singing or athletic societies with large memberships—but had barely got started on a series of conferences with them when Miss Kellor was told that I must hold no more talks in the Interior Department offices in New York with German-American leaders. The Committee on Public Information, it seemed, had got wind of my approach to the German-American question. Its chairman, an able journalist, named George Creel, was inclined, like government propagandists the world over, to paint in blacks and whites, and to see the German-American issue in terms of the bludgeon. To such a mind my efforts to deal with the German-Americans on the basis of compassion, reason and faith, were darkly suspect.

– 4 –

A distorted account of the most recent of the conferences I had held took me to the office of the New York *Tribune*, the morning that my associates and I had selected for the release of our story on the organization of the "Patriotic Council."

By a happy accident, the *Tribune*'s managing editor was a Harvard classmate of mine, Ernest H. Gruening. "I'm so glad you came," he said. "I've had quite a battle over you." An editorial based on the story to which I was objecting had been put on his desk for publication that morning. "On the strength of a wire from Washington, it denounced you as a fraud, and actually a stockholder in disloyal German-language papers. I told the people upstairs that the editorial would be printed only over my dead body, not alone out of justice to you but because it would bring the *Tribune* a libel suit which I knew the paper would be bound to lose."

I thanked my friend as well as I could in the dazed and breathless state into which the interview had plunged me, and went on to my office in the Interior Department's New York headquarters.

That afternoon one of Creel's top assistants called me from Washington. He had seen the story about the formation of the Patriotic Council, he said. "I think you ought to know," he went on, "that if this Council becomes active it will gravely interfere with certain work which the Committee on Public Information has in hand." He was referring, I gathered, to the Friends of German Democracy. "I hope," he went on, "that you will decide not to go ahead with it. I hope it, I might add, for your own good." A sinister note crept into his voice. "For if you go ahead, we shall expose you as an impostor who has falsely represented himself to be an official of the United States government."

I pointed out hotly that I had been appointed by the Commissioner of Education.

"Dr. Claxton will deny your appointment. Moreover, if you persist, you will be exposed as the tool and cat's-paw of the German-language press."

The pleasant places in which my lines had hitherto fallen, the intercourse I had had with decent people in Europe and in my own country and the standards of conduct I had been taught to respect, had not prepared me for this kind of intimidation by an official of the United States government.

I don't know what I said to him. I might have told him, and I assume that I did, of Secretary Lane's approval of our Patriotic Council as "highly important and absolutely practical." But his approval had been verbal, and he was away on government business in Hawaii. I might have told Creel's man to ask the German-language editors and publishers I had enlisted in the struggle for a sound solution of the German-American problem, how pliable a "cat's-paw" they had found me. But that would have done no good; he would not have listened to them.

I was actually too dazed to say much of anything, but I made no promises.

247

I had barely pulled myself together from this second shock when Dr. Claxton himself called me from Washington, denying categorically that he had given me any appointment.

Miss Kellor had no light to shed on the Commissioner's repudiation, not of me only but of herself.

For hours, that afternoon and evening, I walked the streets of New York in humiliation and misery. I had plenty of documentation to prove that I was no impostor. No government sleuth, moreover, would find any record of my owning a single share of stock in any German-language newspaper, loyal or disloyal. I could make a clear case for myself in the press, but what chances would I have against the official propaganda machine of the United States government, or its ruthless engineers?

No, my part was to "take it," keep my mouth shut, and beware in the future of playing marbles with boys who were tougher than I was.

The wisdom of my decision was proved next day. Most of the men in Washington whom we had listed in our press release as supporting our "Patriotic Council" had apparently been tipped off that we were "phony." One after another—happily, for my faith in man, not all!—they disclaimed any sympathy with us.

I was afraid that Colonel Roosevelt would think me a "molly-coddle" for not standing up to the arm-twisters. But the "fightingest man in America" shared Solomon's philosophy of "seasons," and said nothing of fighting. All the advice he gave me was, "Get the record down."

I did it in a letter to the President, asking his counsel in the "dilemma" in which I found myself "because of unwarranted charges brought against me," on the one hand, and my reluctance, on the other, to make a public issue of a case that might "serve to shake the confidence of the public in the sense of responsibility of the heads of important government departments." Might I count on his support? *

The President's secretary acknowledged the letter. That was all.

* H.H. to the President of the United States, June 14, 1918.

No one in the White House could be bothered even to the extent of a perfunctory promise to make inquiries.

Under pressure from Miss Kellor, the falsity of the "impostor" charges was admitted by Dr. Claxton within forty-eight hours and acknowledged by him to the Creel office.

But neither he nor anyone in the Creel office offered any apology.

– 5 –

Recognizing that I might be needing a touch of solace and a word of defense in the New York *Tribune* and the other newspapers that were publishing his syndicated articles, Mr. Roosevelt used my little book, *Where Do You Stand?* as a springboard for his own appeal to his fellow citizens of German descent. With characteristic munificence, he described its author as "an American of the best and bravest and most loyal type," and made that American thereby reach up and out toward the dream of becoming, some day, by God's grace, the kind of American Mr. Roosevelt described him as being.

CHAPTER EIGHT

"And there came a Fiddler, whose name was Truth"

"Night, and a black pall over the city.
  Mist, and the wind's cry, shrill and thin.
Who is he who goes in pity
  With his fiddle under his chin?
His brow is grave, his eyes are stern.
  A slow dawn wreathes his hair,
And the music he makes shivers and shakes
Like hands the high windows where misery wakes.
And, faint as breath on a bubble, breaks
  The dying lamp on the stair.

Winds, and blown fogs over the city.
  Lo, the white-faced, huddled throng!
Who is he who goes in pity,
  Fiddling his terrible song?
The babes in their mothers' arms
  Hear it, wide-eyed;
And the children come in swarms
  And run at his side,
Hearing the silken, sad refrain
Of the fiddler's magical, tragical strain.
Warm as the wind and soft as the rain
  And terrible as the tide.

Out of the houses the women come,
  Mothers and daughters and wives.
From loving and remembering numb,
White through the night, the women come,
  Bearing the shards of their lives.
Lo, the fiddler plays his song
  Of madness and defeat,
And out of the houses the women throng
  And follow him down the street.

And the dead, the dead arise and come!
  Pallid from burden-bearing
The sons of the drum from slumber come
  With eyes like torches flaring.
From their gory bed the battle-dead
  Rise up, resolved and strong;
And follow the shimmering, glimmering thread
  Of the fiddler's terrible song.

The children moan, the women cry,
  The ghosts wail like the wind.
But the fiddler's eye is fixed on high
  And he heeds not the host behind.
But loud as the roaring tide in flood
He plays his terrible chant of God.
And the houses crumble and fall,
  And the steeples reel like ships.
And the rulers rush from the council-hall
  With wild cries on their lips.
Lo, the fiddler plays his high refrain
Over and over and over again . . .

But the rulers and their boasts
Are trampled under the feet of his hosts—
  The feet of fatherless children,
And broken women, and ghosts."

When, sometime during the late summer of 1918, I painted my picture of "the Fiddler, whose name was Truth," I never thought, so far as I now recall, of the effects of his fiddling on Father, or my brother Fred and his family, or on my sisters and their husbands, or on Elsie's two children; on the Aunts, or the beloved von Mauntzes; or on my friend Ruby, who had married an able young baron in the government service and had two or three children. My imagination could encompass the fate of a nation, but it fell short of seeing the consequences in the lives of a dozen people who had a right to look to me for compassion.

For eighteen months my mind and my emotions had been so sharply focused on the ups and downs of American participation in the war and the prospects of victory, that my German ties seemed almost like a memory of another world. Recalling the exultation with which I pulled the long bell rope that sent the tidings of the Armistice pealing across the countryside from the steeple of the Greenfield Hill church, and the ardor with which, that evening, I helped gather fuel for the victory bonfire, I feel humbled at the memory of my heartlessness. If ever there was a time when my devotion to the American cause might rightly have been as passive as my brothers and sisters had expected it to be, it was the day that saw the end of a war that was so tragic for my family and myself.

After forty years, I bow my head in contrition as I read the letters that Father wrote Irma during the desperate days following the German collapse.

"How frightful, what has befallen us! I cannot grasp it. What we here are going through and suffering daily! My heart breaks and I can scarcely breathe for fear and anxiety."

A catastrophe even more overwhelming than military defeat appeared imminent: the moral collapse of a disillusioned people, left suddenly without leadership, their Kaiser in flight, their generals bewildered, frightened and divided, before the upsurge of an unheard-of element in German history, the mob. Revolution—dread word!—breaking out first in the Navy, sweeping the Army; taking hold, now, in the civilian population.

With the Kaiser's abdication, the imperial government had dissolved. A "caretaker" government failed to establish its authority over the bolshevist "soldiers' councils" asserting themselves in every community. The German armies were in retreat toward the Rhine. Any day, Father knew, returning soldiers would be beating at his door. As men under discipline, or as avenging demons?

"Yesterday, two men of the Soldiers' Council were here," Father writes, "claiming quarters for eight horses and forty-six men, besides officers. The officers, too, may belong to the Soldiers' Councils, since distinctions between officers and enlisted men are no longer made. What is going to happen God alone knows!" A week later: "The German armies are crossing the Rhine and we must reckon with the probability that they may reach us today. May they be decent folk!"

German soldiers came, dejected and without hope, and were quartered overnight, behaving themselves better than Father had dared hope. Soon the victors would be coming. If only it might be the Americans! The reports that came from Coblentz were that the American soldiers were courteous, friendly and cooperative. "If we were to have them here, I would have no fear." But it was the French who were taking over the sector!

The French, when they came, found the American flag floating over the house. That was Elsie's doing; her lifetime's single excursion into fraud. It worked. Officers and enlisted men alike proved models of respect and courtesy.

– 4 –

Father's apprehensions were not only for himself and those of his family who were under his own roof. Elsie's husband was commanding a German regiment, deep in Russia; Bensen, trying to run the naval hospital in Wilhelmshafen under a Sailors' Council; Fred, in Berlin, the very heart of the national chaos. As food administrator for Greater Berlin—in effect, food dictator—he was carrying the burden of feeding the huge population of a capital in which the organization of distribution was in collapse and his orders were subject to a Soldiers' Council, jealous of its authority and pathetically ignorant of the business of securing and distributing food.

With characteristic courage, mixed with anger, Fred summoned a representative of the Council to his office and told him that the Council's interference was making his work impossible. If they did not want the people of Berlin to starve, they would have to leave him alone. Shortly after, a group from the Council took him by taxi to a meeting on the other side of Berlin. He had every reason to believe that he was about to be shot. Instead, the Council asked him to state his plans for the distribution of food, and agreed to back him up.

Fred's letters from Berlin, factual and calm though they were, brought little hope. There seemed to be "no strong man in all Germany."

Ah, but there was. Father had a shrewd eye for character and, after a visit to Fred in Berlin, two years before, had written me his impressions of him as he saw him in action on the national scene. Father saw in him "an exceptional man of great energy and enormous capacity for work; a clear, logical thinker, calm in judgment; kindly to all; exacting of his subordinates, but of himself no less."

Besides all the qualities Father had noted, it seems to me that Fred had all the others which a nation, in chaos, required: a realistic mind, understanding of men, imagination, courage, audacity, the capacity for action and decision, and, most important, with these, devotion, devoid of all personal, political ambition. The early nineteenth century German statesman, von Stein, once remarked that effective statesmanship required the strength of the lion joined to the shrewdness of the fox. Fred met the conditions.*

* His subsequent history provided proof of what might otherwise seem merely the expression of a brother's pride. Pursued by Hitler's malevolence, Fred, from the

What flaw was it in Fred's personality or training that kept him from moving in on the wavering leaders of his country and using the determination and courage he had demonstrated in his dealings with the Soldiers' Council to pull the German people together? Was it a lack of initiative or political sense? Or was it some deep-seated self-distrust, planted in his boyhood by Father's conviction that the thoughts of youth are irrelevant, and cultivated by Grandmother Hagedorn's exasperated conviction—ruthlessly expressed to Mother, and no doubt to him—that he would never amount to anything?

Nemesis!

– 5 –

Christmas. . . . Even in desperate times, heartsick as you were, you could not ignore Christmas, not with children in the house, "the dear, sweet innocent children who do not dream of the unspeakable grief that consumes us." Father writes of Elly and Auntie making clothes, and a sewing-woman making dolls' dresses. A gardener has taken a fir tree out of the woods by the roots and planted it in a huge barrel.

"Christmas was nice because the children were happy. But I was grateful when the days were over. The memory of past happy Christmases is too painful."

– 6 –

The Rhine, which had been the background of the romantic dream which had lured Father out of the security and happiness of America, became, under the shadow of French bayonets, the symbol of defeat and bondage. If only he could get away! Back to America? He was

United States, fought him in the German courts and not only defeated him but forced his government to pay the costs of the trial and indemnification besides. "He's a bully," Fred insisted. "Spit in his eye and he cringes." Warned by his friends not to return to Germany, even though he had won his case, Fred took the next steamer home. Hitler never lifted a finger against him again, and Fred lived out his life quietly on his estate in Schleswig-Holstein.

too old "to weather another such journey, bag and baggage," and he knew he would "find everything too greatly changed, so I would be consumed with nostalgia for the happy past." No, not America. Göttingen, perhaps? That would be ideal. "To have a little house there with our beloved Venie, and end my life there, away from the Rhine, away from this big house, away from the loneliness!"

– 7 –

Meanwhile, the world outside his windows was black and daily getting blacker. Political chaos in all the German states and, at the peace table in Paris, the moral chaos of politicians imagining that they could build peace out of vindictiveness and greed, inept idealism and economic moonshine, personal ambition and party politics.

The daily papers were for Father a daily agony, spreading before him their appalling story of violence, bloodshed and official ineptitude within Germany herself. His courage was equal to the anguish of his Fatherland's defeat at the hands of its foes, the bitter dashing of all the high hopes, the frustration of his faith that such resolution, such sacrifice as the German people had shown, could not fail to bear fruit in victory; but the disintegration before his eyes of the great nation, the great people, he had loved; the crumbling of the superb structure of government that had been built up through generations; the prospect of a communist take-over, following the Russian pattern —seemed more than he could bear. "I am brokenhearted, all but in despair, to see our once-wonderful Germany as it is today. I could weep without ceasing, and I tremble when I think what yet may come."

Now and again self-pity overwhelms him, "that I in my old age should have to suffer such terrible experiences." But the issues are too real to him, and too tragic to permit him more than momentary self-concern. In November he had still been capable of lamenting, "It is too frightful how we have been sinned against"; but not, the succeeding July. Was the sin not possibly within Germany itself?

256

Day and night, as he brooded on the tragedy, he was pursued by the insistent, *Why, why, why?*

As, in his pride, he had in the past felt a part of his Fatherland's greatness, so now, in humbleness of spirit, he identified himself with his people in their confusion and guilt. The romantic vision had faded like the mirage it had always been. At last he faced the realities in his people's nature and character.

"We have been weighed in the balance and found wanting," he wrote. "We must have erred deeply, sinned greatly, and we can only hope and pray that God may help us. He is our only hope. When our people shall have found themselves again, He will lead us out of this valley of humiliation."

Between the lines of his letters the moaning on his lips is all but audible. "I think, I brood, I castigate myself, asking myself, over and over, how did it come about that the whole world came to hate us?"

It was in these hours of self-questioning, with all his romantic dreams of the Fatherland in ruins around him, that Father grew at last to his full stature.

CHAPTER NINE

FATHER had his wish to leave the Rhine, the big house, the loneliness, and to return to the house he had built for his sisters in Göttingen. It was good to be where there were people, and his contact with the outer world was not limited to the newspapers that daily exacerbated his sufferings. His sisters fluttered—oh, so busily!—around him, and, to a point, he liked that. Everybody else, Irma noted, had grown in the suffering of the war years, but not the Aunts. They were the same gossipy old maids as ever; but that would not trouble Father. He had never let himself see them as they were, anyway, and he welcomed their devotion.

Auntie, never obtrusive, always there when she was needed, living her own life when she wasn't, was doubly dear to him—for Mother's sake, and her own. The Bensens had moved to the old university town where Willy had been a student, and he was making a new life for himself there in medical research and practice, and they brought Father such cheer as Göttingen could provide. Irma had never ceased to be anything except a transplanted American. She detested what seemed to her Göttingen's petty, small-town atmosphere, the narrow horizons, the gossip; and her indomitable sense of humor had to stretch itself to find any cheer at all.* The Aunts continued to irritate

* One of her life's dearest compensations was the remark made to her by a devoted friend, the great economist, Cohn, on his deathbed: "You have been good for Göttingen." Irma became an American citizen again after her husband's death but had to continue to live in Göttingen in the house that provided her only financial security. She remains, in my memory, the perfect symbol of the family division.

her to the point of fury. But, going in and out of Father's sickroom, she found her feelings soften even toward those exasperating spinsters.

The weeks passed into months, the spring into summer. Relaxed in a bower of devotion, Father gradually withdrew himself from a world struggling to get its bearings after the four-years' disaster. The newspapers dropped from his bed to the floor, unread.

Summer slipped into autumn. The first snow fell. From the house on the Rhine, Elsie came with her cavalry colonel, home from Russia at last; out of uniform, subdued, a little lost, quite different from the dazzling Uhlan who had come to Father, eight years before, to ask him for his daughter's hand. From his estate in Schleswig-Holstein, Fred came, bringing his wife, Marie. All brought Father a love that reflected the love he had ever given them. Beyond that, each brought him something that was individually his or her own: the Aunts, adoration; Auntie, deep-welling tenderness; Fred, balanced judgment; Marie, wit; Elly, the comfort of faith, and of beauty in the way she arranged the flowers that came pouring into his room; Lutz, stability and loyalty; Irma, gaiety, in defiance of an aching heart; Willy Bensen, indomitable courage. Addie and I were not there, in the flesh, but I am sure we were in Father's thoughts, and with no fog of division between us and him.

The late November days were days of happy memories, of harmony and inner peace, for Father and for those who went in and out where he lay. Once only did reality roughly invade his thoughts. In a moment of revived interest, he leafed through a newspaper and noted, to his dismay, that the German mark had been quoted in New York at five cents.

"Children," he gasped, "what have I done to you?"

Happily, the recognition passed quickly, and he was shaken by no presentiment that, within two years, the fortune that he had invested in German war loans would not pay the postage on a letter to the country that had given him the opportunity to acquire it.

"If I didn't live up to what you expected me to make of my life, I am sorry," she wrote me in a letter intended to reach me after her death. "Life wasn't always an easy school. I had so much to learn and was forever kept busy at that."

The turbulent, unhappy world did not again thrust itself into the warm stillness where he lay. The war was forgotten, the abortion that men called "the peace" was forgotten; Germany, America, the past, the future, all were forgotten, in the quiet passing of a greathearted human being who had loved his Fatherland "not wisely but too well," and was going to his rest—a tragic figure, touched, in his final acceptance of reality, with redemption.

At the end, as those he had loved so deeply stood about him, in actuality or in imagining, I have a feeling that all of us children melted for him into a single image, and that it was Mother—no longer aloof, as in his penitential dreams, but with her arms about him and speaking tender words of understanding and comfort—who raised him gently from his bed and led him across the River.

– 3 –

The tragedy of division pursued Father even beyond the gates of death. Because of the chaotic conditions on the German railroads, following the war, the coffin containing his body could not be transported to the tomb he had built in the Protestant cemetery in Wiesbaden, as a last resting place for Mother and himself; but, in accordance with what was believed to have been his own wish, expressed in broken words as he lay dying, his heart was cut out of him and borne there. The body and the brain, the capable, graceful hands, the shoulders that had carried such heavy burdens for us all through the years of his early struggles, and were bent with grief for his country in his old age, were buried in the municipal cemetery in Göttingen.

In the course of time, *Tante* Alma was buried on his right side, and *Tante* Elsbeth on his left. There, beneath a massive granite boulder, they, who always hungered to possess him, have what was mortal of him.

But not wholly. In death, as in life, Mother has his heart.

EPILOGUE

HERE then is the story of the family that tried to live in two countries at once. I have called it a tragedy, and it was such for Father and Mother and, in varying degrees, for us all.

For myself, thanks to Mother, it was something else, also: a challenge to seek the meaning of this high dream that we call America, and, so far as in me lay, to interpret it and to live it.

America, I have learned in the course of the years, is more than these beloved stretches of natural beauty, washed by two great oceans; these multitudes in seething cities and friendly towns on highways leading everywhere or nowhere; more than the free political institutions that dedicated minds and spirits created, and brave and temperate men have maintained; more than the flag which symbolizes both the body of a nation and the soul which gives it meaning.

America is man's highest vision, to this hour, of human society based on the realities of human nature as it is, and the hope of human nature as it might become.

America is an idea, a dream, a perpetual act of faith that man is the child of God and that the forces in him that aspire will ever in the end be victorious over the forces in him that destroy.

America is the many-made-one, the children of feuding races, creeds and nations, united by a conception that shrivels in its glow all lesser loyalties. America is the free association of people, recognizing and basing their lives upon those absolute standards of human conduct that are the pure metal smelted from the experience and dedicated thinking of the most profound and socially-minded spirits on the five continents, through ten thousand years of human history.

To America has been given both the vision of what human society might be and the awful responsibility, as a nation and as individuals, of translating that vision into day-by-day individual, social, national and international conduct.

America today is the fulfillment of the dream of the prophets and seers of a hundred generations, or it is the cynical toss of that dream into the ashcan of history. America is the creative response to the hunger of mankind for hope, self-respect and brotherhood, or it is earth's final disillusionment, its ultimate object of derision and hate, standing, black and alone, against the blaze of thermonuclear fire.

Is it conceivable that the Mind that sets the stars in their cycles, and has given to man the capacity to set stars of his own in orbit, should give a people so compelling a dream, lay upon them so heavy a responsibility, and not give them also the faith, the vision, the courage, the will and the stamina—in a word, the greatness—triumphantly to carry the burden and make the dream come true?

– 2 –

If the forty years since Father's death have given me an ever-deepening sense of the meaning of America, the last decade of those four has given me an admiration for the German people far transcending my boyhood's sentimental attachment to German landscape and German song, German friends and German *Gemütlichkeit*.

In the depths of Father's agony over his country's collapse, the reader will recall, he recognized that the German people—and he identified himself with them—had been "weighed in the balance and found wanting." Somehow they had lost their way, but he never doubted that God would set them on the highroad once more. "When our people shall have found themselves again," he added, "He will lead us out of this valley of humiliation."

His faith has been triumphantly justified. His people's further years in the wilderness were tragic for themselves and for the world, beyond anything which the darkest forebodings of his sleepless nights might have tortured him with. But the redemption, the moral and economic recovery of that portion of his people that was free to be itself, have been, also, beyond the boldest dreams that he might have dared permit himself. A defeated, abject people, facing, fifteen years ago, what seemed to themselves and to their neighbors final annihilation as a great nation; today one of the most respected and prosperous countries in Europe! Once an aggressive, self-centered, bellicose government, the object of universal fear and distrust; today, the protagonist in the struggle for a united European family of nations! Day before yesterday, the glittering symbol of authority and the discipline of power; yesterday the black example of inhuman despotism; today, one of the world's strongest bulwarks in the battle for a free world!

If, on his off-Sundays from Elysium, Father revisits his beloved Fatherland, he has deeper and more genuine reasons for devotion than any he knew in life.

– 3 –

The history of the "hyphenated family" does not end with the final chapter of this book. The next generation has a different and more inspiring story that must some day be told, of a human family losing and finding itself in a world family; of nationalism transcended, not in any blueprint of a supernational government but in the individual's identification, in action, with the peoples of all nations— their problems, their sins, and their hunger to achieve the inner unity, the freedom and the power of the God-centered life; the story of an American prophet's world-encompassing vision that came to palpitating reality for one of Charlotte Hagedorn's great-granddaughters and her husband in Berkeley Square, London, and on Rio de Janeiro's riot-ridden waterfront, in American labor conflict and in African villages and throne rooms; a story of unity in place of division, of a common purpose in men and women of many nations; and of

263

fellowship and growth, instead of sorrow, in the face of racial, cultural and national divergencies; a story, finally, of self-will resolved in the course of common, everyday living under the challenge of absolute moral standards and the guidance of that Spirit which, Dante assures us in the concluding words of his *Paradiso*, "moves the sun and the other stars."